WOODWORKING PATTERNS

By Gayle K. Wood

412 Woodworking Patterns and all material contained therein copyright ©1999, 2004 by Frank W. Cawood and Associates, Inc. All rights reserved. Printed in the United States of America.

This book or any portion thereof may not be reproduced or distributed in any form or by any means without written permission of the publisher.

FC&A Publishing
103 Clover Green
Peachtree City, GA 30269

We have made every effort to ensure the accuracy and completeness of these patterns and drawings. We cannot, however, be responsible for human error, typographical mistakes, or variations in measurements and individual work.

TABLE OF CONTENTS

INTRODUCTION	5
3-D DECORATIONS	11
BIRDHOUSES/FEEDERS	21
CHILDREN AND TOYS	27
CLOCKS	49
FURNITURE	53
GARDEN	67
HOLIDAY/SEASONAL	75
HOUSEHOLD HELPERS	97
LETTERING	107
OUTDOOR PROJECTS	113
PEG RACKS AND SHELVES	123
PLAQUES	131
WALL BRACKETS	145
WESTERN	149
INDEX	159

METRIC CONVERSION CHART

Measurements: Simply apply metric units to most of the pattern grids instead of the inches and feet suggested in the text.

In the U.S.A., lumber generally is measured in inches, such as 2 inches by 4 inches, 1 inch by 2 inches, etc. For example, what you know as a 100 x 50mm (4 inches by 2 inches) stud would be called a 2 x 4 throughout the pattern book. A 2440 x 1220mm sheet of plywood would be a 4 x 8 sheet in this book.

Most building and decorating materials in the UK are sold in metric units, but you may find both metric and Imperial units like inches and feet being used side-by-side in some retail establishments. Here is a table you may use to convert from Imperial to metric units:

To Convert	Into	Multiply by
inches	millimeters	25.4
feet	meters	0.305
yards	meters	0.914
millimeters	inches	0.394
meters	feet	3.28
meters	yards	1.094

INTRODUCTION

CONGRATULATIONS! You made a valuable investment in the art of woodcrafting when you purchased *412 Woodworking Patterns*! This book combines small and large patterns into one useful and informative book that will give you a pattern for every mood and a project for every skill level.

If you've ever been frustrated because the range and type of patterns in a book or pattern collection was too narrow, you won't be disappointed with this purchase. You can get down to the fun part of woodworking — making beautiful, unique crafts AND larger, more useful projects such as furniture and outdoor garden decorations. If you weren't holding this book in your hands, you wouldn't believe the number of pretty and practical patterns we've included.

These 412 patterns come in a wide range of sizes designed to suit any taste or decor. Easy-to-follow instructions ensure that you'll finish with a great looking product every time.

Our patterns include old-time favorites and delightful new creations. Beginning and advanced woodworkers will find designs to challenge and charm them. We've included helpful tips on painting and finishing your products and occasional alternative suggestions for making patterns different.

The feeling of pride and satisfaction you get from creating quality crafts will be well worth the time you invest. The fun doesn't stop until you do. We guarantee you won't be bored.

RULES FOR SAFETY
- Wear goggles or glasses with shatterproof lenses.
- Wear tight-fitting clothes. Loose clothing can be easily pulled into machinery. If you're wearing a long sleeved shirt, keep the sleeves firmly rolled up or buttoned around the wrist to keep material from being pulled into the saw blade.
- Secure all machinery to a workbench or other sturdy stand. Vibrations can cause unsecured saws and other equipment to fall.
- Turn off equipment not in use.
- Position electrical cords so that they cannot be tripped over.
- Keep your workspace organized. Constantly hunting for a tool can cause undue stress and take the enjoyment out of a project.

EQUIPPING YOUR WORKSHOP
- Hammer
- Tape measure. A good tape measure has the first few inches broken down into 32nds for extremely precise measurements.
- Supply of sharpened pencils
- Sandpaper
- Sanding block
- Hand drill and an assortment of bits
- Screwdriver set
- Assorted screws and nails, especially small finishing nails
- Clamps
- Saw

A router and heavy-duty shop vacuum cleaner are optional items. A router will give your projects a finished look. The heavy-duty shop vacuum cleaner will make quick work of cleaning up.

COMMON SENSE FOR SAWS
The saw is the most important tool in your workshop. There are four basic types of saws that we suggest for use with these patterns: a scroll saw, a bandsaw, a table saw and a jigsaw. Three of these saws can be used to cut the patterns in this book. A table saw is necessary for the large woodworking projects and is almost essential when making shelves. Even though the scroll saw is probably the safest and easiest to work with, always use the one that is most comfortable for you. Here are a few simple tips to help you get the most efficient use from your saw.
- Follow all directions and safety procedures in the owner's manual that came with your saw.
- Use both hands and maintain a steady pressure when feeding wood into a saw blade. Forcing the wood may cause the blade to break or push the wood off course. Pushing wood into the side of the blade, or trying to turn a radius too small for the blade, can also break the blade or push it off its course. Breaking blades is dangerous and expensive.
- Keep plenty of extra saw blades on hand. When cutting intricate designs, especially on a scroll saw, the blade could break if too much pressure is applied.
- Keep your blade sharp. The sharper the blade, the finer the cut, which in the end means less sanding time.

TIPS FOR TOOL CARE
The tools you use will help determine how the finished product looks. High-quality tools will perform better and last longer than low-quality tools.

If you don't have the necessary tools to begin woodworking, you can rent them from equipment rental shops. Check the Yellow Pages under Tool and Equipment Rental to find a shop near you.

Remember to keep all tools oiled and clean. Grime and dust buildup impair machine function.

PURCHASING WOOD AND TIMBER
The types of wood are broadly divided into two categories: hard and soft. Generally, the harder the

Introduction

wood, the higher the price. Wood comes in different grades, as joinery fifths or unsorted.

Hardwood is sturdier and more durable than softwood. It does not scar easily, is very heavy and has a tight grain. It is preferred for use in fine furniture and cabinets. The most common types of hardwood are ash, basswood, butternut, beech, birch, cherry, mahogany, maple, oak and walnut.

Some woods, such as basswood, do not stain well but are perfect for painting and have few knots. Most others, such as oak, stain beautifully.

Some types of hardwood are more readily available in certain areas than others. Since hardwood is expensive, you may want to practice with the less expensive woods before putting too much money into a hardwood project.

People often select hardwoods with a specific project in mind. Ash is a flexible wood and is often used for projects that will be subjected to shock and vibration. For projects that will be exposed to water, greenheart and elm work well.

Soft woods work well for projects made for a wall or table display. These woods usually come from the pine or fir families and are usually less expensive than hardwoods.

The cheaper softwoods are more commonly known as deal. You will find pines, firs, cedars and larches among those softwoods commonly stocked at timber supply stores.

White pine is a very good general purpose wood. Many other types of pine are available and are useful for various projects. Pine wins out over all other softwoods because it is plentiful, easy to work with and usually more affordable. Yellow pine is relatively free from warping, shrinking and knots.

Cedar, which often has a reddish color in the grain, is frequently used for outdoor furniture. Cedar is used to construct wardrobes and chests because of its aromatic smell, which is highly prized as a moth deterrent.

TIMBER SELECTION

Choose smooth wood with consistent color and grain markings.

- ❏ Buy heart wood whenever possible. This wood is cut from the center of the tree and is stronger and more durable than wood cut from the outside of a tree.
- ❏ Check for splits, shakes, knots and pitch pockets that would affect the display quality of your project. Buying wood with knots can be good or bad, depending on the situation. If the knots are not in a stress area of wood from which the patterns will be cut, they could lend character and beauty to the finished piece. If the knots are very tightly bound into the wood, the wood will probably be strong enough to withhold stress. However, if the knot has a black ring around it and is loose or has any movement or "give," the board or wooden piece could be too weak to withstand stress and should not be purchased. Use wood like this only when cutting out small objects that will allow you to work around the knots.
- ❏ Position patterns so that any flaws are outside the pattern area.
- ❏ Beware of warped timber! You can work around knots and splits, but warp is almost impossible to overcome.

When buying pine or soft timber, remember that in certain areas, dealers are giving you the size of timber before it was planed (smoothed and evened up). For example a 1"x 4" actually measures 3/4" x 3-1/2". The actual size of hardwood, however, is only 1/8" smaller than the nominal dimension, but there is no standard as there is in softwood. Therefore, a hardwood 1" x 4" measures approximately 7/8" x 3-7/8". This is very important when cutting out wood for a pattern where pieces must be joined because the thickness of the wood determines the outcome of the finished product.

Plywood may be used for some of the projects. It's better to use larger pieces that require no joining. Plywood is usually sold up to a maximum size of 4' x 8' sheets. Be sure to check for smaller sheets and miss-cuts if you only need small quantities. Plywood may also be purchased pre-sanded, so that only light sanding is necessary.

Particleboard (a pressed wood) can also be used but it does not finish well. It is better to use this type of wood only in areas where it will not show.

Luan plywood is inexpensive and finishes well. For most of the patterns that call for 1/4" or thin wood, luan would probably be the best choice. Luan would work well for Christmas ornaments, for example.

Most small patterns may be cut from either 1/2" or 3/4" wood. You can cut thinner items from plywood or particle board and stack them together to create a 3-D effect. Remember that if you cut a pattern from 3/4" wood when it calls for 1/2" wood, it will not fit together correctly. Make sure you check your wood sizes and make all necessary adjustments to the patterns before you begin.

SIZING PATTERNS

Many of the patterns included here are full-sized; however, there may be times when you need to enlarge or reduce a pattern. There are several ways you can do this. Experiment to find the method you prefer.

Photocopying is the easiest and most popular method of pattern sizing. Many available copiers can reduce or enlarge patterns from 50 to 160 percent. Photocopiers are located in many public places, including libraries, and copying is relatively inexpensive. The most obvious advantage of photocopying is that it may be used for exact pattern transfer as well as for enlargements.

You may also transfer patterns by the "grid" method. Graph paper may be purchased and the pattern traced directly onto a grid. Each grid square should then be enlarged to the size needed.

Measure the size of the grid on your grid paper. If the grid size is 1/2 inch square, and you want your finished project to be twice the size of the pattern, lay down grid

Introduction

lines that are one inch square. If you want the item to be three times the size shown, lay down grid lines that are 1-1/2 inches square.

Determine where the pattern lines cross each grid line and mark your grid in the corresponding spot. Repeat this process grid by grid. After putting a dot where the pattern line intersects each grid line, it's simply a process of connecting the dots with curved lines where necessary.

Curved lines are simple to do by hand. Use a pencil to draw your patterns so that corrections will be easy to make. Any pattern that is to be the same size can be traced onto opaque or transparent paper.

Another way to enlarge or reduce your pattern is with a pantograph. An architectural tool, the pantograph looks like four long rulers joined in a zigzag design. This tool can be difficult to work with, but it is very reliable. You can find these useful instruments in craft and hobby shops, craft catalogs and woodworking magazine advertisements.

You may also want to consider using photography for pattern enlargement, although this method can become expensive. Photograph your pattern using a 35 mm camera with slide film. Take the developed slide and project the image directly onto a piece of wood or paper and then trace it. This method has the advantage of an infinite enlargement range, however, its main drawback is the cost of film and developing.

TRANSFERRING PATTERNS TO WOOD

When transferring a pattern to a piece of wood, use tracing, carbon or graphite paper. Graphite paper is preferred as carbon transfers are difficult to remove from wood and the tracing lines are hard to conceal during the finishing process.

Any marks from graphite paper are easy to erase or sand away. Since this transfer paper is available in white colors as well as dark, it's ideal for transferring patterns to darker woods, such as walnut and cherry. You can find graphite paper at most office supply and graphic arts shops.

All of these tracing papers work in essentially the same way. Place the pattern on top of the transfer paper with the pattern facing up and the transfer medium side of the transfer paper down. Then, place the two together directly on top of the wood with the transfer medium against the wood. Trace the pattern, and remove the paper. The image is now transferred to the wood.

If you plan to make a pattern many times, consider making a template. You can make templates using scissors or a knife or saw them out when you saw the pattern. A template can easily be made from lightweight cardboard. If the pattern is to be used many times, the template can be made of thin plastic. Favorite patterns can be reproduced hundreds of times from a sturdy template.

When half patterns are shown (e.g., a heart shape, where each half is exactly the same), fold a piece of paper in half. Draw or trace the half pattern on the paper with the center touching the fold. Cut the pattern on the folded paper. When the paper is opened, the pattern will be perfectly symmetrical.

HOW TO CUT YOUR PATTERN

Don't let a complex pattern discourage you. Most of these cuts only need a steady hand and a little patience.

Examine each pattern before you make any cuts. Use a smaller blade to cut curves and corners if there is no way to change the position of your saw and no waste stock (extra wood around the pattern) to cut into.

Break complicated cuts into simpler curves and lines. Don't be afraid to move your saw to a different position on the wood and approach the line from a different angle.

If your design calls for sharp corners where two lines intersect, cut the first line and keep going past the corner. Cut a loop around in the waste stock and cut the second line. You can also cut the first line and continue cutting to the edge of the wood. Take off the waste and turn the piece, then continue cutting from the edge to the second line.

When cutting sharp interior corners, you can cut the first line up to the corner, then back the blade out of the wood and cut the second line. Another method is to cut the first line up to the corner and back up a few blade widths. Turn into the waste area, leaving the first line, and get into position to cut the second. Cut the second line and take off the waste. Then go back and cut the last part of the second line up to the corner.

Today, with the new constant-tension scroll saws, you can quickly change direction, make right-angle turns, or complete a 360° turn without making extra cuts or breaking a blade. Often the cuts are so smooth that you do not even have to sand after finishing a project.

When cutting small pieces or very thin veneers, tape your wood to heavy poster board or smooth cardboard. If the pieces are very thin, you can sandwich the wood between the two pieces of poster board. This will prevent the pieces from breaking or getting lost.

It is also helpful to cut more than one thin piece at a time. This method is called pad sawing. Stack up the wood pieces and tape them together. The stack should not be thicker than the saw's cutting capability. Saw the whole stack and remove the tape. The pieces will be identical.

JOINERY METHODS

Using a nail and hammer to join two wooden pieces is probably the most common joining method and certainly the easiest. Beginners often find that nails bend and wood splits with unbelievable frequency. If you are having nailing problems, here are some helpful hints.

Ask at the nearest hardware or DIY shop what nail is best for the wood type and wood thickness that you are using. Your problem may be solved by buying a nail of the correct size or type for the job.

Use finishing nails with care when joining a corner piece that will show. They have a tendency to bend very easily when they are longer than needed.

Try buying shorter nails or cutting the

Introduction

point with heavy wire cutters. Punch the nail down below the wood with a nail set so that it doesn't show, and plug the hole with wood putty. Sand the area flush with the wood, and the hole will be unnoticeable.

Hold nails firmly between your thumb and forefinger when hammering. This will keep the nails from going astray or bending so often.

Consider using old-fashioned cut nails when making furniture. These nails, if driven in parallel to the grain, will help to prevent splitting because of their construction and strength.

When hammering into small sections of end grain or side grain, drill small pilot holes before nailing. This will decrease the tendency of the wood to split. Take care not to drill your pilot holes too big. Excessively large pilot holes may weaken the joined area.

Have a helper hold loose ends of the boards while nailing. If you are working alone, use clamps or another device to hold the wood steady. This will help prevent misalignment and the need to remove the nails and begin again.

Screws are very often used in joining. Frequently, screws can be driven into wood more easily and with a greater degree of accuracy than nails. Screws are also less likely to split wood. It is important to use the correct screw type and size for the job.

Many woodworkers use screws in the majority of their joinery projects because they can be power driven. If you decide to use this method of driving screws, buy a power screwdriver or use a drill attachment. Most drills are equipped with a screw bit and are very easy to use.

Be sure that all visible screw holes are counter-sunk (set at or below the surface of the wood). Plug the holes with wood putty or small lengths of dowel. Milled plugs may also be purchased and glued in place.

JOINING WITH GLUE

Glues have been used with great success in wood joinery for a very long time. Many antiques that you see today that are still in very good condition were made from wood veneers (overlays) glued together.

There are many types of glue on the market. Animal glue is a natural glue derived from the by-products of the meat packing industry. This glue, widely used for veneers since the 17th century, is not recommended for outdoor use. One of its chief advantages is that the bond can be broken without damage to the wood when heat and moisture are applied.

Animal glue is available in a cake or granular form. The granular type is preferred by traditional woodworkers, but it is very messy and hard to use because it must be dissolved and warmed in a jacketed glue pot.

For pieces that are used indoors, most woodworkers use a high-quality white wood glue or a yellow aliphatic resin. These synthetic glues form a chemical bond that actually seep into the wood. In some cases, the bond is stronger than the wood itself. The yellow glues are stronger and more resistant to water but still should be used indoors.

Outdoor projects require a waterproof glue such as resorcinol or epoxy. This glue is highly water-resistant and is very good for outside projects, but there are a couple of drawbacks with using resorcinol. It must be used quickly because the drying time is very short and the joints are very noticeable.

Contact cement is widely used when laminating or veneering. Be careful when using contact cement because once a bond is made, it's impossible to break. Therefore, take care not to make mistakes when using this glue. It is also very toxic. Always use in a well-ventilated workshop.

Super glue works well on very small items. It dries very quickly and holds well but is quite expensive. Super glue has also been known to bond skin but is very easy to remove with acetone or nail polish remover.

Urea or plastic resins are widely used for general purpose woodworking. Plastic resins are highly water-resistant and durable. The joints are not very noticeable, and they sand and finish well. Hardwoods do not bond quite as well with plastic resin as softwoods, such as fir, pine or cedar. This type of glue is very popular in the United States, as well as Canada and England . Like contact cement, it is very toxic so use only in a well-ventilated workshop.

There are many other glues on the market, especially those formulated for special purposes that are very good. For best results, follow label directions carefully.

Before gluing, make sure the surfaces to be glued are smooth, dry and free from oil or grease. Clean surfaces take glue much easier than dirty ones.

Apply the glue, then clamp the wood together tightly. Metal or strap clamps can be used. When using metal clamps, be sure to place a wood block between the clamp and the wood to prevent marring. Allow plenty of time for the glue to set and dry completely. Manufacturers usually specify drying times on the glue container.

Make certain that all glue is cleaned from the outer surface of pieces that you are going to stain. Stain will not absorb into any glue spots on your project.

"PICTURE PERFECT" FINISHING

How you finish any project is what will place your individual signature on a piece. So decide how you want the piece to look and get to work.

The first and most important step in finishing is sanding. Sand the piece with a rough grade of sandpaper (100-200 grit) to knock off all large bumps and splinters. Sand again with finer paper or emery cloth (up to 500 grit) until the piece is completely smooth. Steel wool (0000 or 4-0) is best for the final sanding and for smoothing bubbles between coats of finish or polyurethane. This is the secret to all those beautifully finished pieces you find in expensive shops.

If you have any visible knots in your project, you can apply a soft wood filler over the knots before you sand.

There are several different ways to decorate your piece once you've finished sanding. You may paint, stain, stencil or finish with tung oil.

Introduction

When painting a project, make sure you use top quality paint brushes made of camel hair or other natural fibers. These do not lose bristles and spoil the effect as cheaply made brushes do. Applicators on wooden handles are better because they don't leave brush marks. A power sprayer also gives a clean, finished surface. Keep several lint-free rags at hand for clean up as well as for applying stains and sealers.

The most popular type of painting for wooden pieces is tole painting. This is an easy method of applying paint in layers with common designs and shading techniques. Tole painting is probably simpler for a beginner than any other type of painting, and with practice, patience, and proper instructions, anyone can master this technique. You'll find that a large variety of tole painting books are available in craft and hobby shops everywhere. In fact, many of the patterns included already have designs suitable for tole painting.

Acrylic (water-based) paints are easy to use and easy to clean with soap and water. You can use a brush cleaner that contains a conditioner to keep your brushes more supple and make them last longer. Acrylic paints, once dried on the wooden surface, become permanently waterproof. A coat of clear acrylic sprayed or brushed on the painted items acts as a sealer and completes the project.

Stenciling is another very popular finishing technique. Stenciling is the art of dabbing paint, ink or dye through openings in a piece of plastic or cardboard, leaving an impression behind. A great variety of patterns — from flowers and animals to country designs — is available.

Once you have chosen your stencil pattern, tape the pattern down to the wood surface. You may want to practice stenciling on paper before you attempt painting on the wooden piece, just to make sure it's going to turn out the way you're hoping it will.

The "dry brush" method of stenciling works best. Too much paint on your brush will run or drip. Use brushes, sponges or spray paint to stencil.

A new stenciling product on the market is stick paint. Stick paints resemble large children's crayons. You "color" with these stick paints the same way you would with crayons. The stick application is very easy, and it involves less mess than other methods. It is rapidly becoming the favorite method of many first time stencilers.

If stenciling requires too much patience, many craft stores now carry wood decals which can be found in several attractive patterns.

Staining is another popular finish for wood crafts. Color variety is an added advantage of wood stain. Just so you won't be surprised or disappointed, make sure you test your stain on a piece of scrap wood to check the color before applying to the wood.

Stain is easy to apply. Brush or wipe it on with a lint-free soft cloth. Always apply the stain with the grain of the wood, then against the grain. Wipe off excess with the grain.

After staining, rub the piece with 0000 grit sand paper. Brush on a coat of polyurethane over the dried stain, brushing along with the grain, forcing out the bubbles. After it has dried thoroughly, rub with steel wool to eliminate any bubbles that may have formed.

For best results, use a tack cloth (found at paint and DIY shops) to remove dust after each sanding. Polyurethane forms a hard, bright, waterproof finish. It comes in a high gloss or satin finish. Make sure you are in a well-ventilated, dust-free environment when applying polyurethane.

Tung oil is also a great finish. Tung oil is a thick, heavy liquid applied directly to the wood by hand or with a lint-free cloth. Apply several coats to form a stain and water-resistant finish.

USEFUL, DECORATIVE FINISHING ITEMS

Keep these additional items on hand to help you finish each project. Be sure to check the instructions with each pattern for items not listed.

- ❑ Twine or ribbon for enhancing certain patterns
- ❑ Dowel rods of various sizes, shaker pegs
- ❑ Polyurethane, used to protect most outdoor patterns and some indoor patterns
- ❑ Hot glue
- ❑ Door harp, lamp and whirligig assemblies. Ask at hardware or craft shops or order from woodworking supply shops and mail order companies.
- ❑ Hangers to display your finished pieces
- ❑ Cup hooks, L-hooks, screw eyes and coat hangers. Available at hardware shops
- ❑ Small pliers and cutters

TURNING WOODCRAFTING INTO A PROFITABLE HOBBY

Once you've completed a few projects, you may want to try making money from your woodcrafting projects. Here are ten easy steps to get you started.

1. Look for places to sell your products. This will help you decide if a woodcrafting business would be profitable in your area. Possible markets include craft shows, craft shops, boutiques, antique shops, frame shops, tourist attractions, convenience stores, club or church functions and markets. If you have trouble convincing people to buy your crafts and display them in their shops, ask them about working under consignment. This means that for a small percentage of your profits, a shop would let you display your crafts.

   You may also want to consider selling your products through the mail or post. You can advertise in national or regional magazines. All publications have numbers you can call to get more information about advertising rates.

2. Identify best-selling woodcrafts by visiting shows or shops where such item are sold. Note current prices. Choose a handful of pieces

Introduction

you think will sell the best.

3. Set up shop in a well-ventilated and well-lit area. Make sure you have the proper tools and necessary woods on hand. You don't want to waste time gathering supplies. Buy a good grade of wood to make your projects. This will save you time in the long run, and you will be able to offer your customers a better quality product. Buy materials in small quantities to help cut start-up costs. As your business grows, you will be able to purchase materials in larger quantities, which will save you money. Lower expenses mean higher profits.

4. Keep records. Record every purchase you make for your woodworking venture. Enter supplies, rental fees, transportation, etc. These records will be a big asset when tax time comes around. Once you start selling products, record each item sold and its selling price. This will help you determine your best-selling products.

5. Open a separate bank account for your crafts. Pay for everything by check and deposit all receipts into this account. It will be a good double-check against your records when calculating the year's net profit and estimating taxes.

6. Make only a few of each item at first. If you did not pick hot sellers, you won't be stuck with a huge inventory that won't move.

7. Check with local authorities and make sure you have the proper licenses and tax numbers to fulfill legal requirements.

8. Decide on a selling price. Make sure your rates are competitive with other woodcrafters. Your expense records will help you determine a profitable price.

9. Display your crafts attractively whether you've set up a booth at a craft show or are marketing your products through the mail. When you display your products directly to the public, make sure you have enough inventory to fill your space.

10. Be friendly and courteous to your customers. You're more likely to make a sale and have repeat business. If you don't have exactly the product the customer is looking for, you may be able to suggest one of your items as an alternative that the customer would like just as much or better.

With a little preparation and practice, you should soon be able to carve out a profit from your woodcrafting.

CRAFT FAIRS: FUN AND PROFITABLE

Craft fairs and shows are a very popular way to display and sell woodwork creations. You can find craft shows by checking your local newspapers or by asking in local craft shops. Small, local shows are often free or only require a small fee to enter. With good quality products and our hints in hand, you'll be able to pocket a nice profit.

Make your display stand out from the rest. Keep your space open and well-lit. Use long, narrow folding tables to exhibit your wares. They take up less room than square card tables. Rent or borrow such tables before you purchase them. These tables are difficult to transport, and you may decide to stop selling woodcrafts quicker than you had planned.

Cover your tables with long cloths. Store extra items underneath. Don't use table coverings that clash with your products.

Take plenty of inventory. Use boxes or crates to display your items at various heights. This will make your display more appealing and encourage people to give attention to each individual product.

Use products to accentuate your products. Put candles in the candlesticks you designed or real fruit in the fruit bowl you crafted. Using your imagination, you will discover plenty of household items that will show the beauty and usefulness of your woodcrafts.

Take a small wood piece to work on when business is slow. Often people will stop near your display just to watch. You may even want to custom paint a piece to suit your customer's wishes.

Carry a thermos, cooler and some sandwiches. This will prevent you from eating up all your profits at the concession stands.

Be prepared for unusual weather if the show will be held outside. Take sunscreen, umbrellas, heavy-duty plastic to cover your products in case of rain and the proper clothing so that you will be comfortable.

Selling a quality product you feel good about is easy. What are you waiting for?

REMEMBER

It's a great big world of woodworking out there, so have fun!

CHAPTER ONE
3-D Decorations

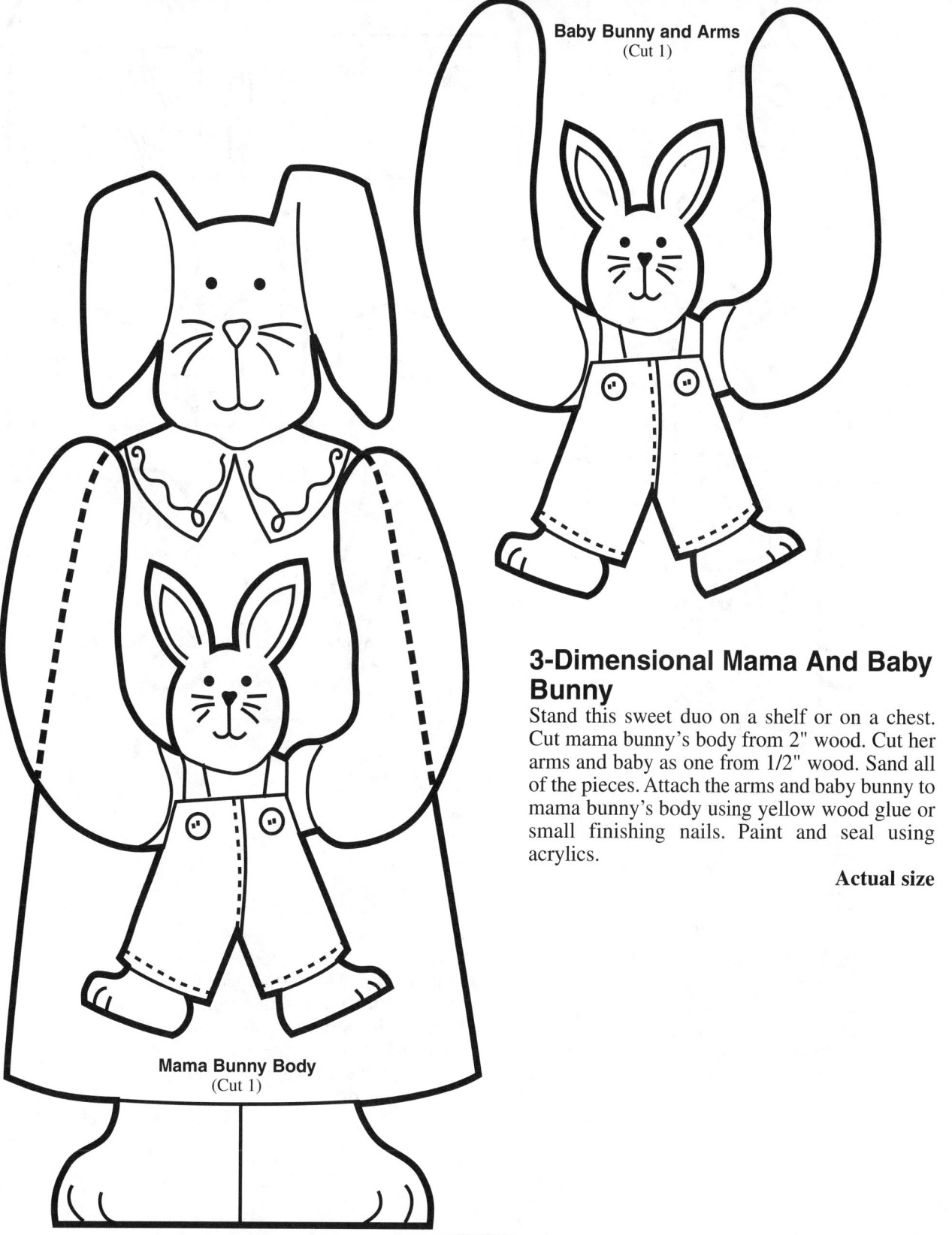

Baby Bunny and Arms
(Cut 1)

Mama Bunny Body
(Cut 1)

3-Dimensional Mama And Baby Bunny

Stand this sweet duo on a shelf or on a chest. Cut mama bunny's body from 2" wood. Cut her arms and baby as one from 1/2" wood. Sand all of the pieces. Attach the arms and baby bunny to mama bunny's body using yellow wood glue or small finishing nails. Paint and seal using acrylics.

Actual size

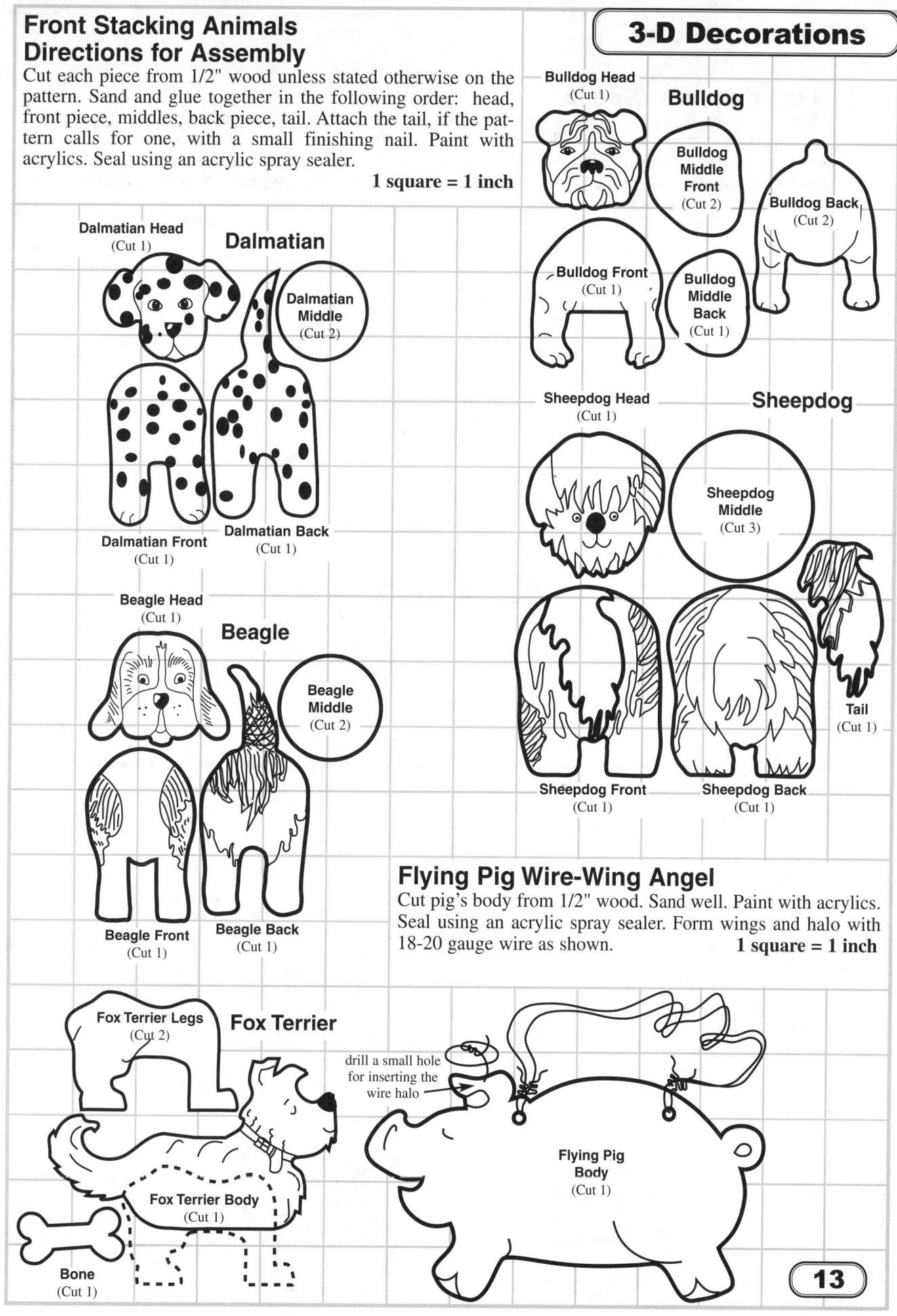

3-D Decorations

"I Love Apples" Mobile

Cut the plaque and apples from 3/4" wood. Cut the heart from 1/4" wood. Drill a hole in each place marked with an "X". Sand all of the pieces. Paint the same design on both sides of each apple and hanger. Seal using acrylic paints. Glue the heart in place with yellow wood glue. Insert screw eyes into the tops of the apples. Suspend the apples from the top piece using twine, jute or clear nylon fishing line.

1 square = 1 inch

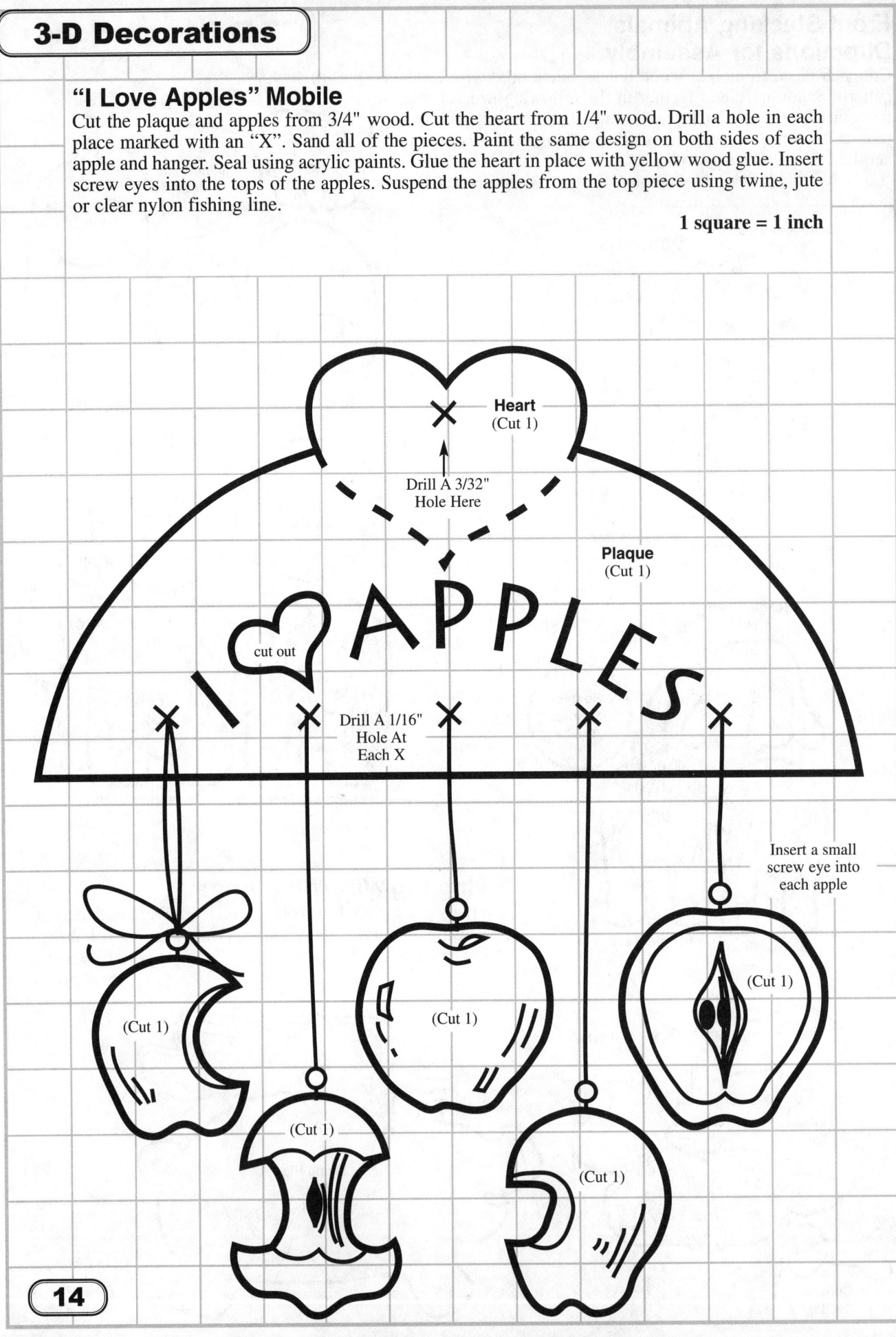

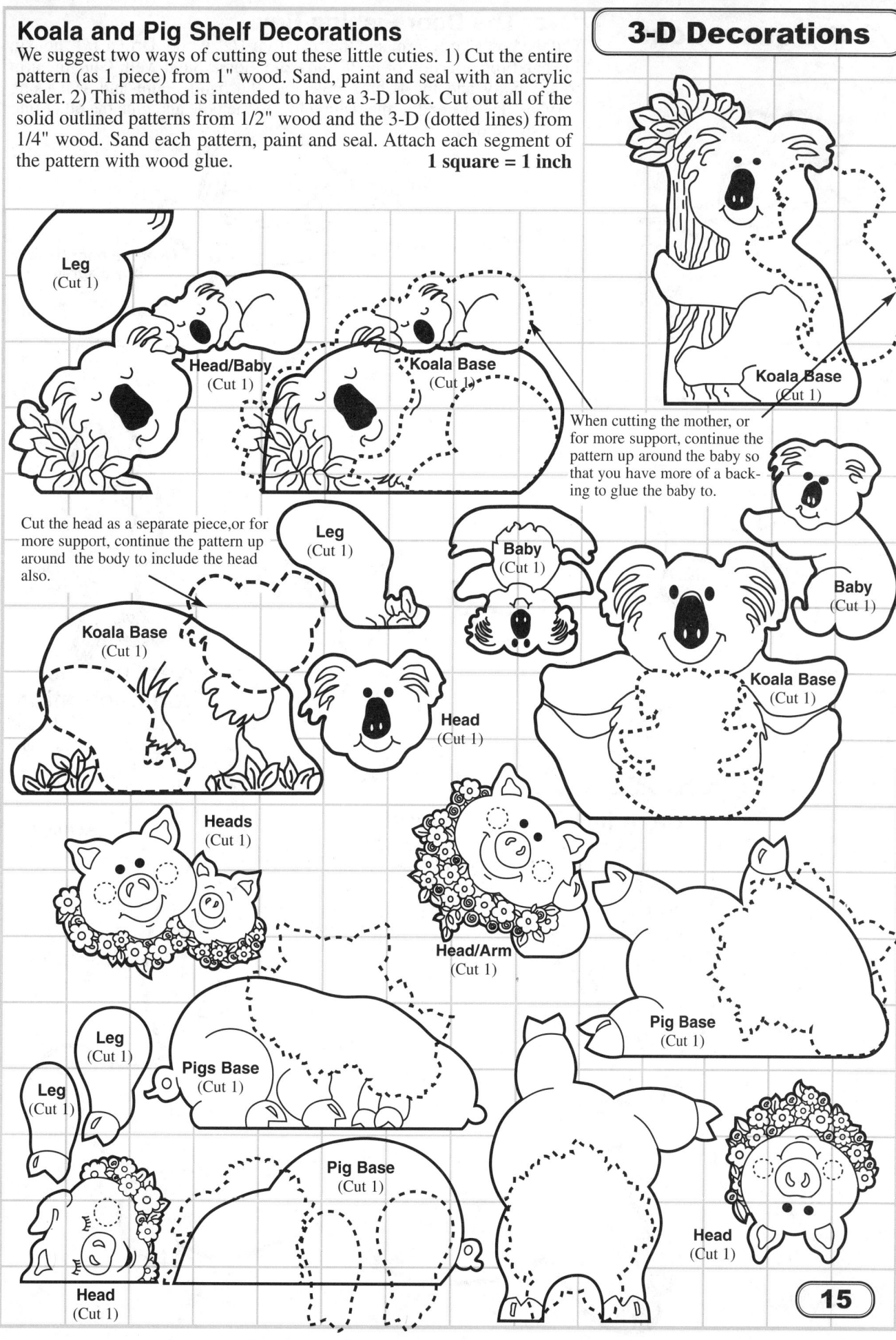

3-D Decorations

Over The Door Fishing Boy
Cut the boy's body, arm and the fish from 1/2" wood. Drill a 1/4" hole in his hand for insertion of a 1/8" dowel 5" long. Sand well. Glue the arm to the body and the fishing pole into the hand. Paint and seal using acrylics. Tie one end of the fishing line to the pole and glue the other into the fish's mouth.

Actual size

Over The Door Frog Decoration
Cut the frog's body and leg from 1/2" wood. Sand well. Glue the leg to the body. Paint and seal using acrylics.

Actual size

Capering Cat On A Stand
Cut the cat from 3/4" wood. Cut a 3" x 3" base from 3/4" wood. Drill a 1/4" hole 1/2" deep in the cat and base for insertion of a 1/4" dowel 4" long. Sand the pieces. Glue the dowel into the cat and base. Paint and seal using acrylics.

Actual size

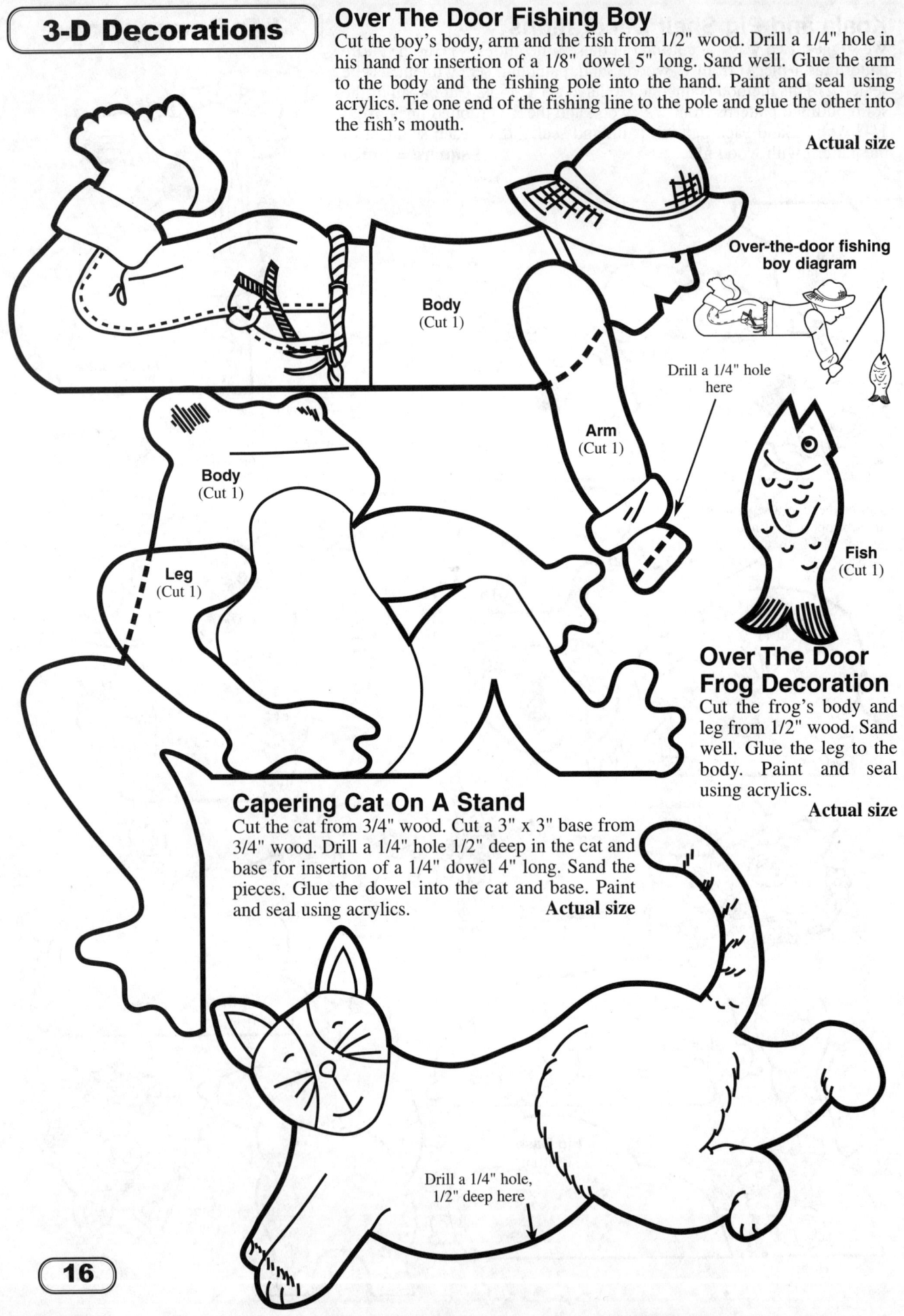

16

3-D Decorations

Ribbons And Hearts Merry-Go-Round

Painted fancy or simple, this merry-go-round will delight everyone. Purchase one ball knob with a pre-drilled 3/8" hole for the top. Cut the platform from 1/2" wood. Drill holes in places indicated. Drill the 1/4" holes 1/4" deep. Drill the 3/8" hole in the center all the way through. You will need 1, 3/8" dowel 13" long. Cut the base from 1" wood. Drill the 3/8" hole in the center 3/4" deep. Cut 4 carousel horses from 1" wood. Drill a 1/4" hole through each horse as indicated. Cut 4 hearts from 1" wood and drill a 1/4" hole in the bottom of each one 1/4" deep. Insert a 5" long 1/4" diameter dowel through each horse. Glue the dowels into the platform after you have painted everything. You will need 4 pieces of 1/4" ribbon cut 7" long to attach to the hearts and the ball knob. Assemble all of the pieces as shown in the diagram. There is a 1 1/2" space between the base and the platform. The platform will be supported by the ribbons; therefore, you will need to place several blocks of wood 1 1/2" tall as temporary spacers between the base and platform. Remove the spacers after the glue dries.

1 square = 1 inch

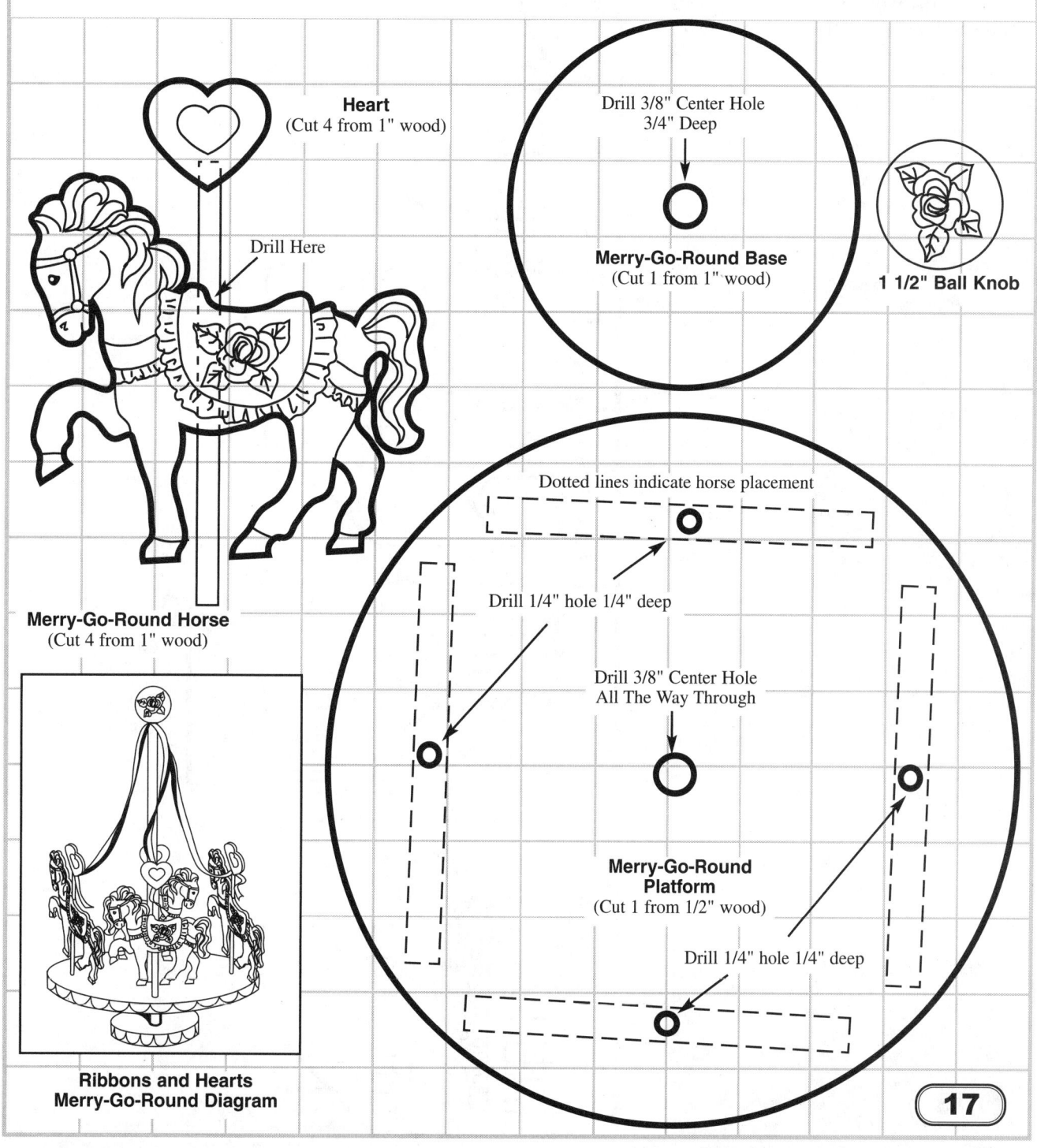

Heart (Cut 4 from 1" wood)
Drill Here

Drill 3/8" Center Hole 3/4" Deep
Merry-Go-Round Base (Cut 1 from 1" wood)

1 1/2" Ball Knob

Merry-Go-Round Horse (Cut 4 from 1" wood)

Dotted lines indicate horse placement
Drill 1/4" hole 1/4" deep
Drill 3/8" Center Hole All The Way Through
Merry-Go-Round Platform (Cut 1 from 1/2" wood)
Drill 1/4" hole 1/4" deep

Ribbons and Hearts Merry-Go-Round Diagram

17

3-D Decorations

Layered Village

Adorn a shelf with this layered village. Cut the buildings from 3/4" wood. Sand all of the pieces. Glue in layers as shown. Paint with acrylic paint. Glue layers using yellow wood glue. Seal dry pieces with spray or brush on acrylic varnish.

Actual size

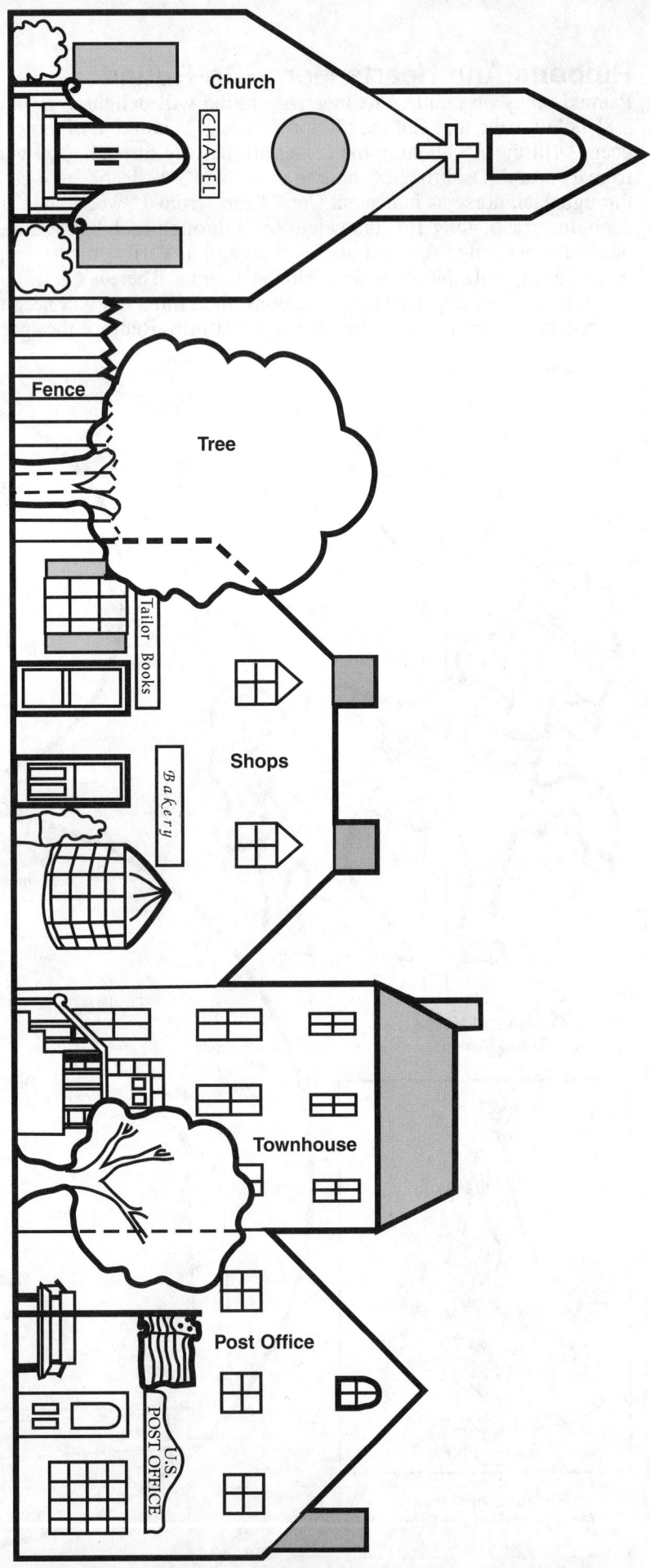

18

3-D Decorations

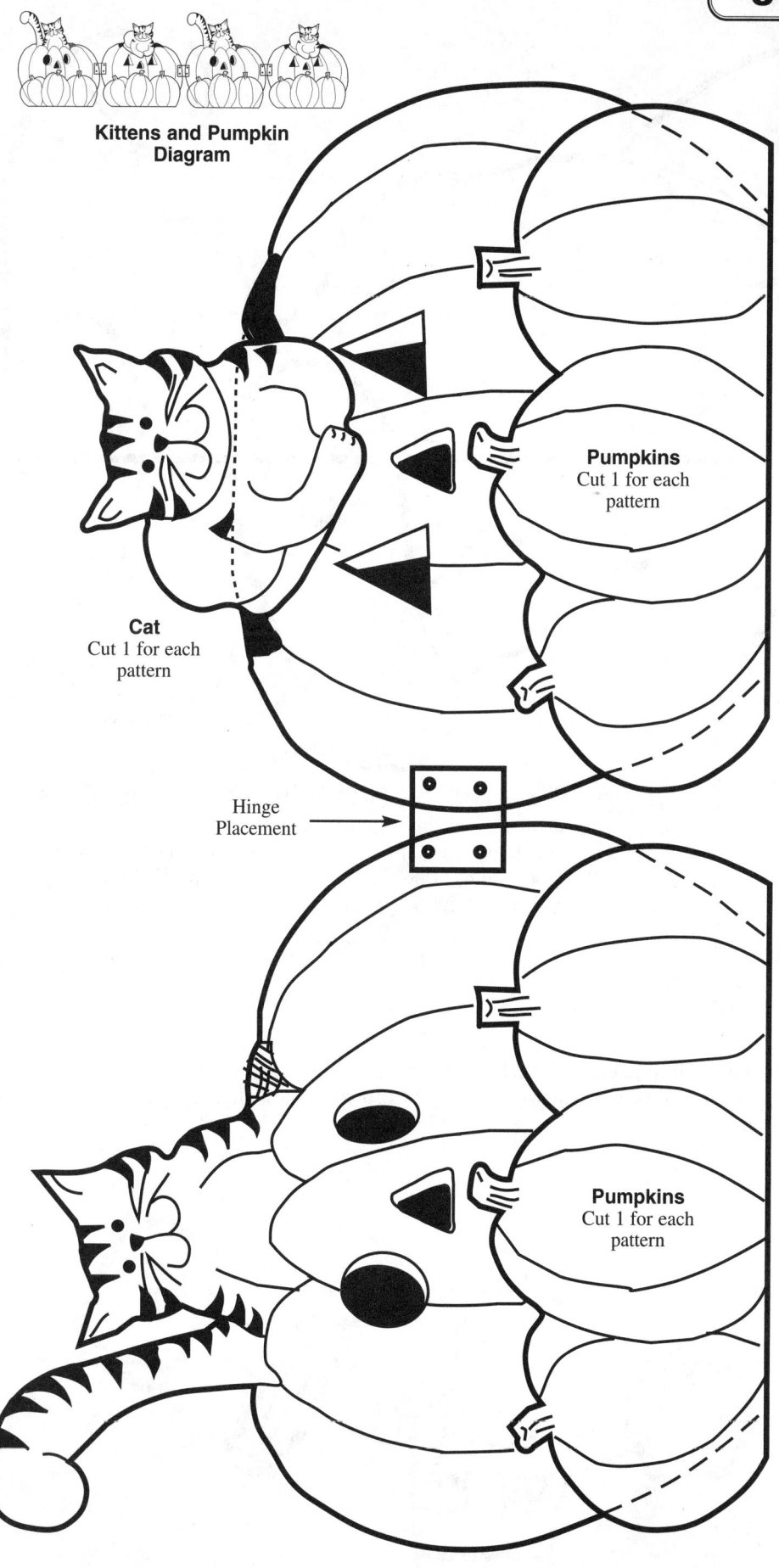

Kittens and Pumpkin Diagram

Kittens and Pumpkins Windowsill Decoration

Cut as many pieces of each pattern as desired from 1/2" wood. Sand and basecoat. Transfer the detail with graphite paper. Paint with acrylic paints. Lightly sand the areas where the additional pieces will be attached. Attach those pieces with craft or wood glue. Connect the finished designs with 1/2" hinges. Seal with an acrylic spray or brush-on varnish.

Actual size

Pumpkins Cut 1 for each pattern

Cat Cut 1 for each pattern

Hinge Placement

19

3-D Decorations

Body (Cut 1)

Leg (Cut 1)

Arm (Cut 1)

Ear (Cut 1)

Sleepy Time Rabbit Shelf Or Windowsill Sitter
After a feast of carrots this bunny needs to rest on your shelf or windowsill. Cut his body from 3/4" wood. Cut his arm and carrot, leg and ear from 1/2" wood. Sand. Glue the 1/2" wood parts to the body with wood glue. Paint and seal using acrylics.

Actual size

Teacher Garland
Cut patterns from 1/2" wood. Drill a small hole through each pattern for insertion of a thin wire. Transfer the detail using graphite paper. Paint with acrylic paints and seal with a spray or brush-on varnish. Pull the wire through the holes and dab glue on the openings.

Actual size

— CHAPTER TWO —
Birdhouses & Feeders

Lighthouse Birdhouse

Cut 1 front piece from 1/2" wood, 1 back piece from 1/2" wood, 2 side pieces 1/2" x 7 3/16" x 6" (bevel the top edges), 2 roof pieces 1/2" x 4" x 6" and 1 bottom piece 1/2" x 8" x 8". Cut 2 fence pieces from 1/2" pine. Drill a 1 1/4" entrance hole. Drill a 1/4" hole 3/8" deep for insertion of a 1/4" dowel. Assemble the pieces using brass screws and all weather wood glue. Do not glue the bottom so it is easily removable for once a year cleaning. Sand and paint with acrylics. Seal the outside only with several coats of exterior grade polyurethane.

1 square = 1 inch

Back Diagram

Front Cut 1 1/2" wood

Roof

Side 1/2" x 8-1/2" x 5-1/2"

Side 1/2" x 8-1/2" x 5-1/2"

Drill a 1 1/4" hole here

drill a 1/4" hole, 3/8" deep here for insertion of a 1/2" dowel 2" long

Fence Cut 2 1/2" wood

attach a fence here

attach a fence here

Bottom 1/2" x 7" x 7"

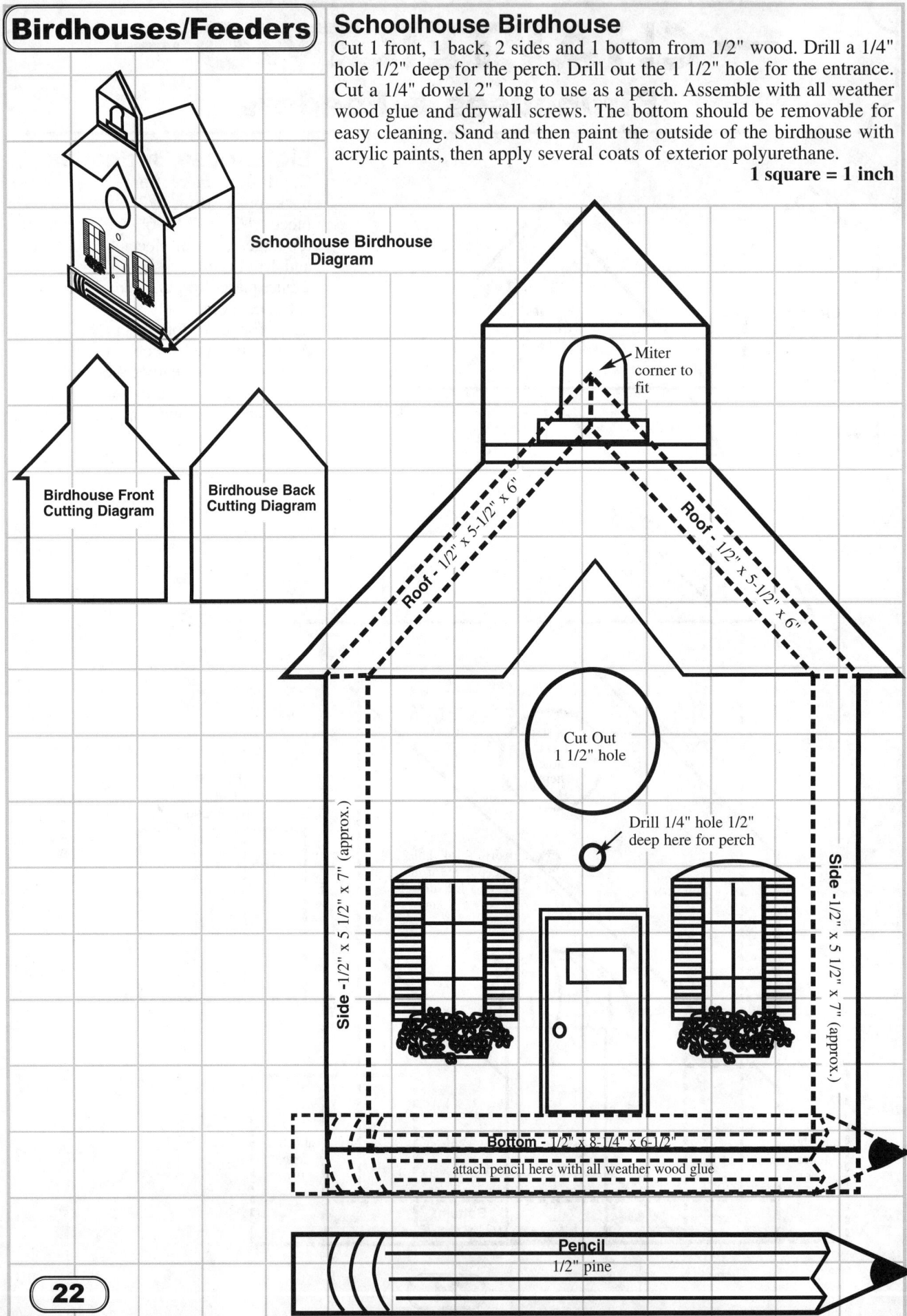

Birdhouses/Feeders

Schoolhouse Birdhouse

Cut 1 front, 1 back, 2 sides and 1 bottom from 1/2" wood. Drill a 1/4" hole 1/2" deep for the perch. Drill out the 1 1/2" hole for the entrance. Cut a 1/4" dowel 2" long to use as a perch. Assemble with all weather wood glue and drywall screws. The bottom should be removable for easy cleaning. Sand and then paint the outside of the birdhouse with acrylic paints, then apply several coats of exterior polyurethane.

1 square = 1 inch

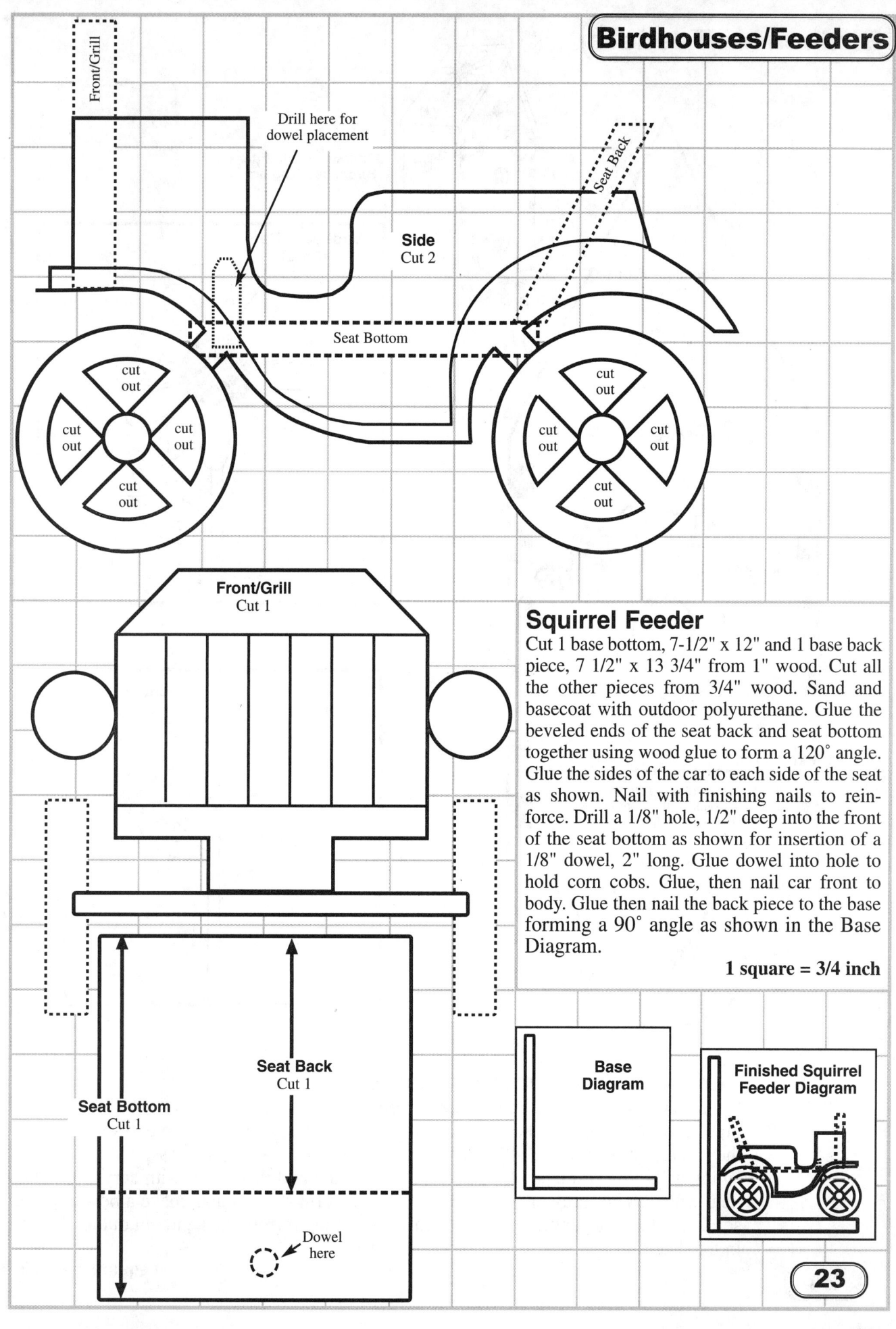

Birdhouses/Feeders

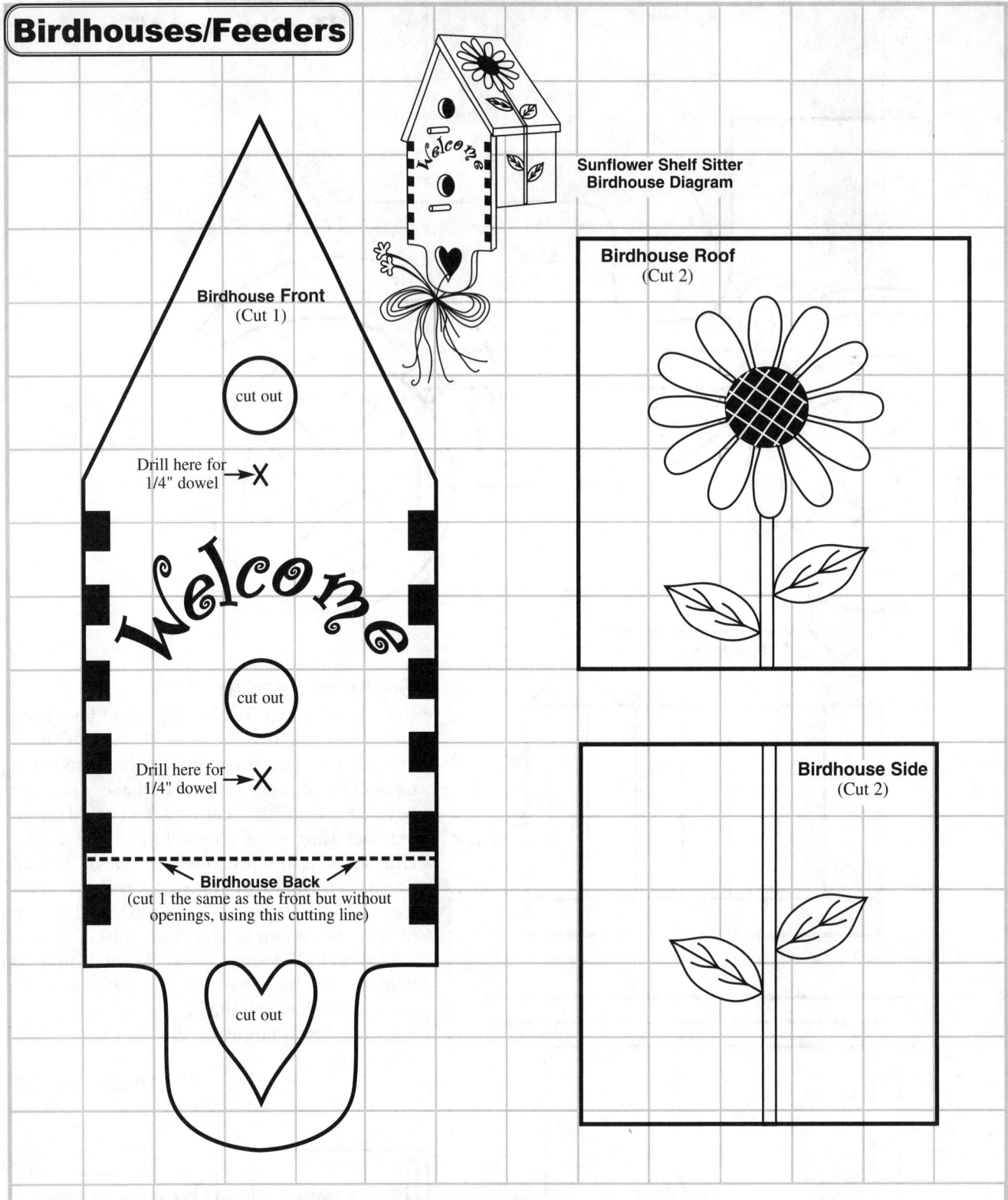

Sunflower Shelf Sitter Birdhouse Diagram

Birdhouse Front (Cut 1)

cut out

Drill here for 1/4" dowel

Welcome

cut out

Drill here for 1/4" dowel

Birdhouse Back (cut 1 the same as the front but without openings, using this cutting line)

cut out

Birdhouse Roof (Cut 2)

Birdhouse Side (Cut 2)

Sunflower Shelf Sitter Birdhouse

Cut a front and a back, 2 sides, 2 roof pieces and 1 bottom (4-1/4" x 4-1/4") from 1/2" pine. Drill a 1" entrance hole through the front piece. Drill a 1/4" hole 3/8" deep into the front as shown for a 1/4" dowel 2" long to be used as a perch. Assemble with finishing nails. Insert the perch with wood glue. Sand and then paint with acrylic paints. Seal with acrylic spray or brush on varnish. For a finishing touch, make a bow around some dried or silk flowers with some raffia and hang it from the heart cut out as shown in the diagram.

1 square = 1 inch

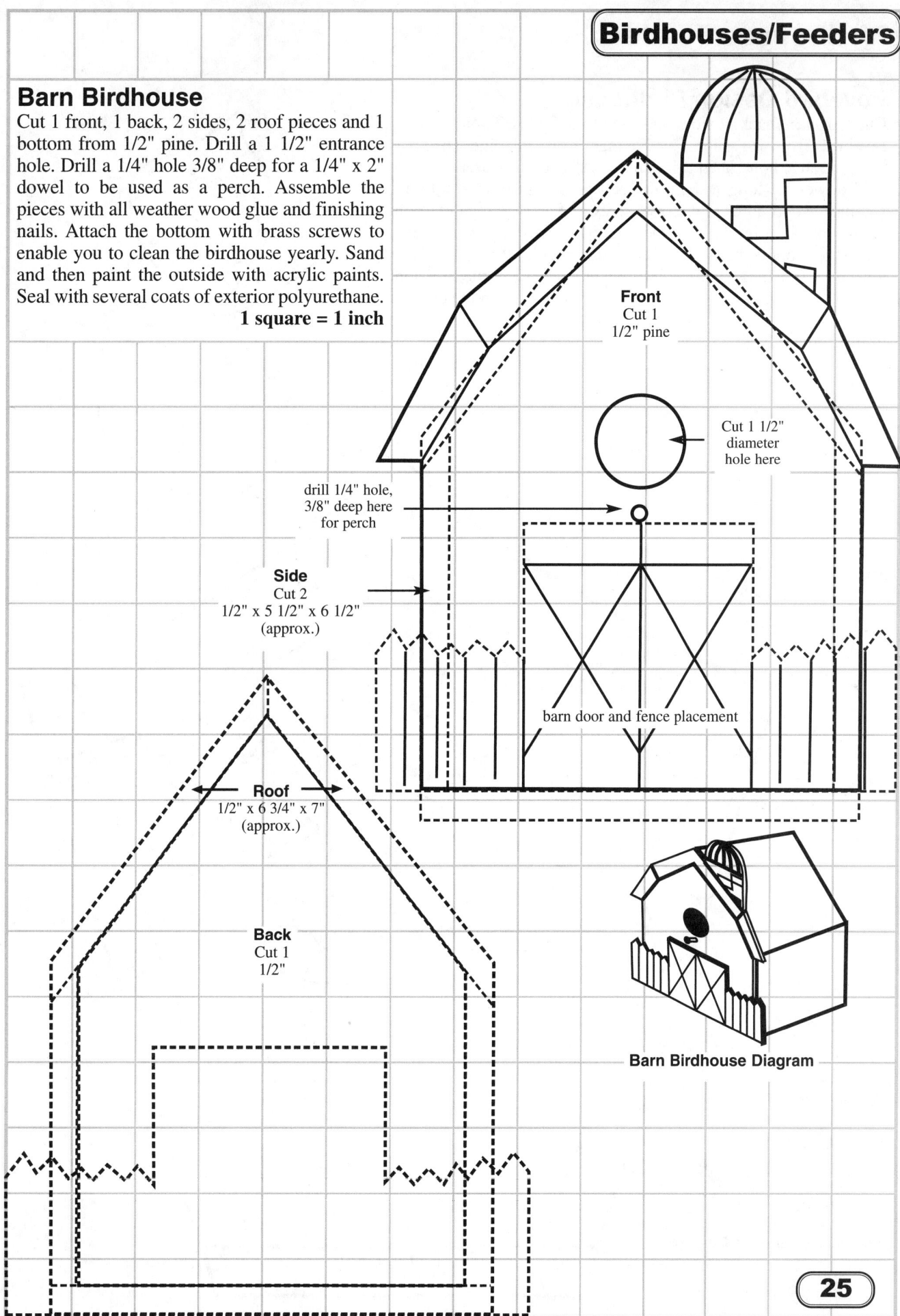

Birdhouses/Feeders

Barn Birdhouse

Cut 1 front, 1 back, 2 sides, 2 roof pieces and 1 bottom from 1/2" pine. Drill a 1 1/2" entrance hole. Drill a 1/4" hole 3/8" deep for a 1/4" x 2" dowel to be used as a perch. Assemble the pieces with all weather wood glue and finishing nails. Attach the bottom with brass screws to enable you to clean the birdhouse yearly. Sand and then paint the outside with acrylic paints. Seal with several coats of exterior polyurethane.

1 square = 1 inch

Front Cut 1 1/2" pine

Cut 1 1/2" diameter hole here

drill 1/4" hole, 3/8" deep here for perch

Side Cut 2 1/2" x 5 1/2" x 6 1/2" (approx.)

barn door and fence placement

Roof 1/2" x 6 3/4" x 7" (approx.)

Back Cut 1 1/2"

Barn Birdhouse Diagram

25

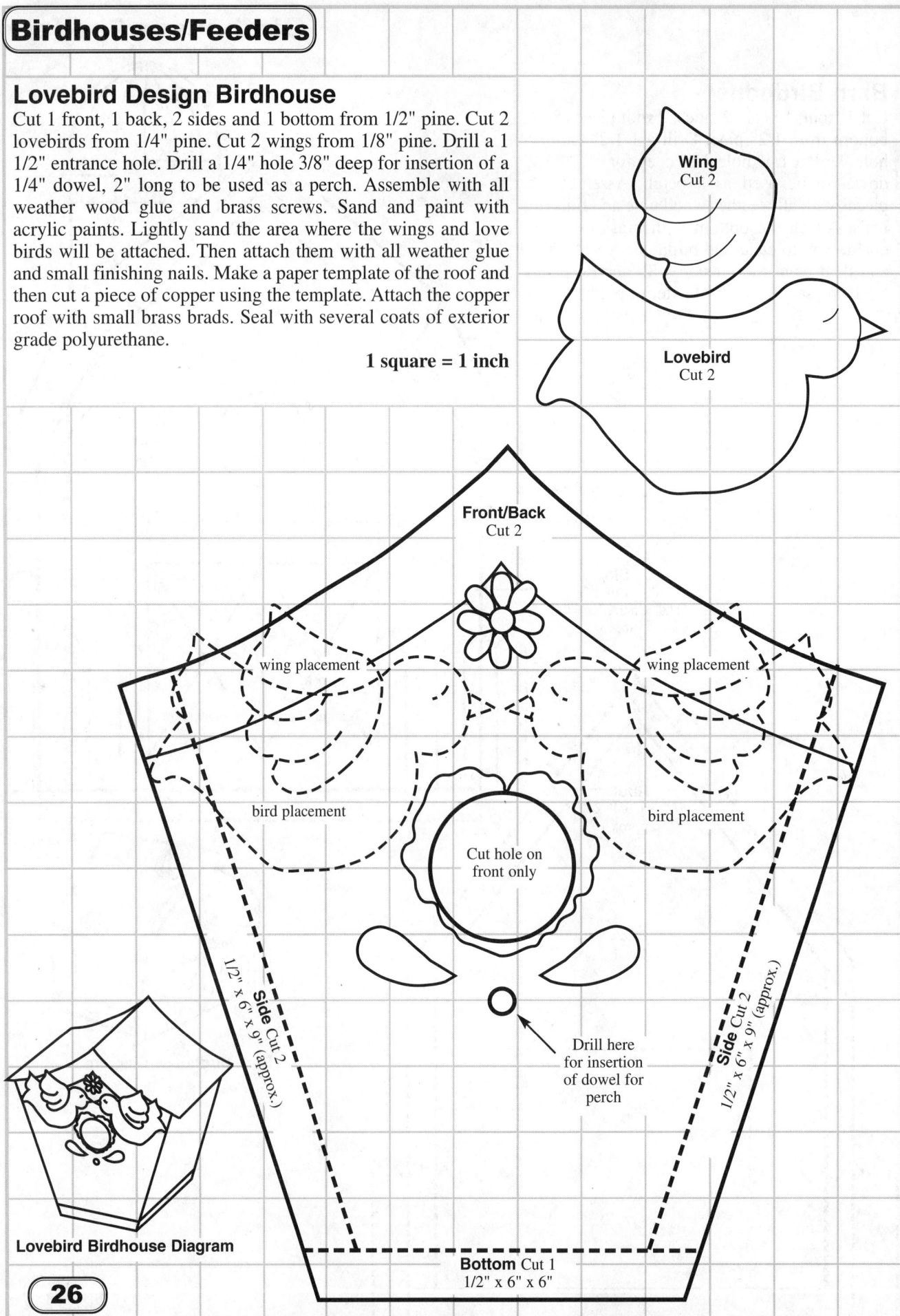

— CHAPTER THREE —
Children & Toys

Elizabeth And Jonathan Victorian Dress-Up Dolls

Cut the dolls from 3/4" wood. Cut a 3" x 5" base from 3/4" wood for each one. Cut the outfits from 1/8" wood. Sand all of the pieces. Attach the dolls to base from underneath using #10 wood screws. Paint all of the pieces, then seal using a spray or brush-on varnish. Glue 2, 8" long 1/8" wide ribbons to the back of the neck of each outfit to allow a bow to be tied paper-doll style.

Actual Size

Elizabeth
Victorian Dress-Up Doll

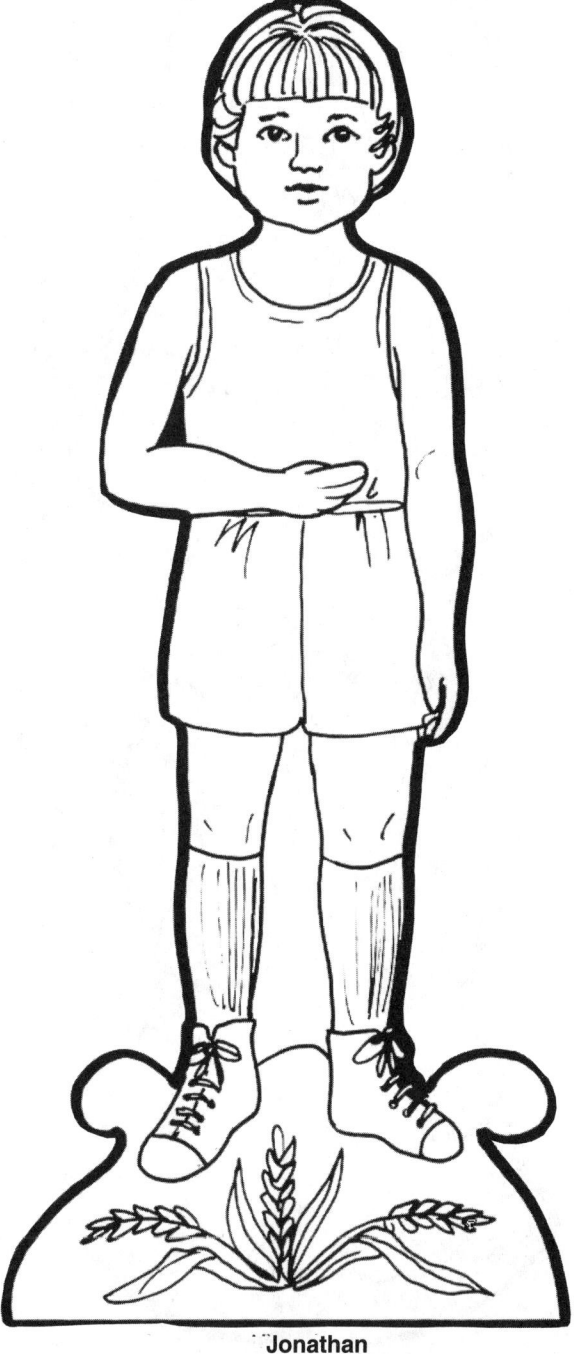

Jonathan
Victorian Dress-Up Doll

Children/Toys

Sunday Best

Play Suit

At the Beach

Going to Grandma's

Time For Bed

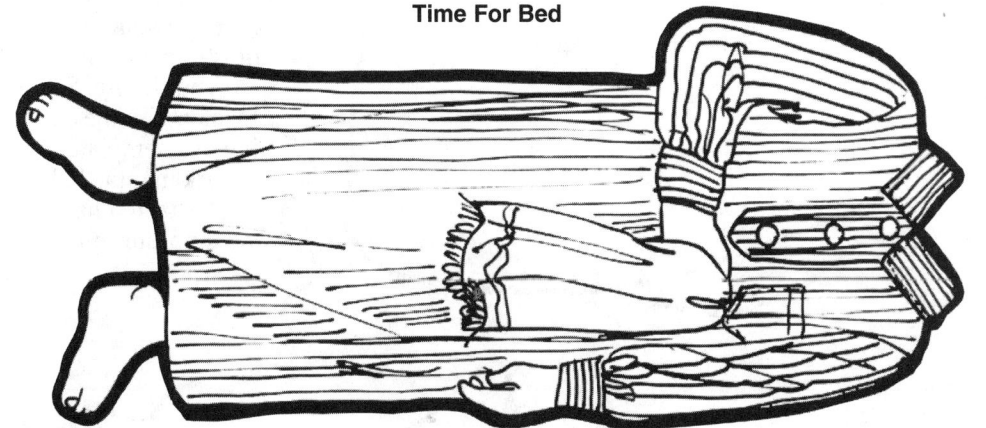

29

Children/Toys

"Three Little Kittens Lost Their Mittens" Plaque

Never lose your mittens again. Hang them and the wooden decorative mittens on the shoulder hooks. Cut the plaque and mittens from 1/2" wood. Sand well. Paint and seal using acrylics. Insert brass shoulder hooks in places marked with an "X". Tie raffia to the wooden mittens and hang from a hook.

1 square = 1 inch

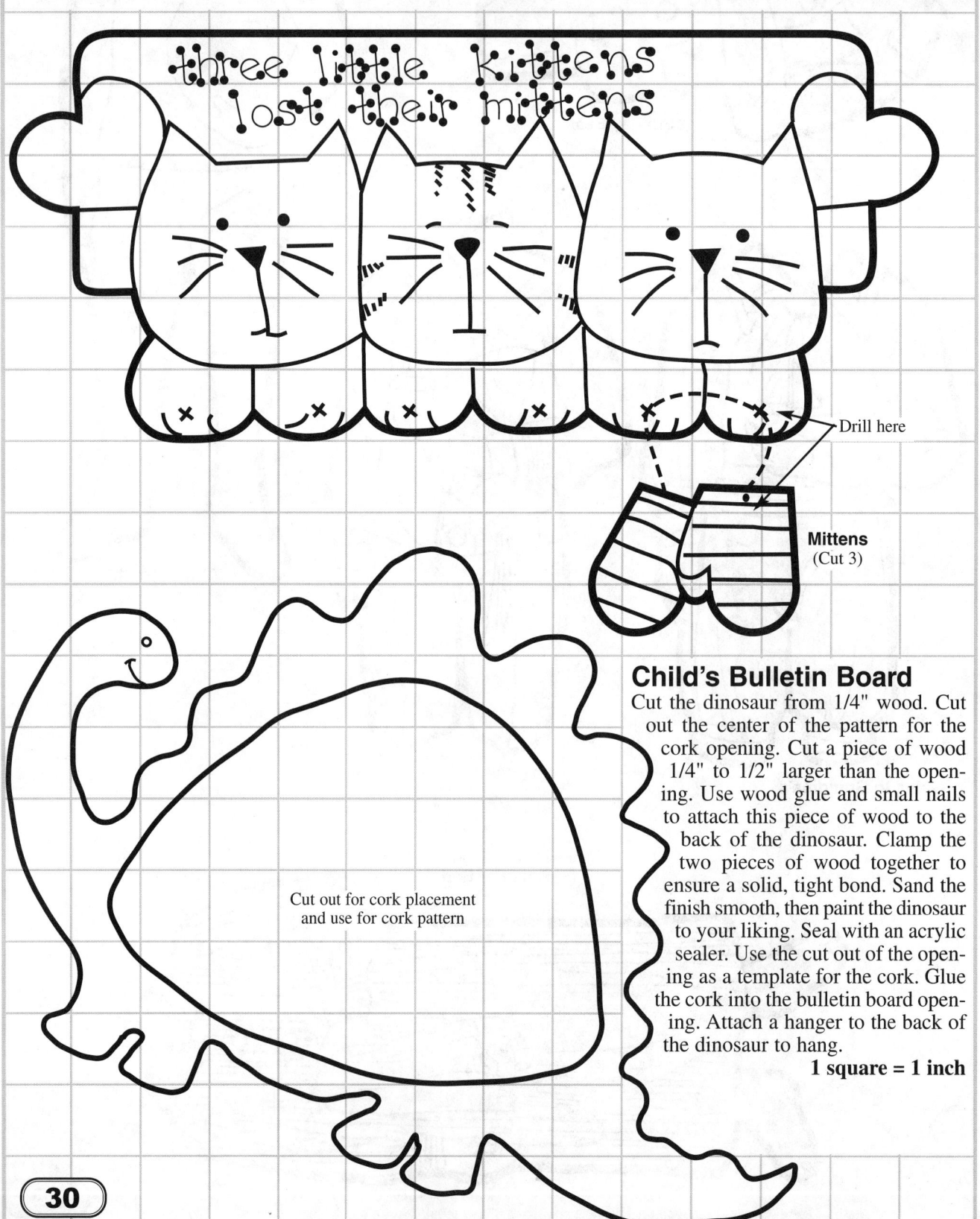

Mittens (Cut 3)

Drill here

Cut out for cork placement and use for cork pattern

Child's Bulletin Board

Cut the dinosaur from 1/4" wood. Cut out the center of the pattern for the cork opening. Cut a piece of wood 1/4" to 1/2" larger than the opening. Use wood glue and small nails to attach this piece of wood to the back of the dinosaur. Clamp the two pieces of wood together to ensure a solid, tight bond. Sand the finish smooth, then paint the dinosaur to your liking. Seal with an acrylic sealer. Use the cut out of the opening as a template for the cork. Glue the cork into the bulletin board opening. Attach a hanger to the back of the dinosaur to hang.

1 square = 1 inch

Children/Toys

3-D "Two By Two" Book End

Cut 1 back piece (entire pattern), one 6 1/2" x 4" base and two sets of waves from 1/4" wood. Cut 1 ark and 2 giraffes from 1/2" wood. Sand all of the pieces. Paint the front and sides of the pieces with acrylic paints. Attach all of the pieces with glue and finishing nails. Seal with a coat of acrylic spray or brush-on varnish.

Actual Size

"Two by Two" Bookend Diagram

Children/Toys

Child's Bear Chair

Cut the entire pattern from 3/4" pine board which is free of knots or at least has only a few small knots. Sand all the pieces. Attach together with glue. Countersink 2" flathead drywall screws for strength. Glue plugs into the holes. Sand the chair again. Sand the plugs flat. Stain the chair using water based walnut stain. Outline the arms, claws on the paws and smile with dark brown paint. Paint the ears and snout light tan, the nose black, the bow bright red, the eyes white and black with a little white glint in the black of each eye. Seal the chair with brush on acrylic lacquer.

1 square = 1 1/2 inches

Bear Chair Diagram

Bear Chair Back
(Cut 1)

Seat placement

32

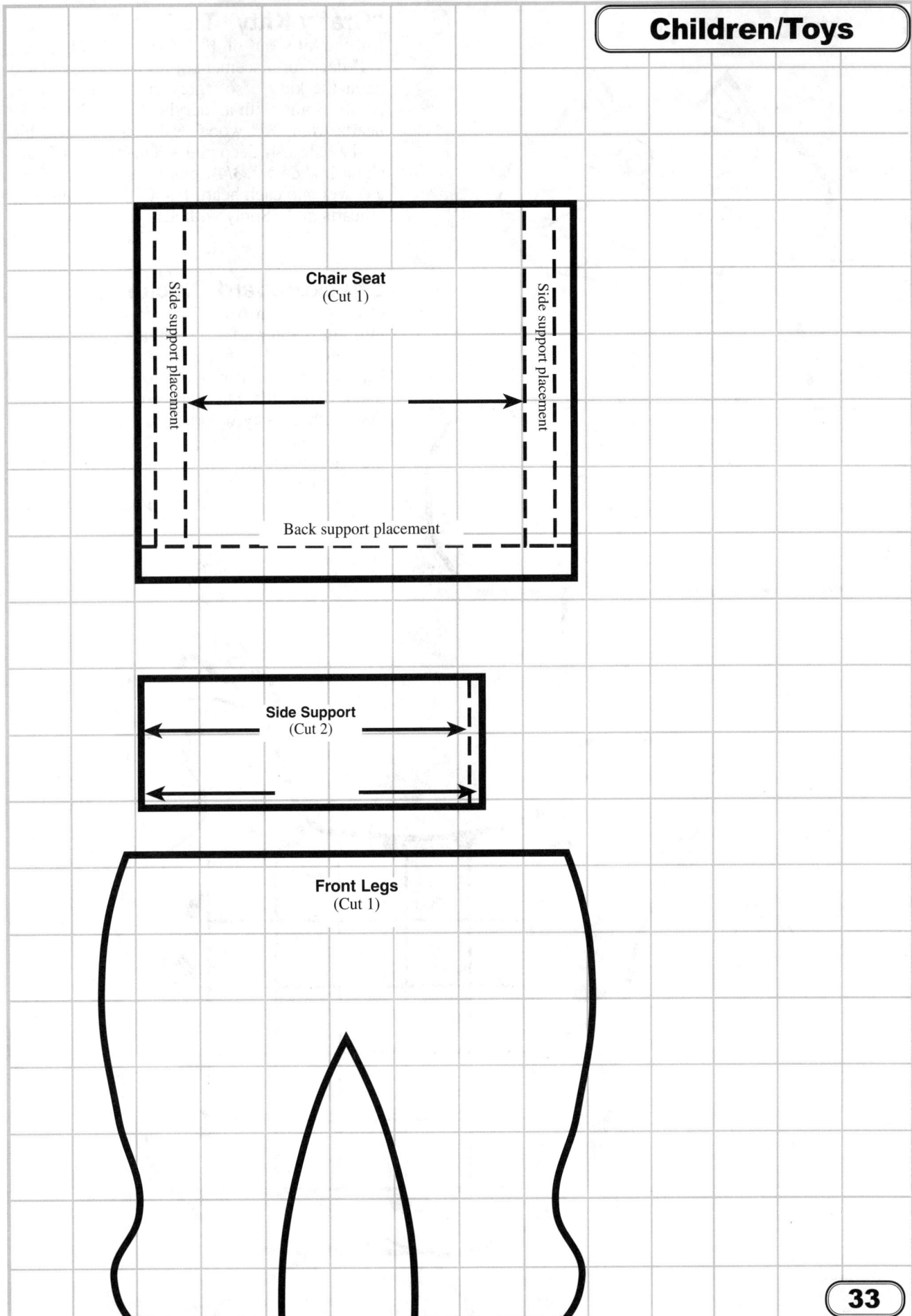

Children/Toys

Hearts (Cut 9)

Drill 1/4" hole here

Drill 1/4" hole at each circle

"Crafty Kitty" Tic-Tac-Toe

Cut the kitty out of 1" wood. Drill 1/4" holes, 1/4" deep for placement of heart pegs. Sand and paint the kitty a soft grey color using acrylic paints. Spray with an acrylic sealer. Cut out 10 hearts from 1/2" wood. Using a 1/4" drill bit, drill a hole 1/4" deep in the center of each heart. Cut a 1/4" dowel, 3/4" long for each heart. Glue a dowel into each heart. Paint 5 hearts blue and 5 hearts pink. Spray with acrylic sealer.

1 square = 1 inch

Checkerboard Chicken

Cut the chicken from 3/4" wood. Drill a hole into the center of 12 purchased, unfinished checkers. Drill a hole through the chicken's beak for insertion of a 10" long piece of jute. Sand. Paint the checkerboard and checkers. Seal with a spray or brush on acrylic varnish. When the checkers have dried, string them onto the jute. Insert the jute into the chicken's beak and tie in a bow.

1 square = 1 inch

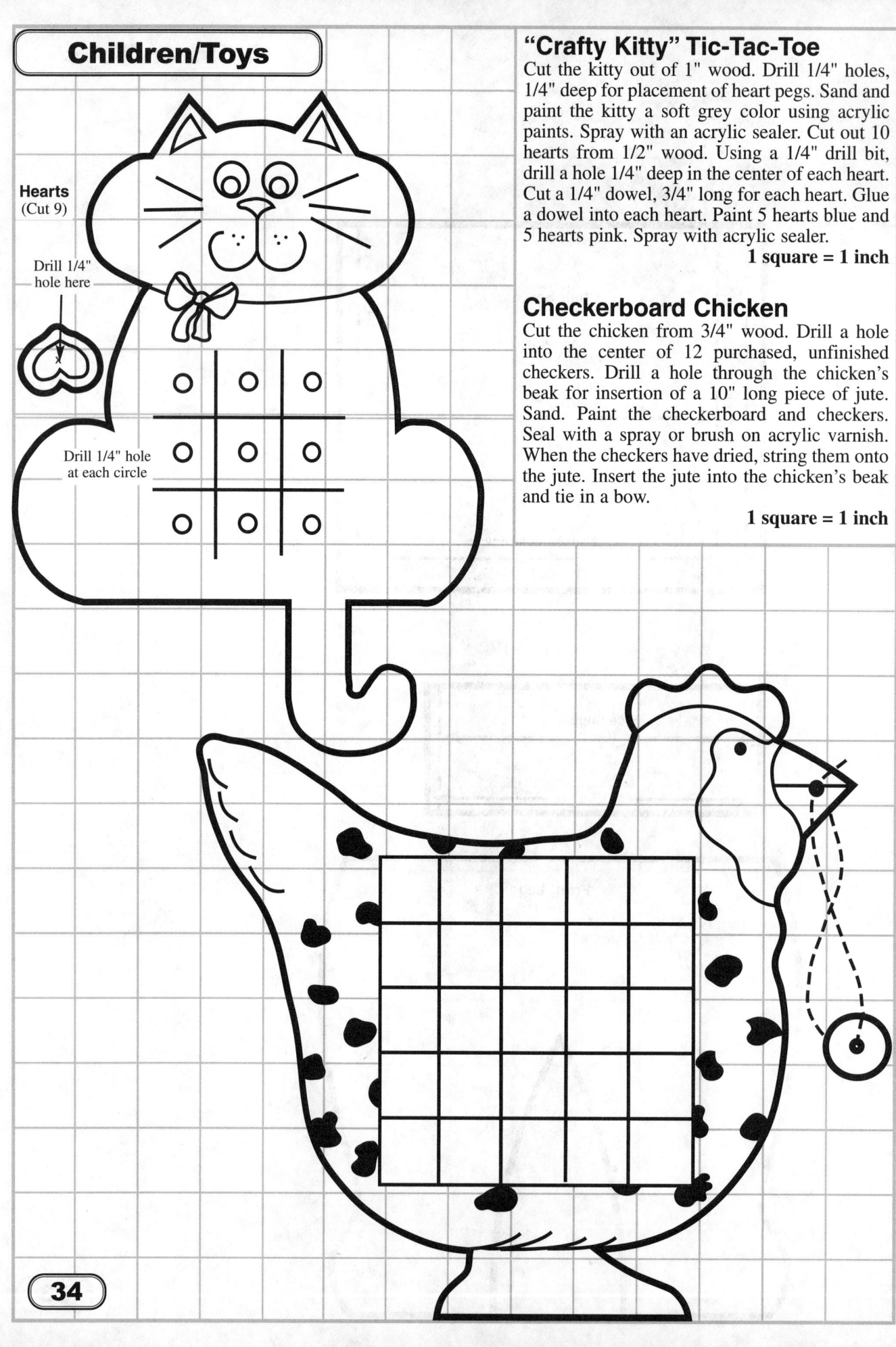

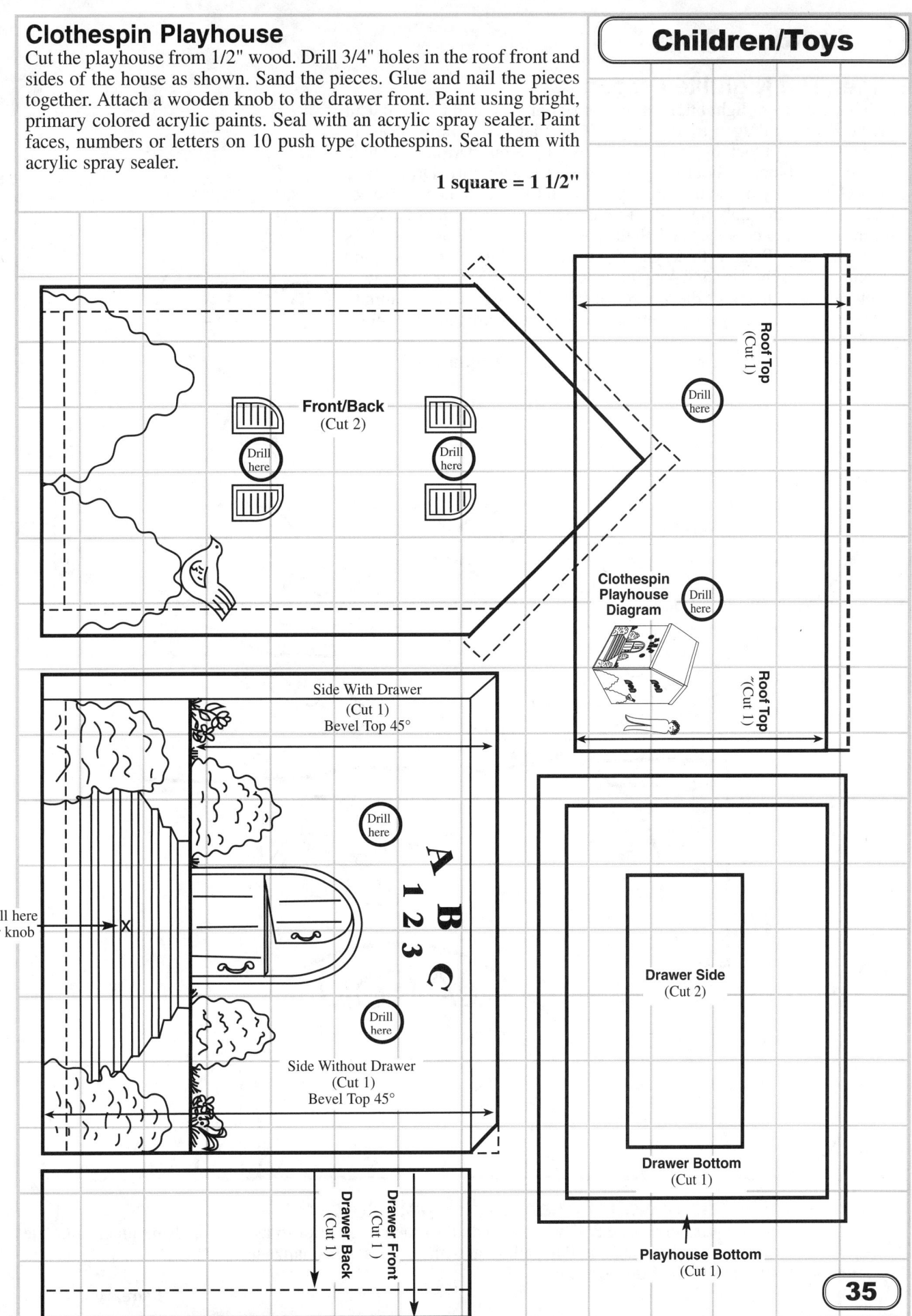

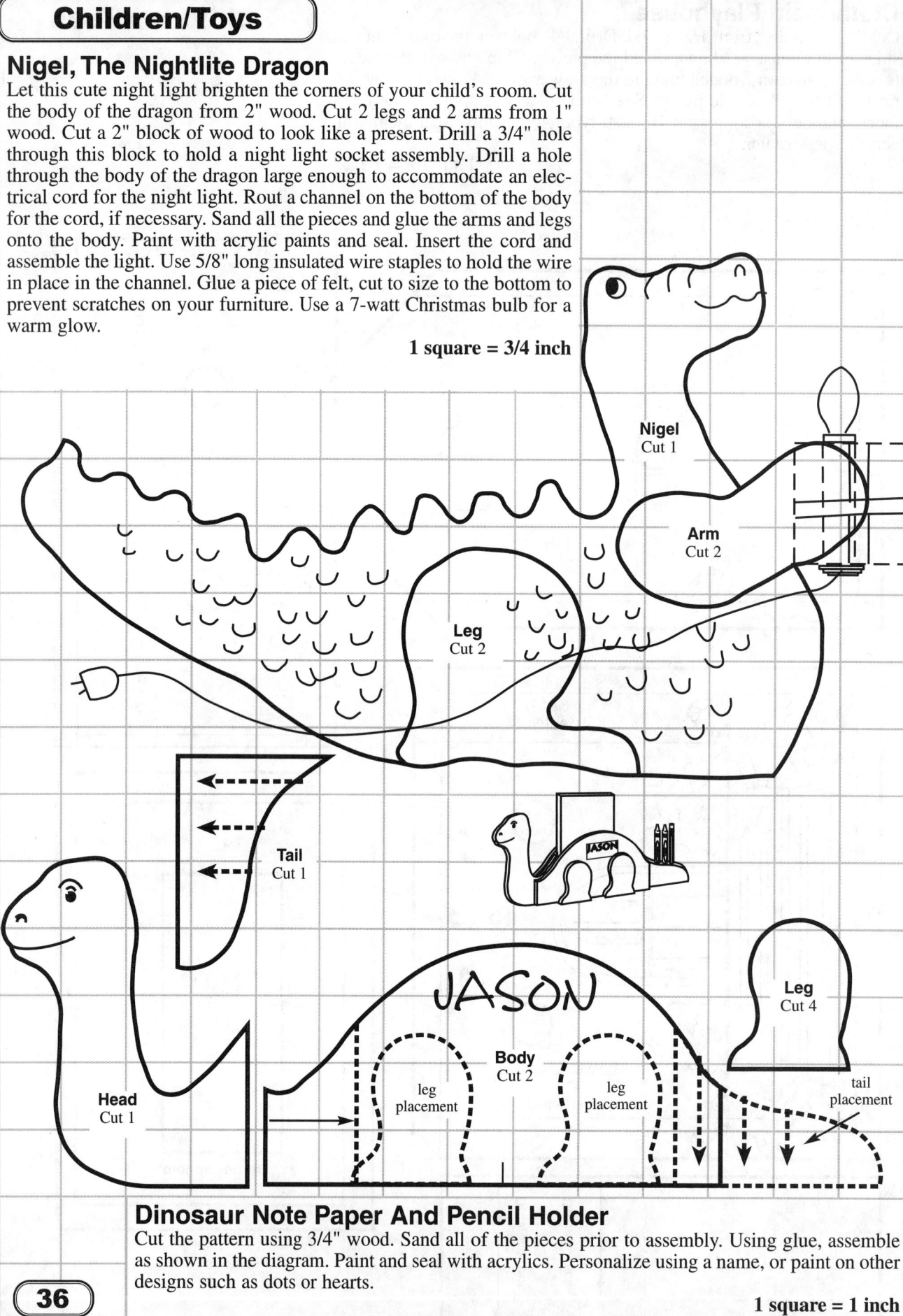

Children/Toys

Toddler-Sized Rocking Horse

We have found the most durable wood for this project to be yellow pine.

Materials Needed
(All sizes are rough cut sizes)

Description	Dimension (in inches)	Qty
Mid-Section	2" x 15" x 34"	1
Side-Section	2" x 15" x 26"	2
Saddle	1" x 4" x 8"	2
Front Legs	2" x 5" x 18"	2
Back Legs	2" x 7" x 20"	2
Rockers	2" x 9 1/2" x 48"	2
Braces	1" x 2 1/2" x 14"	5

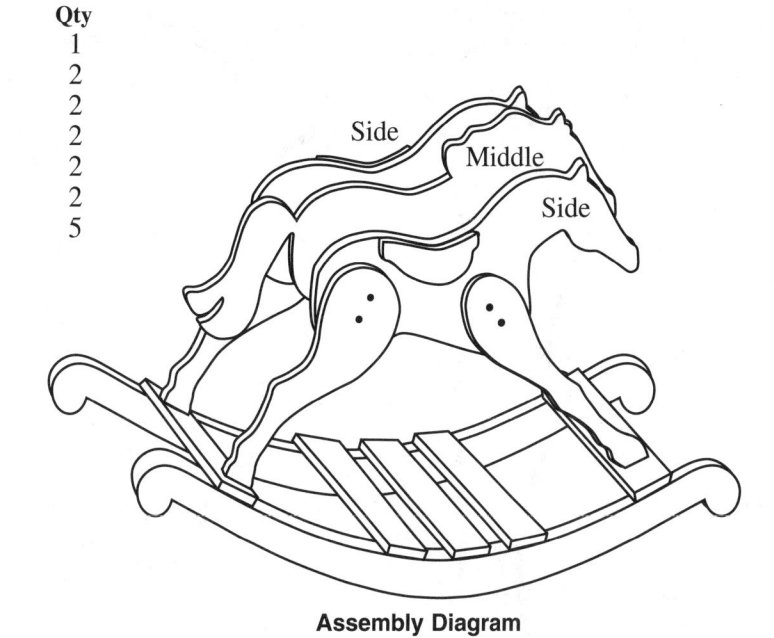

Miscellaneous
1 Handle Dowel, 3/4" x 9 1/2"
4 Alignment Dowels, 1/4" x 5 1/2"
Miscellaneous screws
Wood glue

Tools Required
Band Saw
Router with a round-over bit
Sander
Clamps
Drill

Assembly Diagram

Assembly Instructions for Rocking Horse

Make scale drawings of all pieces. Trace onto wood. Position all pattern pieces to avoid any unusually rough spots or knots. Cut out all pieces, using the round-over router bit on exposed edges. Sand each piece until smooth.

1) Drill a 3/4" hole in the head of the middle section for the handle dowel.
2) Drill 1/4" holes completely through the middle section and the two side sections for the dowels.
3) Fit all these parts together to make sure they are properly cut and drilled. When complete, use glue and 1/4" wooden dowels to build the body section. Clamp tightly until completely dry. See pattern details and assembly diagram.
   Note: When using screws to help hold the body together, make sure that the screws will be hidden behind the front and rear legs.
4) Drill 1/4" holes through the four leg pieces per pattern detail.
5) Test fit legs to the assembled body and when complete, use glue and alignment dowels to attach the front and rear legs to the body section.
   Note: Two #10, 2 1/2" counter-sunk wood screws in each leg, covered by a wooden button, make the horse much more stable.
6) Attach the seat to the completed body section using glue and #10, 2" screws.
7) Center the front feet onto a 1" x 2 1/2" x 14" brace. Attach with glue and a #10, 2" screw into the bottom of each brace and through the foot.
8) Repeat above instruction for the back feet.
9) Set the completed body on the rockers and reposition the body back and forth on the rockers until the unit is balanced.
10) Attach the front and rear braces to the rockers using #10, 1 1/2" screws.
11) Center the remaining braces on the rockers to provide a step and attach using #10, 1 1/2" screws.
12) Use your favorite primer, stain, and finish to taste.

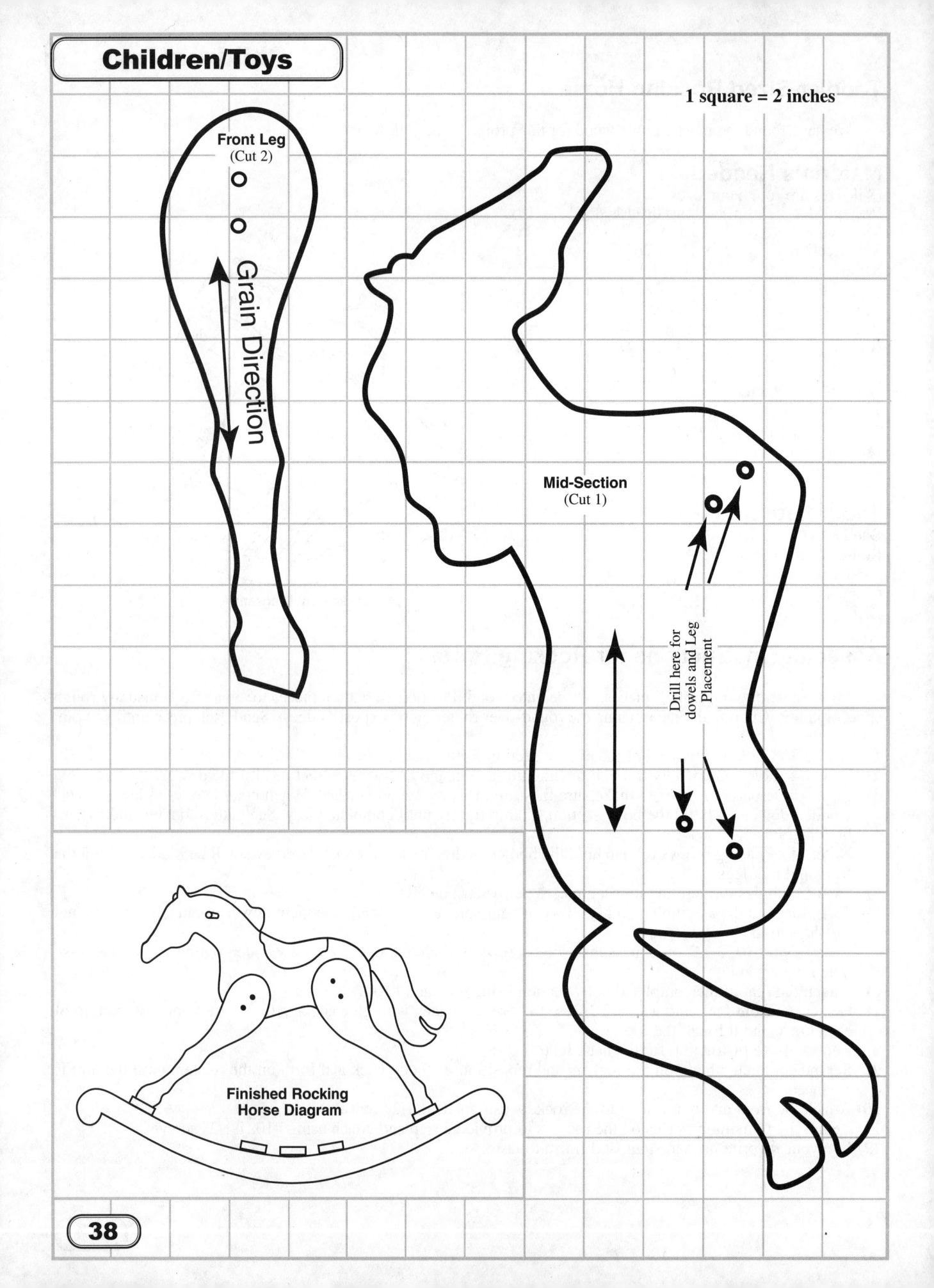

Children/Toys

1 square = 2 inches

Front Leg
(Cut 2)

Grain Direction

Mid-Section
(Cut 1)

Drill here for dowels and Leg Placement

Finished Rocking Horse Diagram

38

1 square = 2 inches

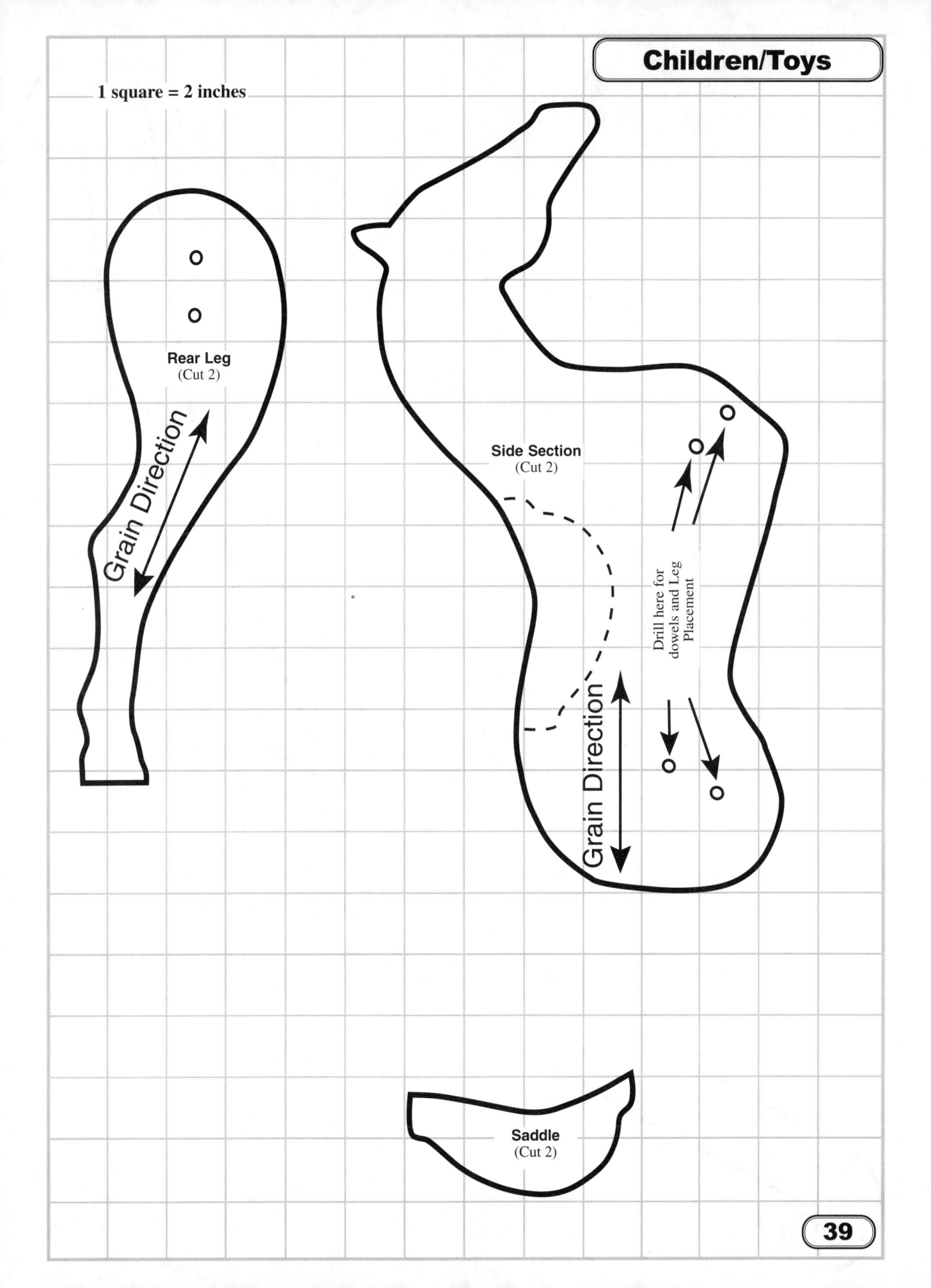

Children/Toys

Rear Leg
(Cut 2)

Grain Direction

Side Section
(Cut 2)

Grain Direction

Drill here for dowels and Leg Placement

Saddle
(Cut 2)

39

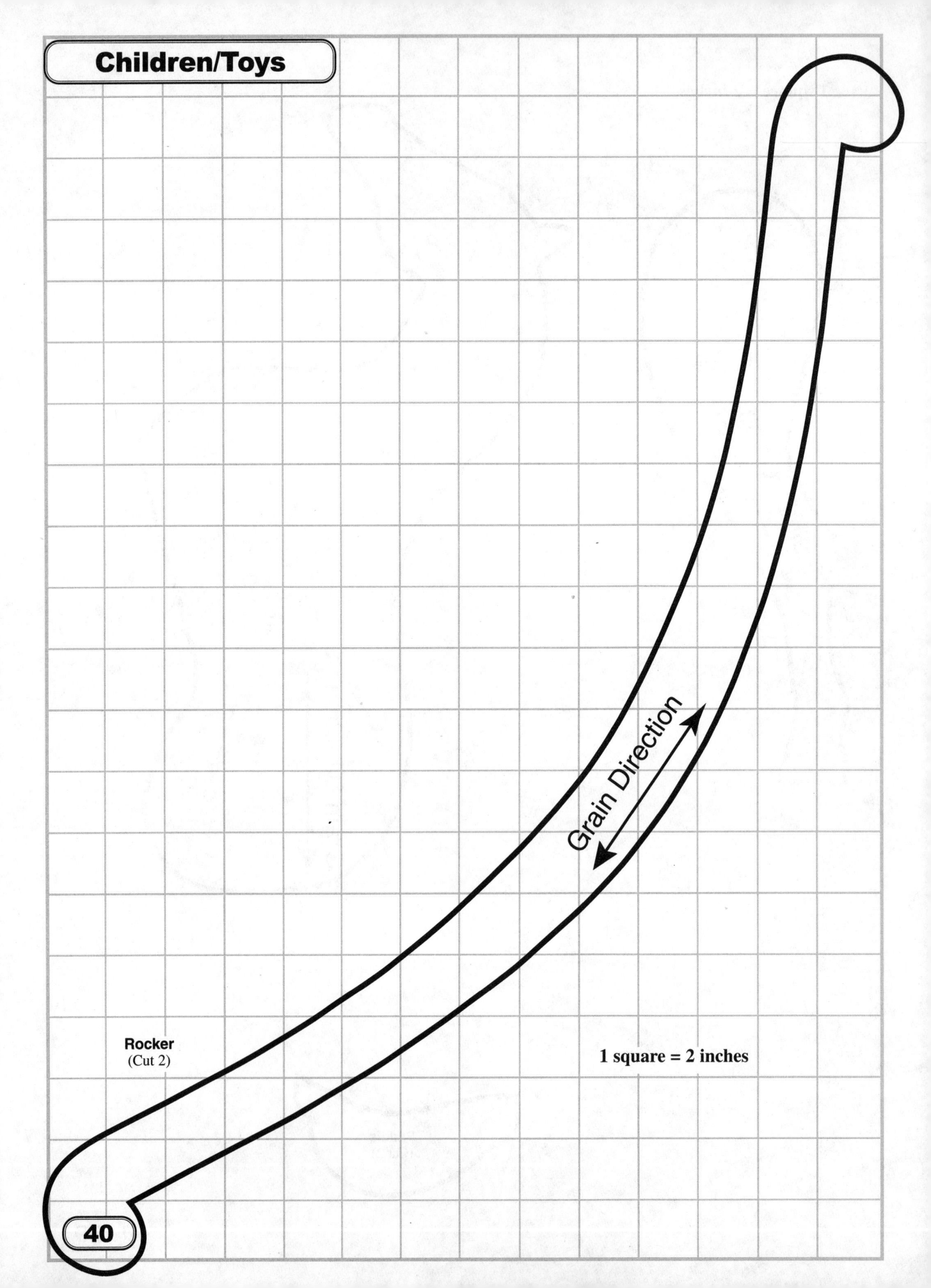

Children/Toys

Rocker
(Cut 2)

Grain Direction

1 square = 2 inches

40

Dinorockasaurus

Children/Toys

- Check all components for splits and cracks
- Use a 1/4 inch round-over router bit on all exposed edges
- Sand all surfaces to remove any splinters

The most critical pieces in the rocking horse are the rockers. These two pieces should be cut out at the same time. Clamp two pieces of wood together before cutting and keep them clamped until the bottom and top surfaces have been sanded. Make sure rockers are cut along the grain for added strength. Test the rockers as a unit to ensure a smooth rocking action.

We have found the most durable wood for this project to be yellow pine.

Materials Needed
(All sizes are rough cut sizes)

Description	Dimension (in inches)	Qty
Body Middle	2" x 19 1/4" x 28"	1
Body Sides	2" x 11 1/4" x 22 1/2"	2
Seat	1" x 9" x 9"	1
Seat Back	1" x 4 1/2" x 6 1/4"	1
Front Legs	2" x 5 3/4" x 10 3/4"	2
Back Legs	2" x 6 3/4" x 10"	2
Rockers	2" x 11 3/4" x 45"	2
Braces	1" x 4" x 12"	3
Leg Braces	1" x 6" x 12"	2

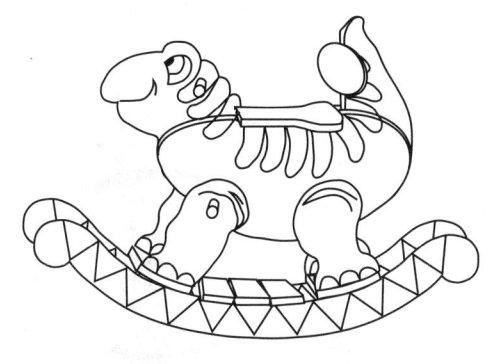

Rocking Dinosaur Diagram

Miscellaneous
2 Handle Dowels, 3/4" x 10"
4 Alignment Dowels, 1/4" x 6"
Miscellaneous screws
Wood glue
3/4" Masking tape

Tools Required
Band Saw
Router with a round-over bit
Sander
Clamps
Drill

Assembly Instructions
Enlarge all pieces. Trace onto wood. Position all pattern pieces to avoid any unusually rough spots or knots. Cut out all pieces, using the round-over router bit on exposed edges. Sand each piece until smooth.

1) Drill a 3/4" hole completely through the head for the handle dowel. Drill 1/4" holes through the two body sides and the middle body section for the alignment dowels.
2) Fit all these parts together to make sure they are properly cut and drilled. When complete, use glue and 1/4" wooden dowels to build the body section. Clamp tightly until completely dry.

Note: When using screws to help hold the body together, make sure that the screws will be hidden behind the front and rear legs.

3) Drill the 1/4" holes in the back side only of the four leg pieces.
4) Test fit legs to the assembled body and when complete, use glue and alignment dowels to attach the front and rear legs to the body section.

Note: Two #10, 2-1/2" counter-sunk wood screws in each leg, covered by a wooden button, make the horse much more stable.

5) Attach the seat to the completed body section using glue and #10, 2" screws.
6) Center the front feet onto a 1" x 4" x 12" brace. Attach with glue and a #10, 2" screw in each foot.
7) Repeat above instruction for the back feet.
8) Drill a 3/4" hole completely through the front legs, sides and body for the foot rest dowel. Set the completed body on the rockers and reposition the body back and forth on the rockers until the unit is balanced.
9) Attach the front and rear leg braces to the rockers using #10, 1-1/2" screws.
10) Center the remaining braces on the rockers to provide a step and attach using #10, 1-1/2" screws.
11) Using acrylic paints, color it to your tastes. Seal with a clear acrylic finish.

Children/Toys

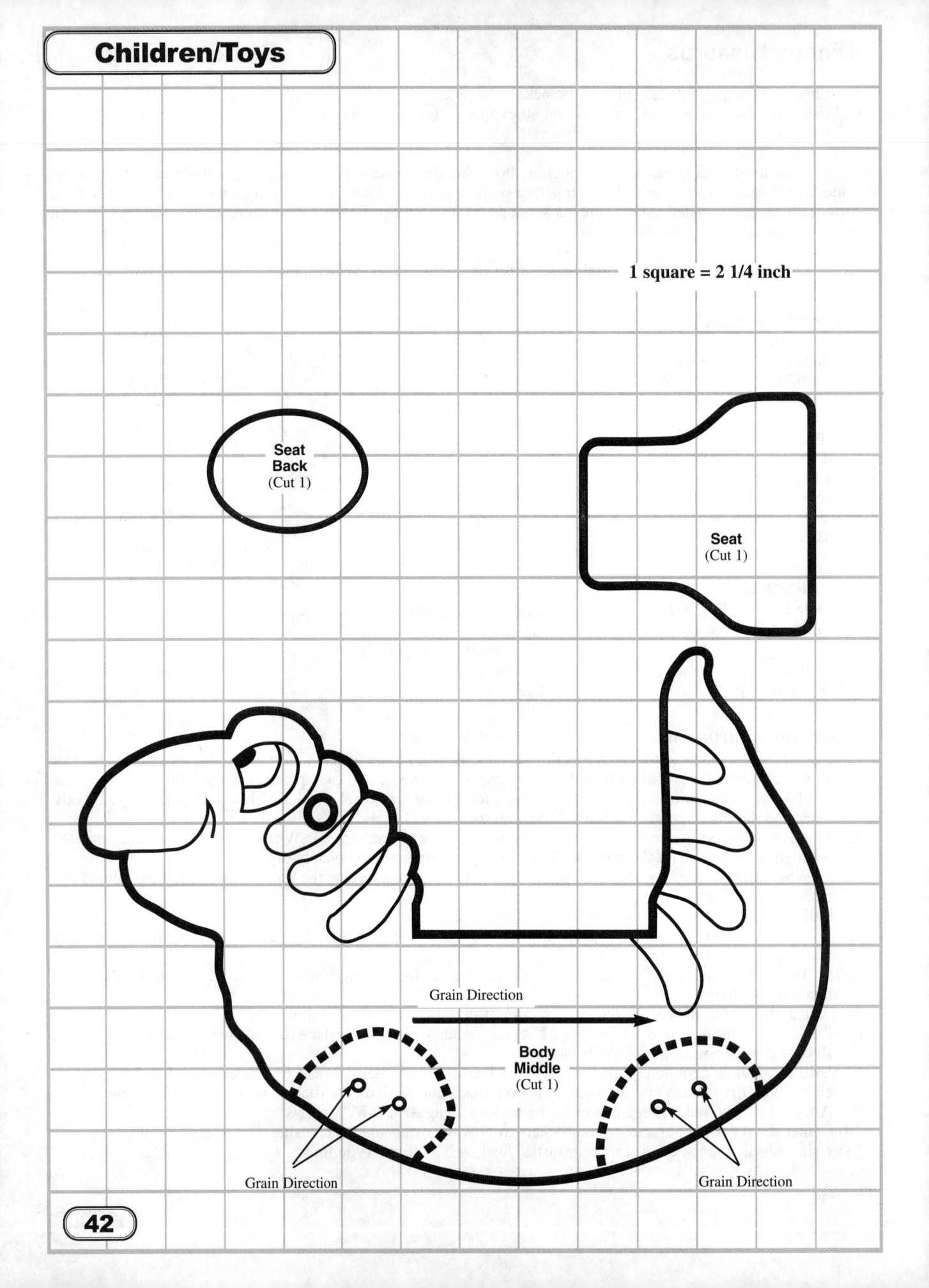

1 square = 2 1/4 inch

Seat Back (Cut 1)

Seat (Cut 1)

Grain Direction

Body Middle (Cut 1)

Grain Direction

Grain Direction

42

1 square = 2 1/4 inches

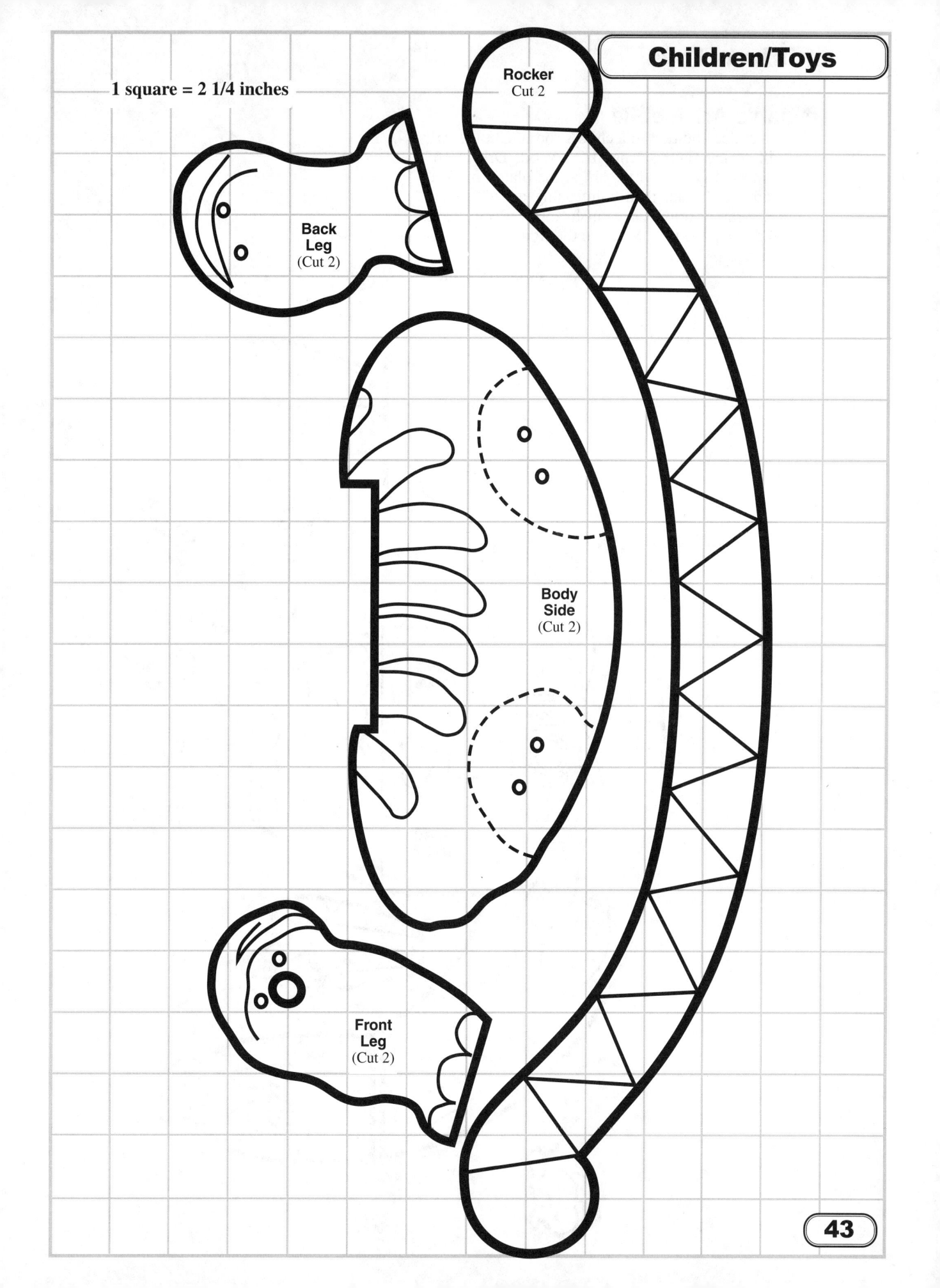

Rocker Cut 2

Back Leg (Cut 2)

Body Side (Cut 2)

Front Leg (Cut 2)

Children/Toys

43

Children/Toys

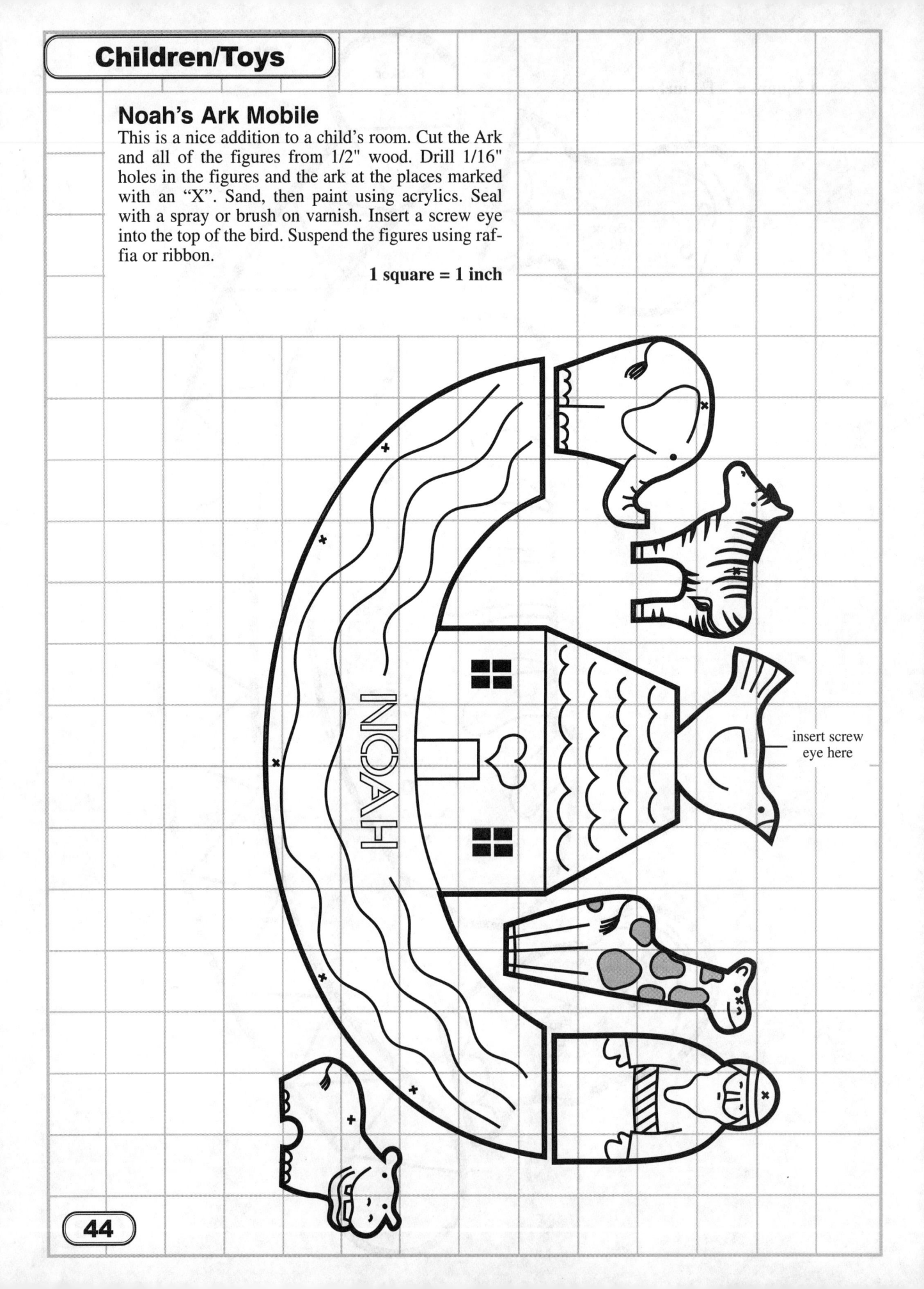

Noah's Ark Mobile

This is a nice addition to a child's room. Cut the Ark and all of the figures from 1/2" wood. Drill 1/16" holes in the figures and the ark at the places marked with an "X". Sand, then paint using acrylics. Seal with a spray or brush on varnish. Insert a screw eye into the top of the bird. Suspend the figures using raffia or ribbon.

1 square = 1 inch

insert screw eye here

Children/Toys

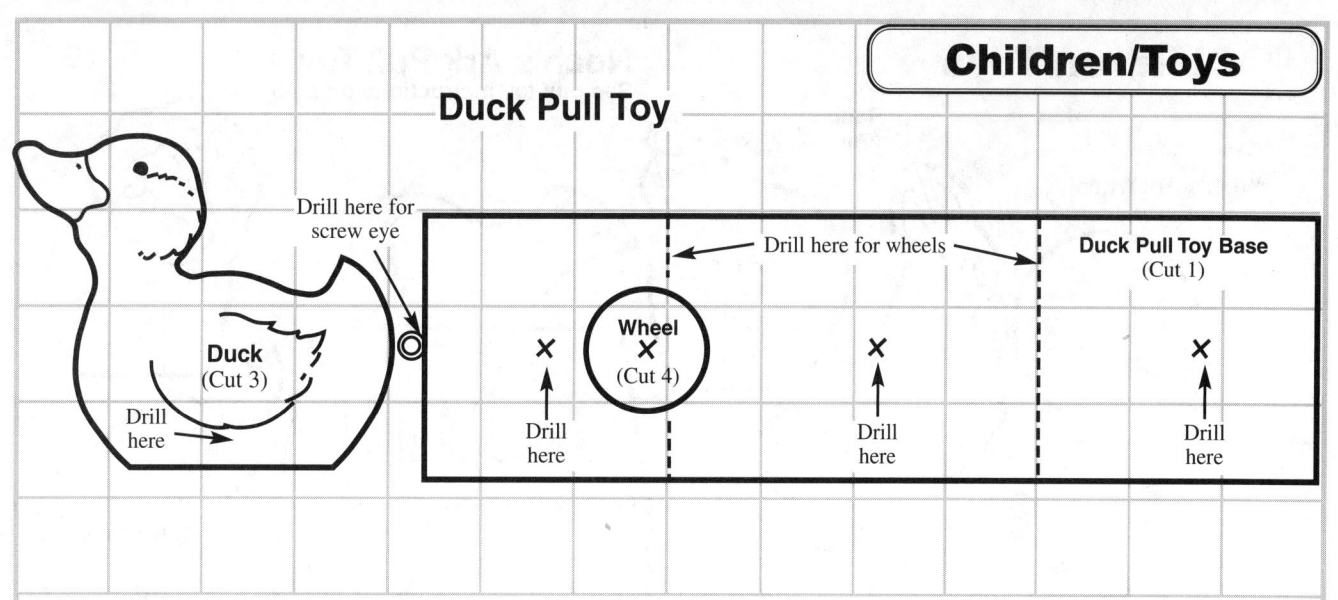

Duck Pull Toy

Duck (Cut 3)

Drill here for screw eye

Drill here

Drill here for wheels

Duck Pull Toy Base (Cut 1)

Wheel (Cut 4)

Drill here

Drill here

Drill here

Instructions For Pull Toys

Cut the base and other applicable patterns from 3/4" wood. Cut 4 wheels from 1/2" wood or purchase toy wheels from a craft or wood shop. You may use a dowel as an axle. Drill two holes through the width of the pull toy base 1/32" larger than the dowel. In this case you should use a 1/4" dowel. The length of each dowel needs to be the width of the base plus the width of two wheels plus 1/4". Insert the dowels through the drilled holes and glue a wheel at each end. Drill 1/4" holes 1/2" deep for dowels in both the base at the places marked with an X and the bottom of the pieces to place on the platform. Glue a 1" long 1/4" dowel into the bottom of each animal. Pre-drill a hole for a screw eye at the one end of the platform. Sand all the pieces. Paint and seal with acrylics.

1 square = 1 inch

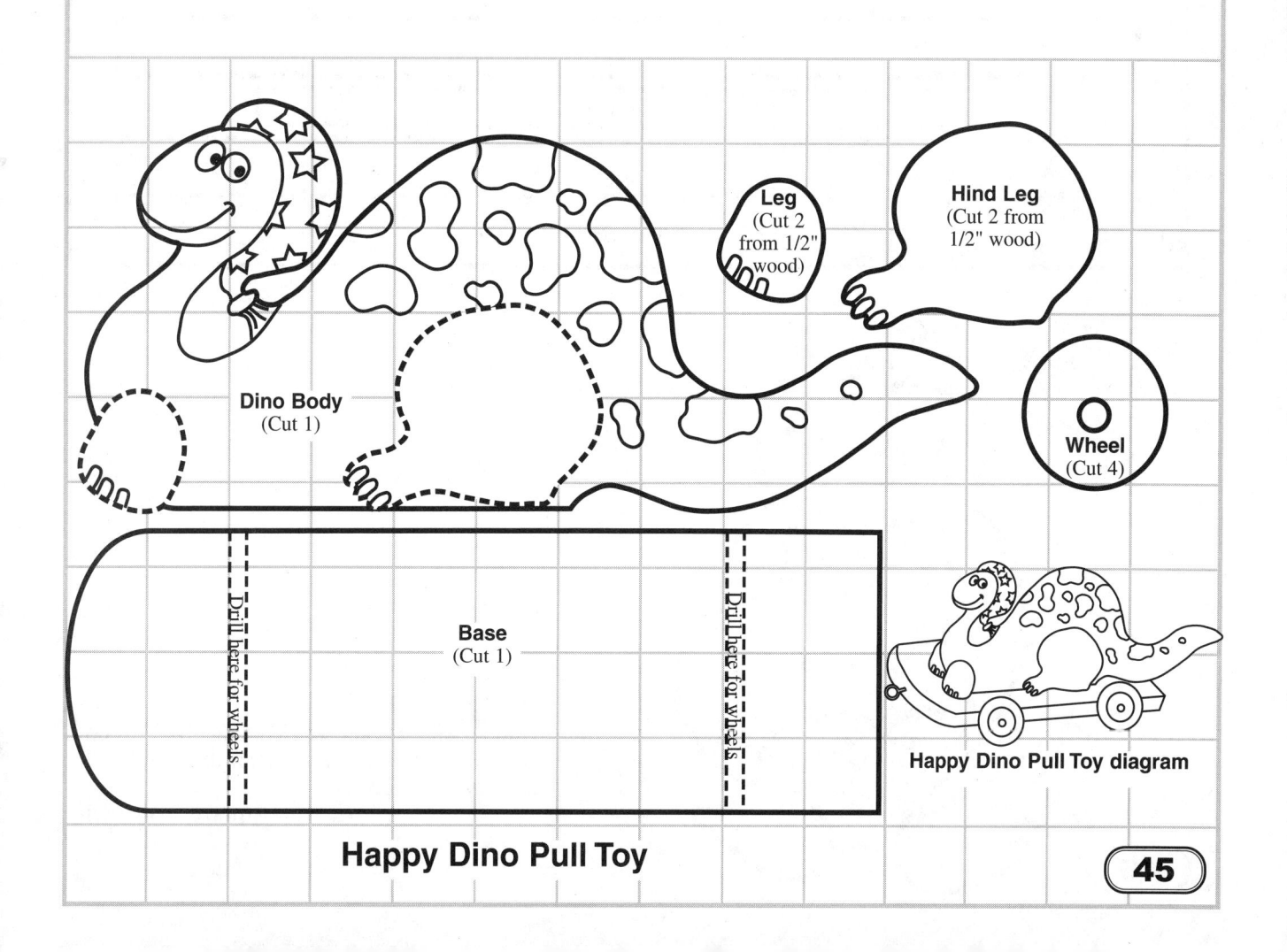

Dino Body (Cut 1)

Leg (Cut 2 from 1/2" wood)

Hind Leg (Cut 2 from 1/2" wood)

Wheel (Cut 4)

Base (Cut 1)

Drill here for wheels

Drill here for wheels

Happy Dino Pull Toy diagram

Happy Dino Pull Toy

45

Children/Toys

Noah's Ark Pull Toy
See pull toy instructions on p.45

Noah's Ark Wheel (Cut 4)

Rabbit (Cut 2)

Bear (Cut 2)

Lion (Cut 2)

Giraffe (Cut 2)

Monkey (Cut 2)

Elephant (Cut 2)

Noah and His Ark (Cut 1) from 1/2" wood

Noah's Ark Pull Toy Base (Cut 1)

Ark placement

Drill at each "X"

Drill here for wheels

Drill here for screw eye

Frog Puzzle
Cut around darker lines using 1/4" wood. Sand lightly. Paint or use craft dye. Seal with an acrylic sealer.

1 square = 3/4 inch

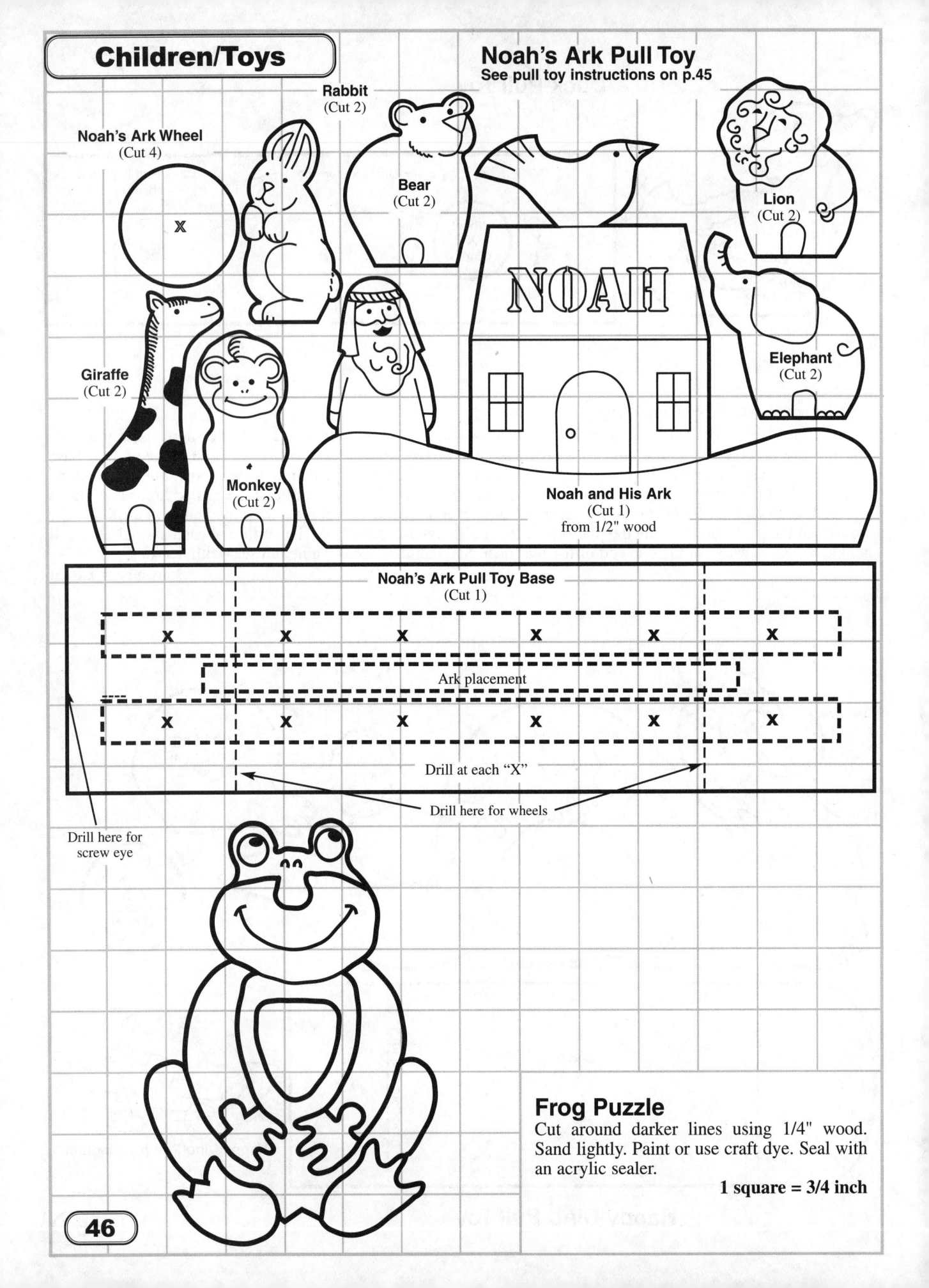

46

Children/Toys

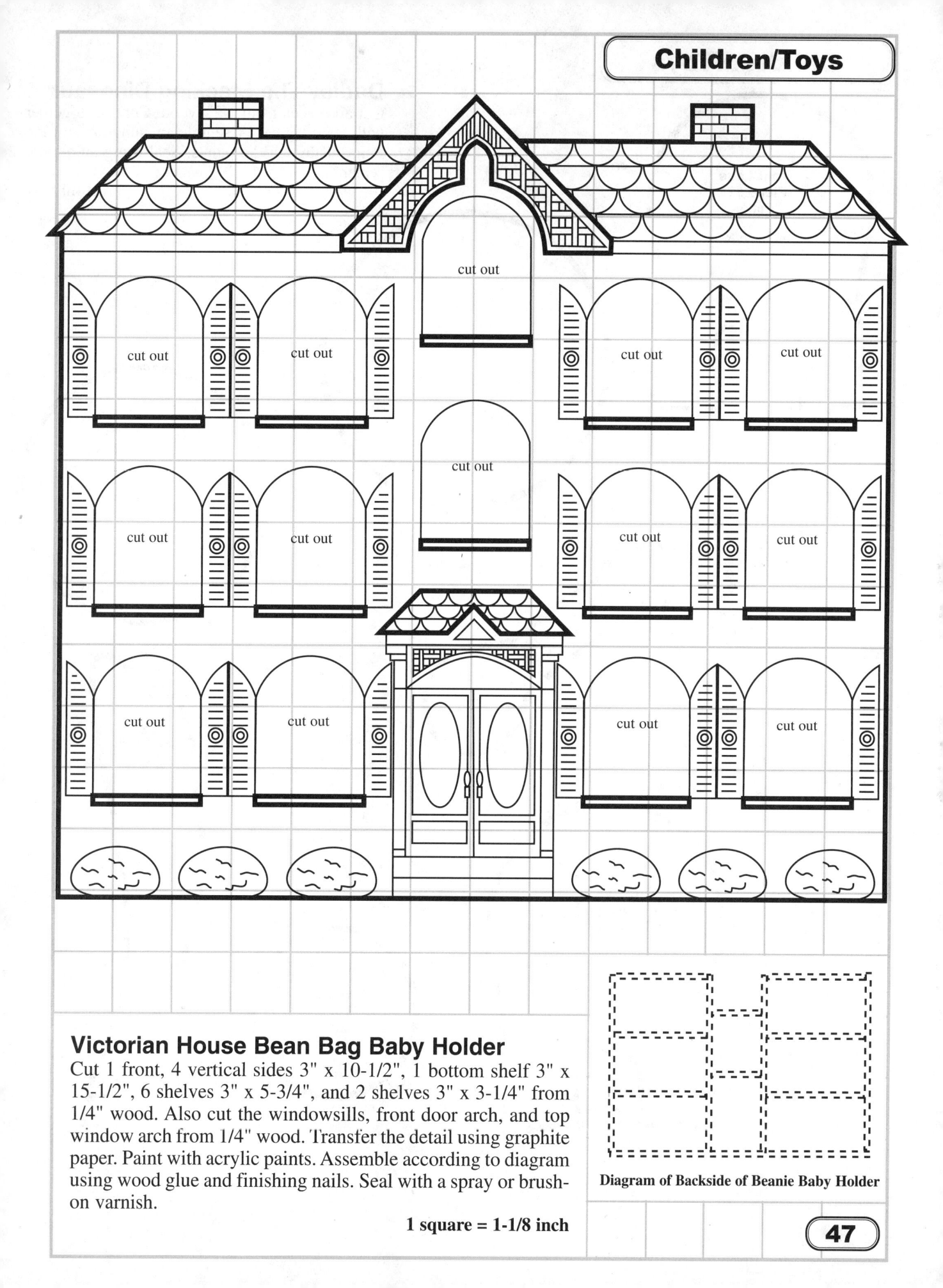

Victorian House Bean Bag Baby Holder

Cut 1 front, 4 vertical sides 3" x 10-1/2", 1 bottom shelf 3" x 15-1/2", 6 shelves 3" x 5-3/4", and 2 shelves 3" x 3-1/4" from 1/4" wood. Also cut the windowsills, front door arch, and top window arch from 1/4" wood. Transfer the detail using graphite paper. Paint with acrylic paints. Assemble according to diagram using wood glue and finishing nails. Seal with a spray or brush-on varnish.

1 square = 1-1/8 inch

Diagram of Backside of Beanie Baby Holder

47

Children/Toys

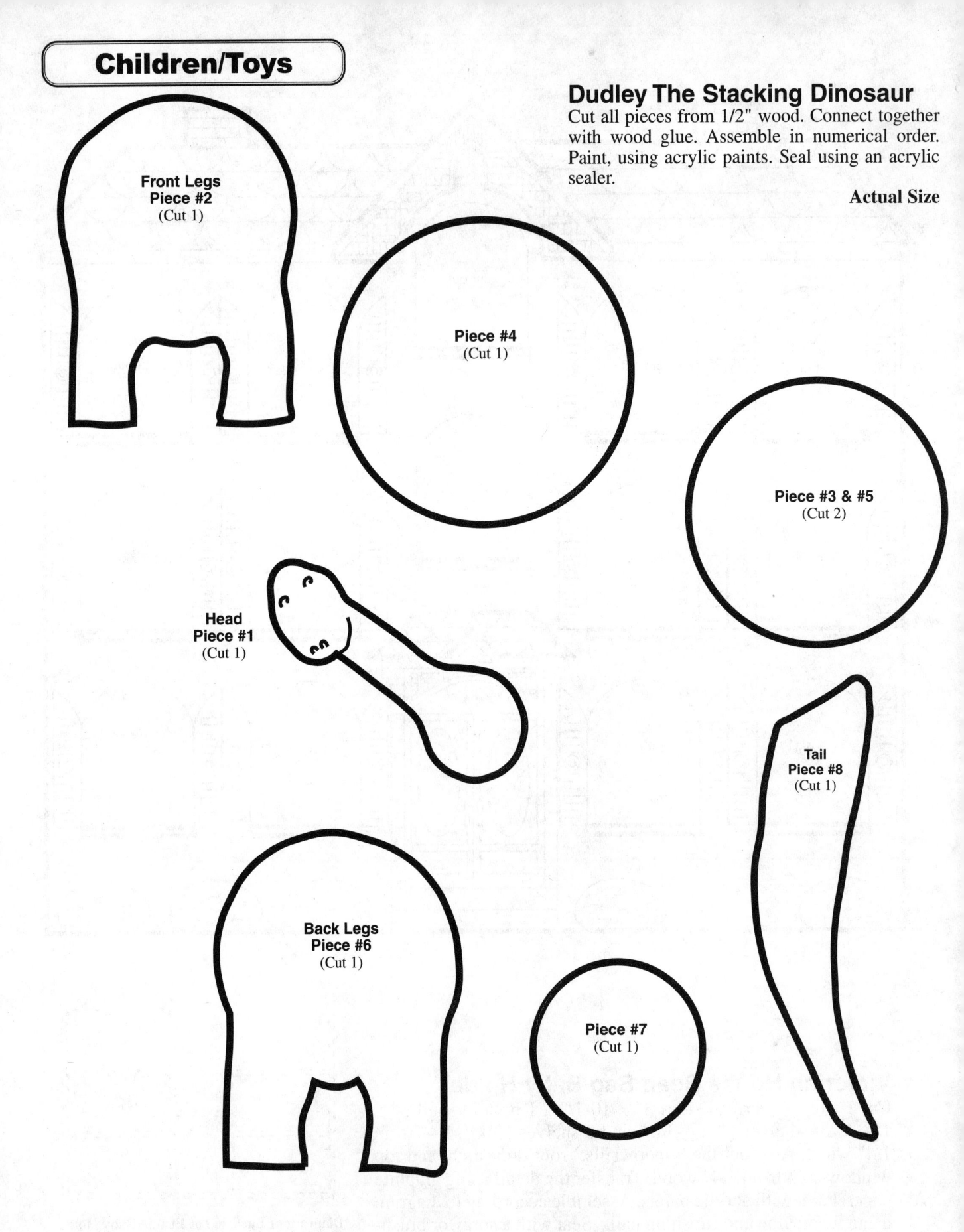

Front Legs Piece #2 (Cut 1)

Piece #4 (Cut 1)

Piece #3 & #5 (Cut 2)

Head Piece #1 (Cut 1)

Tail Piece #8 (Cut 1)

Back Legs Piece #6 (Cut 1)

Piece #7 (Cut 1)

Dudley The Stacking Dinosaur

Cut all pieces from 1/2" wood. Connect together with wood glue. Assemble in numerical order. Paint, using acrylic paints. Seal using an acrylic sealer.

Actual Size

— CHAPTER FOUR —
Clocks

Clock Bird (Cut 1)

Tower Front/Back (Cut 2)

Clock Bird (Cut 1)

Sunflower and Bird Clock Diagram

Drill here for dowel

Clock front placement

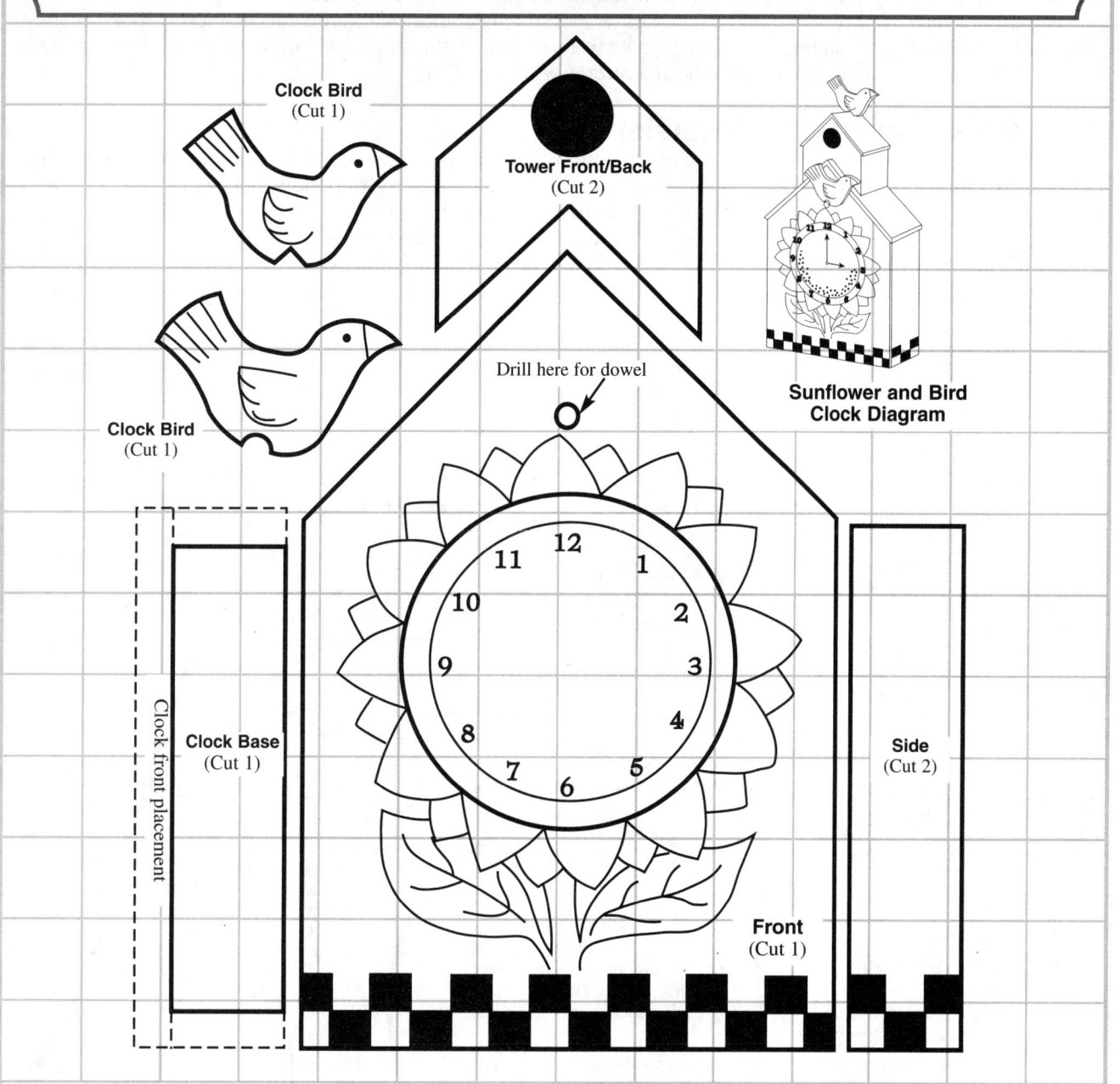

Clock Base (Cut 1)

Side (Cut 2)

Front (Cut 1)

Bird and Sunflower Clock

Cut the pieces as specified for this enchanting clock. Drill a 3/8" hole for a 3/8" dowel 2" long. Sand all of the pieces lightly. Assemble using small finishing nails and glue. There is no back piece to this clock. Adjusting the clockworks will be easier this way. Paint with acrylic paints. Paint the sunflower face and numbers onto the front of the clock or purchase numerals with your clock works. Seal with a brush-on or spray varnish.

1 square = 1 inch

Materials List:
- 1 clock front from 1/2" wood, cut as shown in the pattern
- 1 base 5 3/4" x 1 1/2" from 1/2" wood
- 2 sides 6 1/2" x 1 1/2" from 1/2" wood
- 2 roof pieces 6" x 2" from 3/8" wood, bevel both ends at 45° angles
- 2 tower pieces cut as shown in the pattern, one for the front and one for the back from 3/8" wood
- 2 sides 2 1/8" x 3/4" from 3/8" wood,
- 2 roof pieces 3" x 1 3/4" from 3/8" wood, bevel both ends at 45° angles
- 2 birds cut from 3/8" wood

Clocks

Intarsia Instructions:
Intarsia involves cutting pieces of a pattern from varied wood for color and grain to give the piece interest. Or you can use a single kind of wood and paint it for a special appearance. After you cut the pieces, round the top edges either by routing or sanding. Cut a back piece from 1/8" stock the size of the original pattern. Paint or stain the round edged pieces and glue to the back in a puzzle or mosaic form.

"A Stitch in Time" Clock (Intarsia)
Cut 1 clock back pattern from 1/8" wood. Cut the pattern again from 3/4" wood, following the darker cut lines. Drill the area for a clock insert. An extra-thin clock insert may be purchased from the Klockit Company, P.O. Box 636, Lake Geneva, WI 53147 (1-800-556-2548) <www.klockit.com>. Round the edges of the 3/4" pieces. Paint with acrylic paints. Glue the pieces onto the 1/8" back. Spray with a clear spray or brush-on acrylic varnish. Insert a piece of brass wire through the eye of the needle. Dab a bit of glue into the eye to keep the wire from coming out. Make small holes in the pincushion and then glue real needles and large ball-end pins into the holes. Install the clock works.

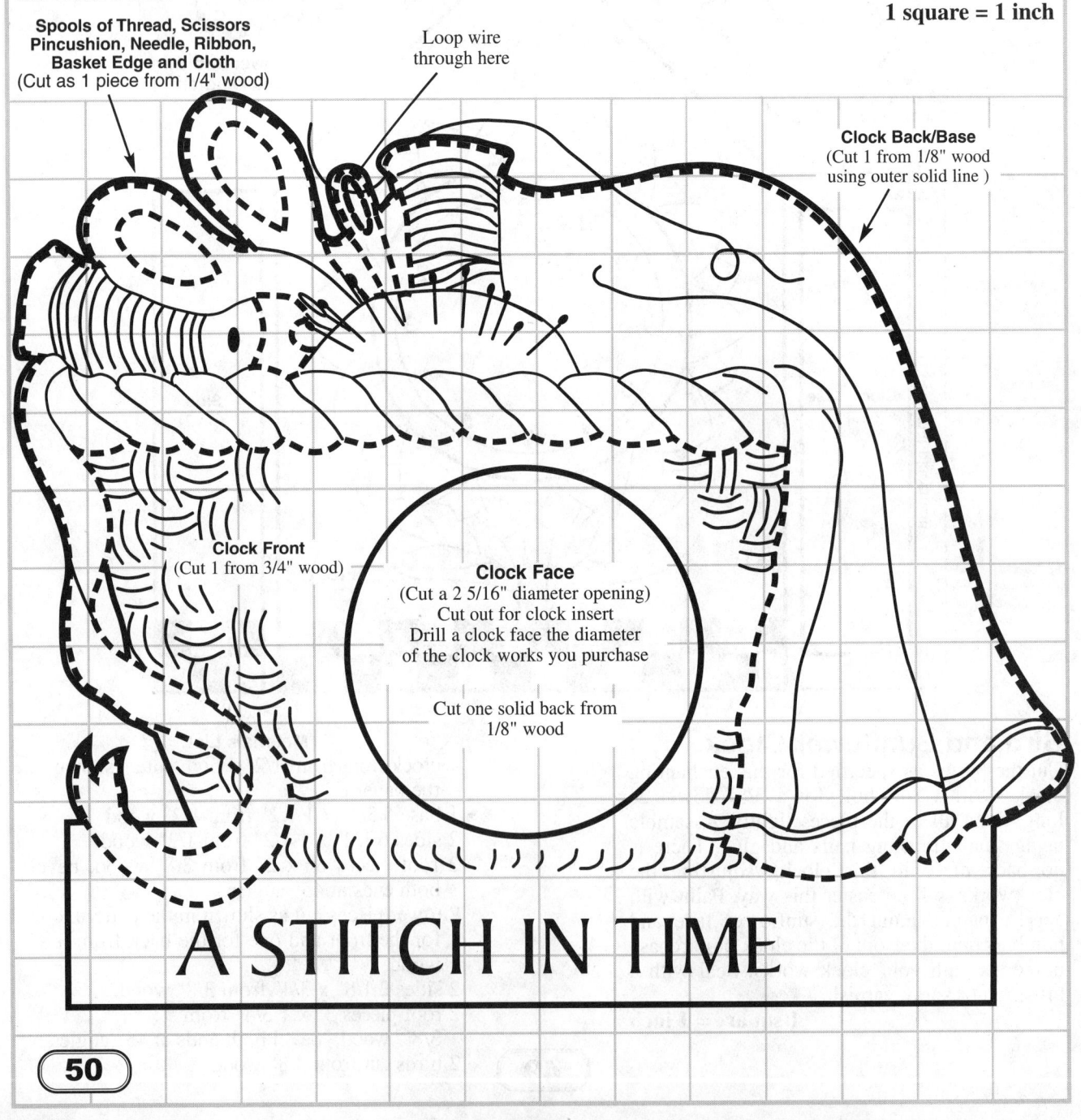

1 square = 1 inch

Spools of Thread, Scissors Pincushion, Needle, Ribbon, Basket Edge and Cloth
(Cut as 1 piece from 1/4" wood)

Loop wire through here

Clock Back/Base
(Cut 1 from 1/8" wood using outer solid line)

Clock Front
(Cut 1 from 3/4" wood)

Clock Face
(Cut a 2 5/16" diameter opening)
Cut out for clock insert
Drill a clock face the diameter of the clock works you purchase

Cut one solid back from 1/8" wood

A STITCH IN TIME

Clocks

Clock Face

Village (Cut 1)

CITY HALL

Tree (Cut 1)

PUBLIC LIBRARY

Shrub (Cut 1)

Tiny Village Clock Base (Cut 1)

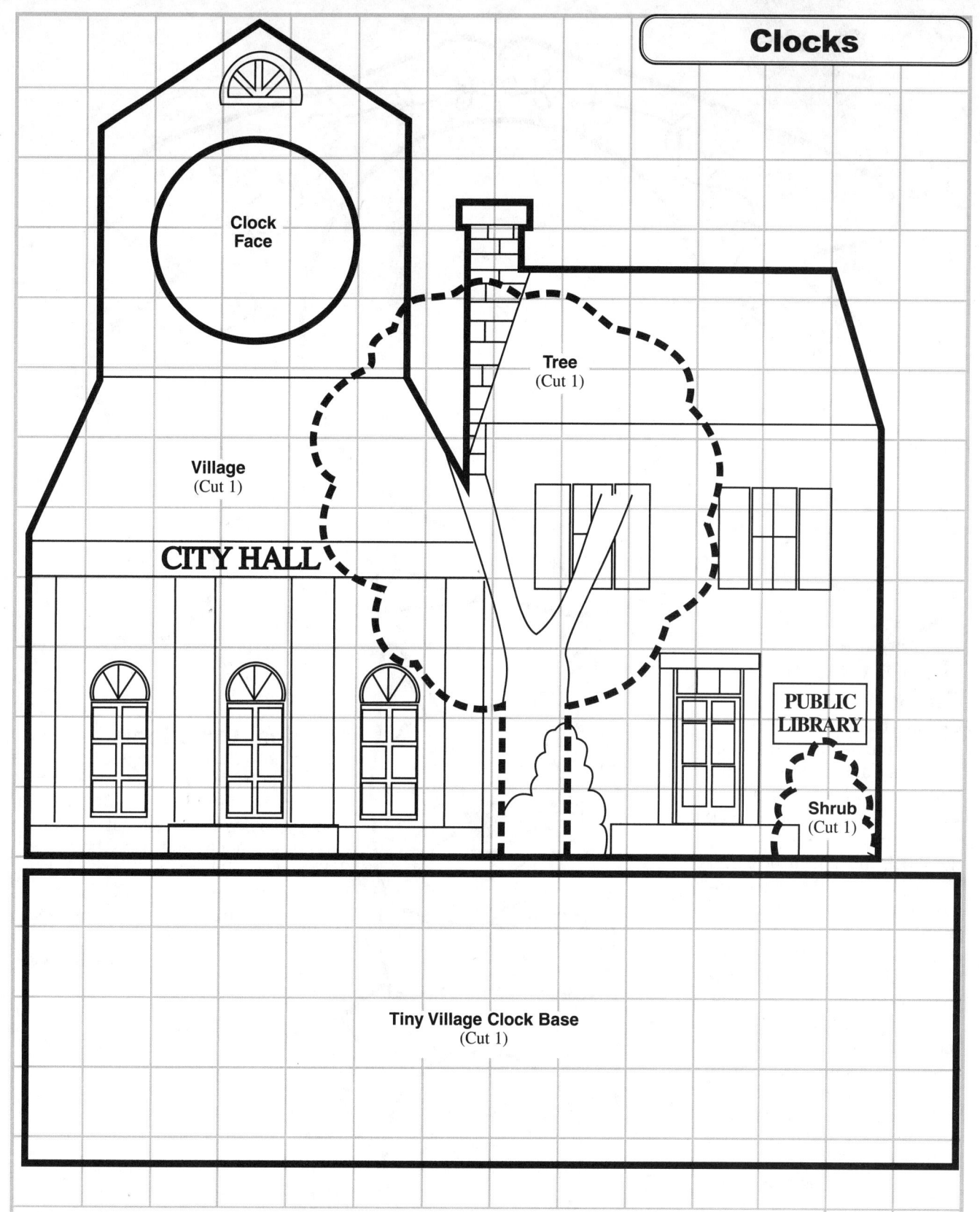

Tiny Village Clock

Cut 1 base and buildings from 1" wood. Cut the tree and shrub from 1/4" wood. Rout an area directly opposite the clock face on the back of the clock tower, large enough to accommodate battery operated clock works. Sand all of the pieces before assembly. Glue the buildings to the base and nail them from the bottom of the base for stability and strength. Paint the buildings, tree and shrub. Glue the tree and shrub to the base and buildings. Seal with an acrylic sealer. Attach a clock assembly to the city hall tower.

1 square = 1 inch

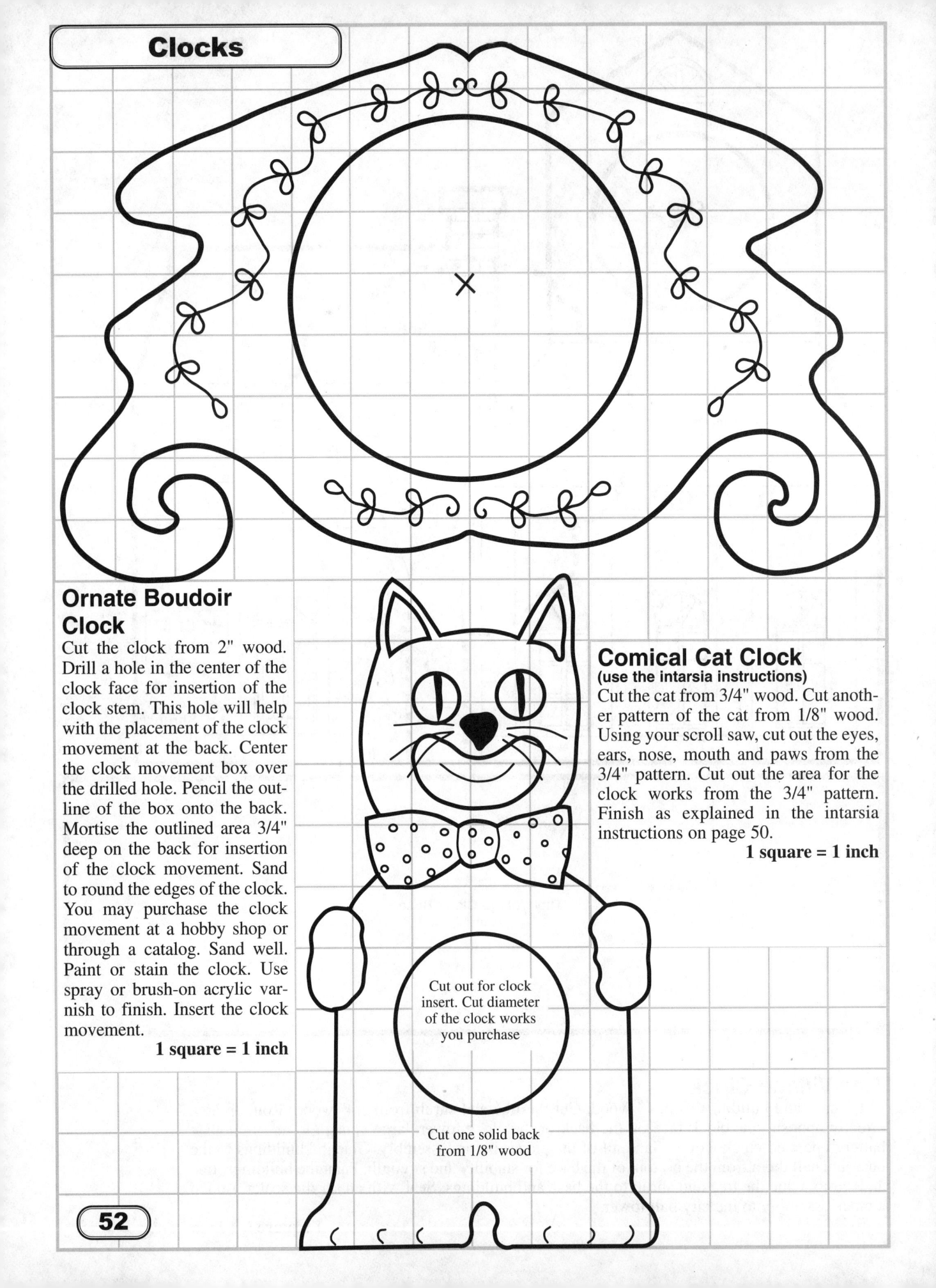

Clocks

Ornate Boudoir Clock

Cut the clock from 2" wood. Drill a hole in the center of the clock face for insertion of the clock stem. This hole will help with the placement of the clock movement at the back. Center the clock movement box over the drilled hole. Pencil the outline of the box onto the back. Mortise the outlined area 3/4" deep on the back for insertion of the clock movement. Sand to round the edges of the clock. You may purchase the clock movement at a hobby shop or through a catalog. Sand well. Paint or stain the clock. Use spray or brush-on acrylic varnish to finish. Insert the clock movement.

1 square = 1 inch

Comical Cat Clock
(use the intarsia instructions)

Cut the cat from 3/4" wood. Cut another pattern of the cat from 1/8" wood. Using your scroll saw, cut out the eyes, ears, nose, mouth and paws from the 3/4" pattern. Cut out the area for the clock works from the 3/4" pattern. Finish as explained in the intarsia instructions on page 50.

1 square = 1 inch

Cut out for clock insert. Cut diameter of the clock works you purchase

Cut one solid back from 1/8" wood

CHAPTER FIVE
Furniture

Adirondack Rocker

This is a classic and so very comfortable. You will want to make at least two for the patio and two for the deck. You can make this project from any type of wood, but if you want it to last, use pressure treated lumber or heartwood redwood.

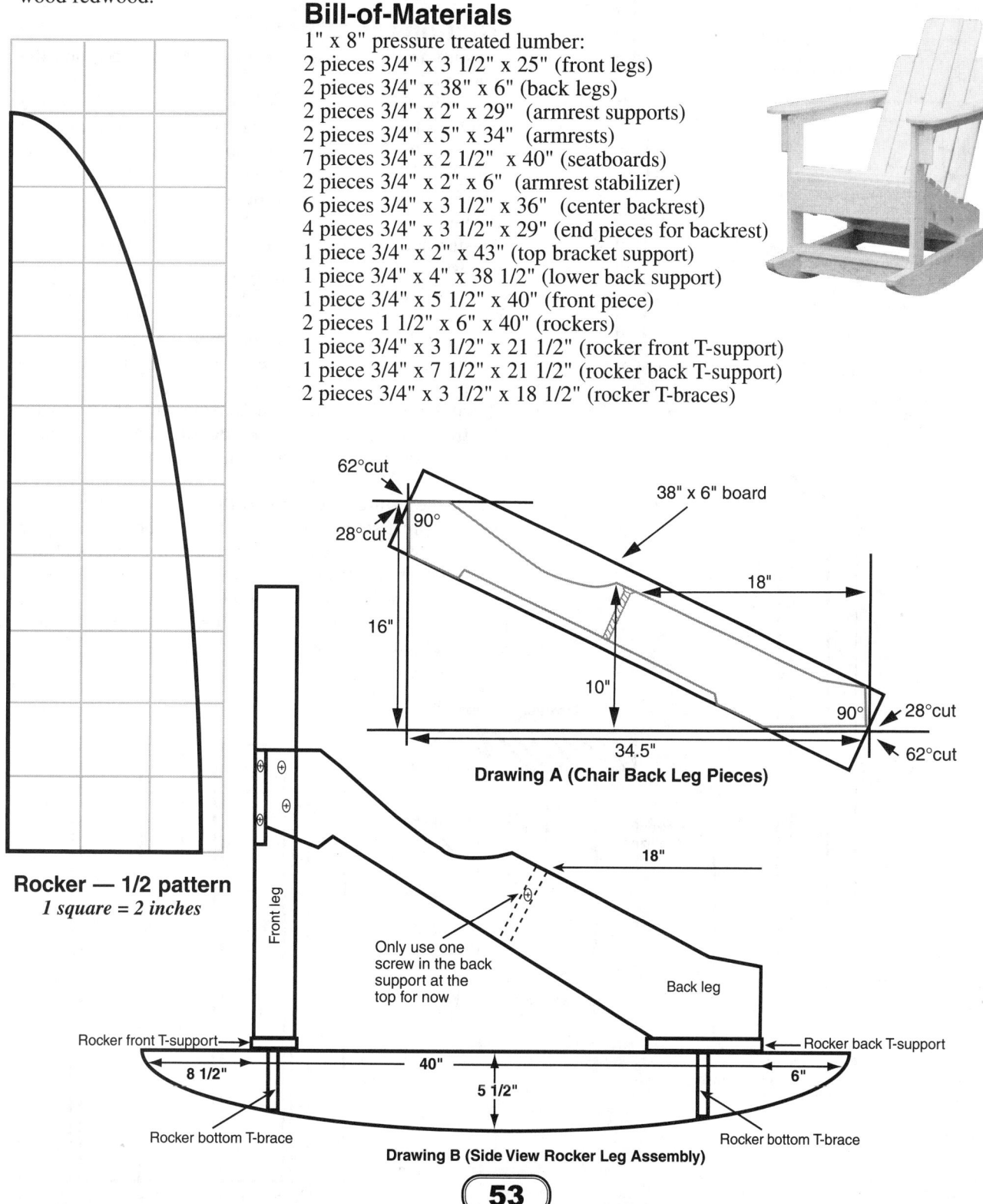

Bill-of-Materials

1" x 8" pressure treated lumber:
2 pieces 3/4" x 3 1/2" x 25" (front legs)
2 pieces 3/4" x 38" x 6" (back legs)
2 pieces 3/4" x 2" x 29" (armrest supports)
2 pieces 3/4" x 5" x 34" (armrests)
7 pieces 3/4" x 2 1/2" x 40" (seatboards)
2 pieces 3/4" x 2" x 6" (armrest stabilizer)
6 pieces 3/4" x 3 1/2" x 36" (center backrest)
4 pieces 3/4" x 3 1/2" x 29" (end pieces for backrest)
1 piece 3/4" x 2" x 43" (top bracket support)
1 piece 3/4" x 4" x 38 1/2" (lower back support)
1 piece 3/4" x 5 1/2" x 40" (front piece)
2 pieces 1 1/2" x 6" x 40" (rockers)
1 piece 3/4" x 3 1/2" x 21 1/2" (rocker front T-support)
1 piece 3/4" x 7 1/2" x 21 1/2" (rocker back T-support)
2 pieces 3/4" x 3 1/2" x 18 1/2" (rocker T-braces)

Rocker — 1/2 pattern
1 square = 2 inches

Drawing A (Chair Back Leg Pieces)

Drawing B (Side View Rocker Leg Assembly)

53

Furniture

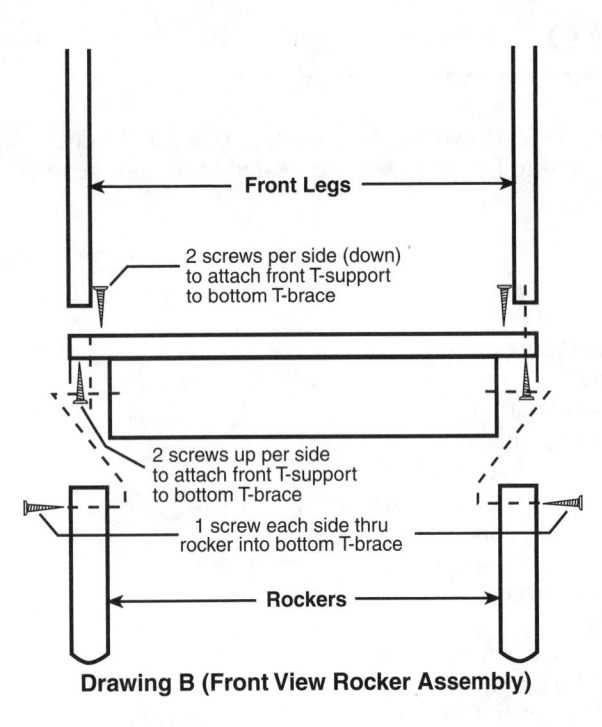

Hardware and Miscellaneous
Silicone glue
50 screws 1 1/4" Dacrotized
1 pint exterior stain

Tools Required
Circular saw
Saber saw
Drill with countersink bit
Screwdriver
Router with rounding-over bit
Flap wheel sander

Instructions for Chair

1) Measure and cut the leg pieces, the front piece and the lower back support.
2) Attach the front piece to the back legs as shown, using screws and glue. Attach the back support 18 inches from the end of the back legs. At this point only, put one screw in the top of the board on both sides. This will allow for minor adjustments later as the lower part of the back is attached.
3) Measure and cut the armrest, the armrest support and the armrest stabilizer.
4) Center the armrest stabilizer on the outside top of the front legs. Attach, using glue and screws from the inside of the leg. Remember to countersink the screws.
5) Measure and cut the back pieces and the upper back support piece.
6) Attach the two back end boards using only one screw (at this time) to the lower back support. They will hang loosely. You may need some help for these next few steps.
7) Attach the armrest support to the front leg. Attach the upper armrest support to the end of the armrest support using screws and glue. Do not tighten the screws at this point. Attach the armrest (as shown) to the armrest support. Position the two back end boards on the back support against the armrest and attach using screws and glue. Tighten all screws.

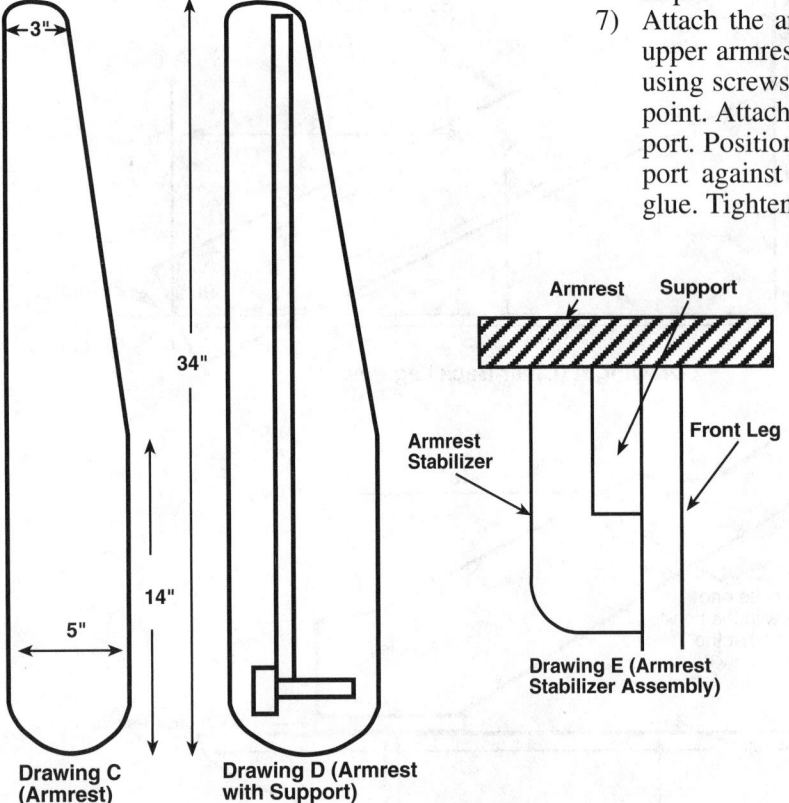

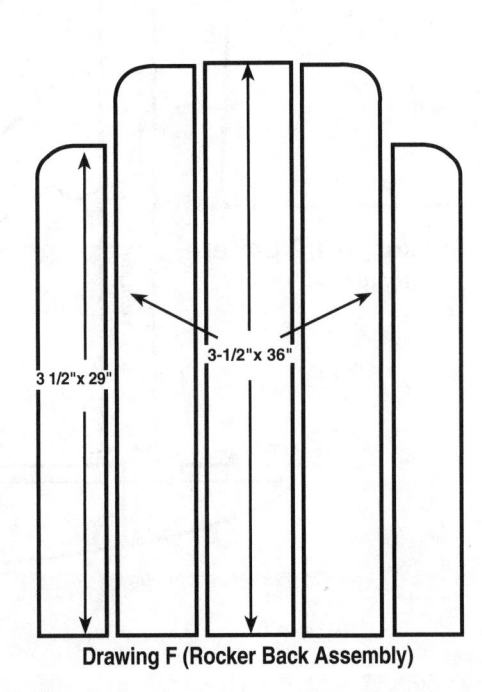

Drawing B (Front View Rocker Assembly)

Drawing C (Armrest)

Drawing D (Armrest with Support)

Drawing E (Armrest Stabilizer Assembly)

Drawing F (Rocker Back Assembly)

8) Attach the remaining three back boards by evenly positioning them across the back. There should be a slight gap between the boards. Add all of the remaining screws and tighten.
9) Finish the project by routing the front seat area and the inner and outer sides of the armrest with a router and a rounding-over bit. If you want all sides of the armrest routed, do this before attaching it to the support. Rout the top of the back boards and continue down the sides as far as the router can reach.
10) Rout all of the top edges of the seat boards.
11) Evenly position the seat boards and attach using glue and screws.

Instructions for Rocker

1) Measure and cut the rocker pattern full-scale, the front and back T-supports, and the bottom T-braces.
2) Assemble according to Drawing B (front & side view diagrams). Note: The back T-support and the bottom T-brace attach the same as the front, except on the outside instead of the inside.
3) The bottom T-braces and the front and back T-supports should be nailed or screwed together with the bottom T-braces offset from the front/back T-supports by 1-1/2" on both sides (width of rocker).
4) Stain the project using an exterior-rated stain product. Sit back and enjoy the rewards of your labor.

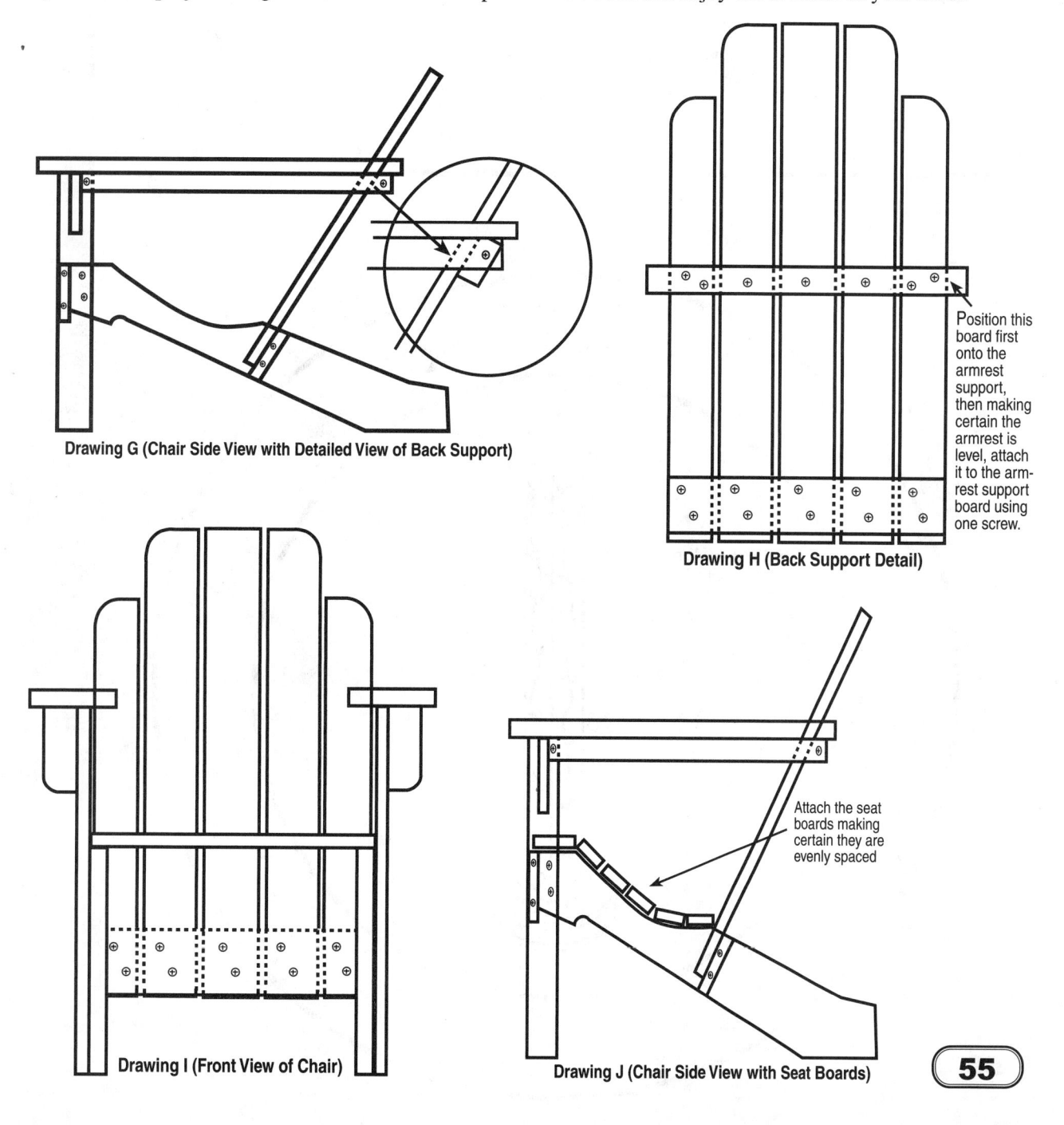

Drawing G (Chair Side View with Detailed View of Back Support)

Drawing H (Back Support Detail)

Position this board first onto the armrest support, then making certain the armrest is level, attach it to the armrest support board using one screw.

Drawing I (Front View of Chair)

Drawing J (Chair Side View with Seat Boards)

Attach the seat boards making certain they are evenly spaced

Furniture

Heart & Vine Coat Tree (Overall finished height: 60")

Cut 1 upper base and 1 lower base. Cut 1 coat rack post from 4 x 4 stock. Drill 1" holes, 1" deep and at 45 degree angles for insertion of 1" dowels as shown in the diagram. Assemble, using the diagram as a guide. Wooden spheres may be purchased for the dowel ends and the coat rack top. Drill holes through base pieces to make rests for walking canes and umbrellas (see diagram). Stain or paint coat rack and paint on heart and vine design. Coat with clear acrylic finish or polyurethane.

1 square = 1 1/4 inch

60"

Coat Rack Post
(Cut 1)
4"x 4"x 60"

Coat Rack Lower Base
(Cut 1)

Coat Rack Upper Base
(Cut 1)

Coat Rack Diagram

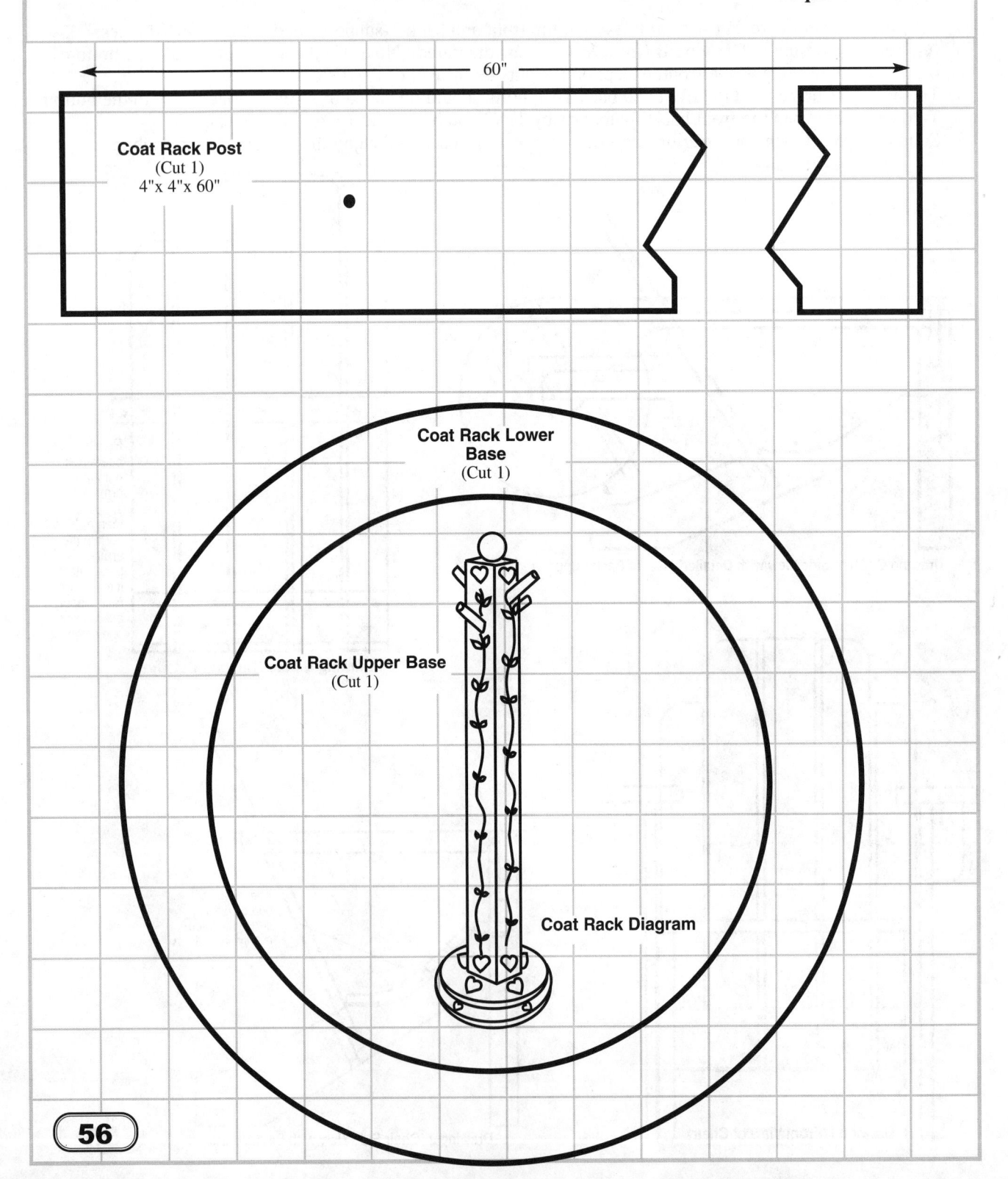

56

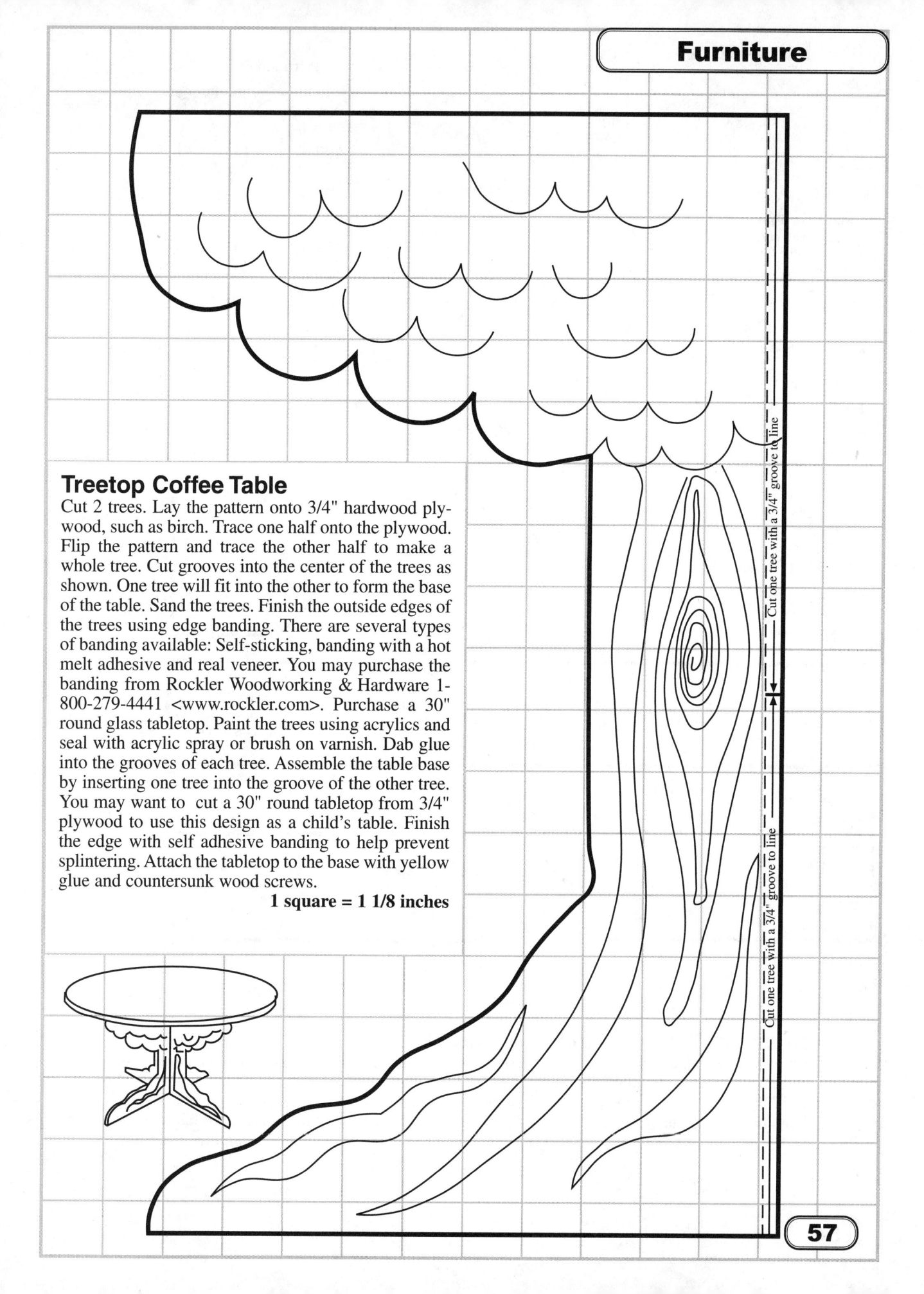

Furniture

Treetop Coffee Table

Cut 2 trees. Lay the pattern onto 3/4" hardwood plywood, such as birch. Trace one half onto the plywood. Flip the pattern and trace the other half to make a whole tree. Cut grooves into the center of the trees as shown. One tree will fit into the other to form the base of the table. Sand the trees. Finish the outside edges of the trees using edge banding. There are several types of banding available: Self-sticking, banding with a hot melt adhesive and real veneer. You may purchase the banding from Rockler Woodworking & Hardware 1-800-279-4441 <www.rockler.com>. Purchase a 30" round glass tabletop. Paint the trees using acrylics and seal with acrylic spray or brush on varnish. Dab glue into the grooves of each tree. Assemble the table base by inserting one tree into the groove of the other tree. You may want to cut a 30" round tabletop from 3/4" plywood to use this design as a child's table. Finish the edge with self adhesive banding to help prevent splintering. Attach the tabletop to the base with yellow glue and countersunk wood screws.

1 square = 1 1/8 inches

Cut one tree with a 3/4" groove to line

Cut one tree with a 3/4" groove to line

57

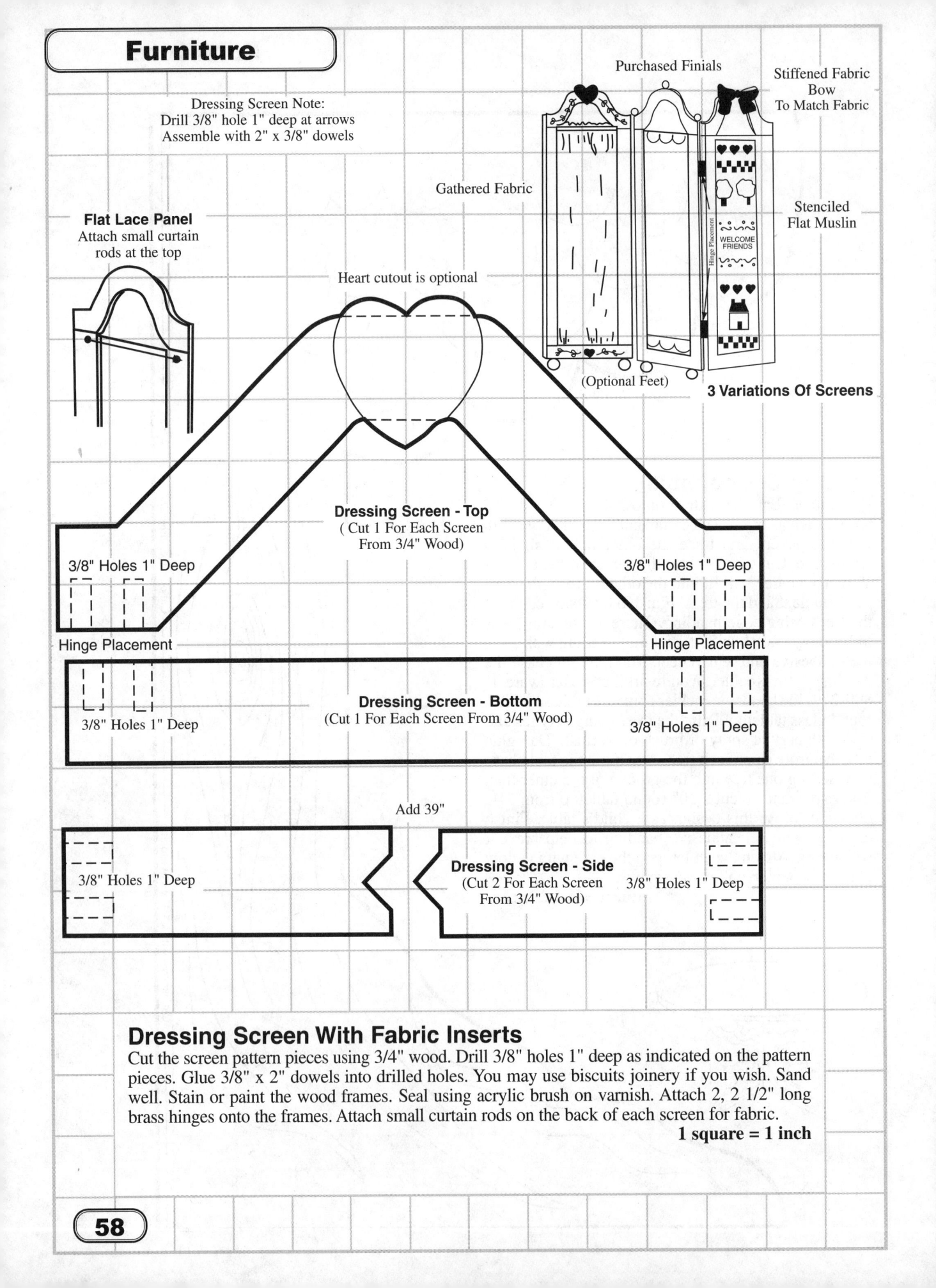

Furniture

Dressing Screen Note:
Drill 3/8" hole 1" deep at arrows
Assemble with 2" x 3/8" dowels

Purchased Finials

Stiffened Fabric Bow To Match Fabric

Gathered Fabric

Flat Lace Panel
Attach small curtain rods at the top

Stenciled Flat Muslin

Heart cutout is optional

(Optional Feet)

3 Variations Of Screens

Dressing Screen - Top
(Cut 1 For Each Screen From 3/4" Wood)

3/8" Holes 1" Deep

3/8" Holes 1" Deep

Hinge Placement

Hinge Placement

Dressing Screen - Bottom
(Cut 1 For Each Screen From 3/4" Wood)

3/8" Holes 1" Deep

3/8" Holes 1" Deep

Add 39"

3/8" Holes 1" Deep

Dressing Screen - Side
(Cut 2 For Each Screen From 3/4" Wood)

3/8" Holes 1" Deep

Dressing Screen With Fabric Inserts

Cut the screen pattern pieces using 3/4" wood. Drill 3/8" holes 1" deep as indicated on the pattern pieces. Glue 3/8" x 2" dowels into drilled holes. You may use biscuits joinery if you wish. Sand well. Stain or paint the wood frames. Seal using acrylic brush on varnish. Attach 2, 2 1/2" long brass hinges onto the frames. Attach small curtain rods on the back of each screen for fabric.

1 square = 1 inch

Furniture

Child's Chest and Cradle
Bill of Materials

	T	L	W	#	Diagram
Chest Cabinet					
Back	1/4"	48"	21 1/4"	1	
Bottom Front Trim	3/4"	22"	3"	1	O
Cabinet Bottom Pieces	3/4"	21"	6 7/8"	2	H
Decorative Top Piece	3/4"	24"	7"	1	N
Hanging Bar Supports	3/4"	2 3/4"	2"	2	K
Optional Hanging Bar	1"	19 1/2"	1"	1	
Optional Shelf Pieces	3/4"	20 1/4"	6 3/8"	4	
Shelf Support Strips	1/4"	18"	5/8"	4	
Side Front Trim	3/4"	45"	1 1/2"	2	
Sides	3/4"	45"	13 1/4"	2	J
Top Pieces	3/4"	24"	7 1/8"	2	
Chest Doors					
Rails	3/4"	7 7/8"	2 1/2"	4	I
Stiles	3/4"	23 1/8"	1 1/2"	4	C
Chest Drawers					
Back	1/2"	17 7/8"	5 1/4"	3	
Bottom	1/4"	18 3/8"	13 1/4"	3	
Front	3/4"	18 7/8"	5 7/8"	3	E
Sides	1/2"	13 3/8"	5 5/8"	6	F
Support Frames					
Back/Front Rails	3/4"	21"	2 1/2"	8	L, H
Drawer Guides	3/4"	13"	3/4"	6	
Stiles	3/4"	10 1/4"	2 1/2"	12	I
Cradle Floor					
Floor	3/4"	36"	18"	1	AA
Headboard/Footboard					
Bottom Rails	3/4"	16 1/2"	2 1/2"	2	R
Panel (Foot)	1/4"			1	U
Panel (Head)	1/2"			1	U
Stiles	3/4"	18 3/4"	2 1/2"	4	X
Top Rail (Foot)	3/4"	20"	6 1/2"	1	S
Top Rail (Head)	3/4"	20"	9 1/2"	1	S
Sides					
Bottom/Top Rail	3/4"	37"	1 1/2"	4	W,Y,Z
Spindles	1/2"	17 1/4"		22	
Base					
Bottom End Piece	3/4"	24"	7"	2	
Decorative Wooden Balls	2"			4	
End Piece Support	3/4"	28 3/4"	6"	2	
Horizontal Supports	3/4"	39 1/4"	3 1/2"	2	
Locking Peg	3/8"	2 1/2"	3/8"	1	Q
Support Rods	5/8"	2 1/2"	5/8"	2	Q
Top End Piece	3/4"	22 1/2"	6"	2	

Diagram A

Diagram B

Diagram C

Attach two rails into the top and bottom dados of one stile. Attach another stile to the two attached rails. Square up assembled door, glue, clamp and let dry. Assemble the other door in the same manner.

Drawers
Attach two drawer sides to the rabbeted edges of a drawer front, making sure the dado grooves near the bottom of these pieces are even and bottom edges are flush. Slide the drawer bottom into the dado grooves of the drawer sides, gently tapping it into the groove on the drawer front. Attach drawer back to the drawer sides. Note that the drawer back will fit inside the edges of the drawer sides and on top of the drawer bottom. Square up assembled drawer, glue, clamp and let dry. Assemble the remaining drawers in the same way.

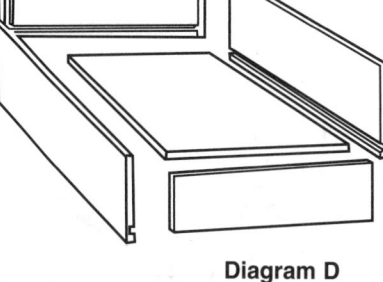

Diagram D

Furniture

Support Frames
Attach three stiles to one front rail (with front corners notched per Diagram H). Make sure the middle stile is in the center of the rail, and the end stiles are flush with the ends of the rail. Attach one back rail to the rabbeted ends of the three stiles (do not notch corners). Make sure the middle stile is centered and the end stiles are flush with the ends of the back rail. Square up assembled frame, glue, clamp and let dry. Assemble the remaining three frames in the same way. After the frames are dry, attach the drawer guides as shown in Diagram G. The fourth frame will be used at the top of the chest cabinet.

Cabinet
Glue and clamp the two top pieces edge to edge to form the main top piece. Do the same with the cabinet bottom pieces and the shelf pieces for the optional shelves. Recommendation: If you have a jointer, you may want to square up the edges to assure an evenly glued joint. Be sure to allow extra width for jointer-work. The finished shelf pieces should be 7 1/8". Alternate edge grain patterns to avoid warping. (Looking at the end of the piece, if the grain on the edge curves upward, the piece next to it should curve downward.) Lay one side piece on a flat work surface with dados facing upward. Attach the support frames in the dados on the side piece. Make sure the notches in the frames face the front (the back of the chest rabbet for the back piece). The drawer guides must face up and the frame, without the drawer guides, is at the top. Also attach the assembled cabinet bottom with the notches facing front, as before. Attach the remaining side piece to the support frames. Turning the whole assembly on its front, square up the assembly and attach the back piece in the rabbet on the side pieces and glue. Clamp and let dry. Turn the assembly on its back and attach the side front trim and bottom front trim pieces. Setting the assembly upright, attach the decorative top piece to the back edge of the top assembly. Attach the completed top to the chest, making sure the back edge is flush with the chest back. The top should overlap the sides and the front by 1".

Final Touches
Attach hinges to doors, line up doors in openings, mark and drill pilot holes and attach doors to side front trim pieces. Attach your choice of hardware for the doors and drawers or the plain wooden pulls as illustrated in Diagram A. Door stops or magnetic latches may need to be installed if you choose to use plain wooden pulls. Do any final sanding necessary, stain and/or finish as desired. Attach fabric to insides of doors to cover openings. Fabric can be glued, stapled, or hung on small rods. Insert drawers, optional shelves and/or hanging bar.

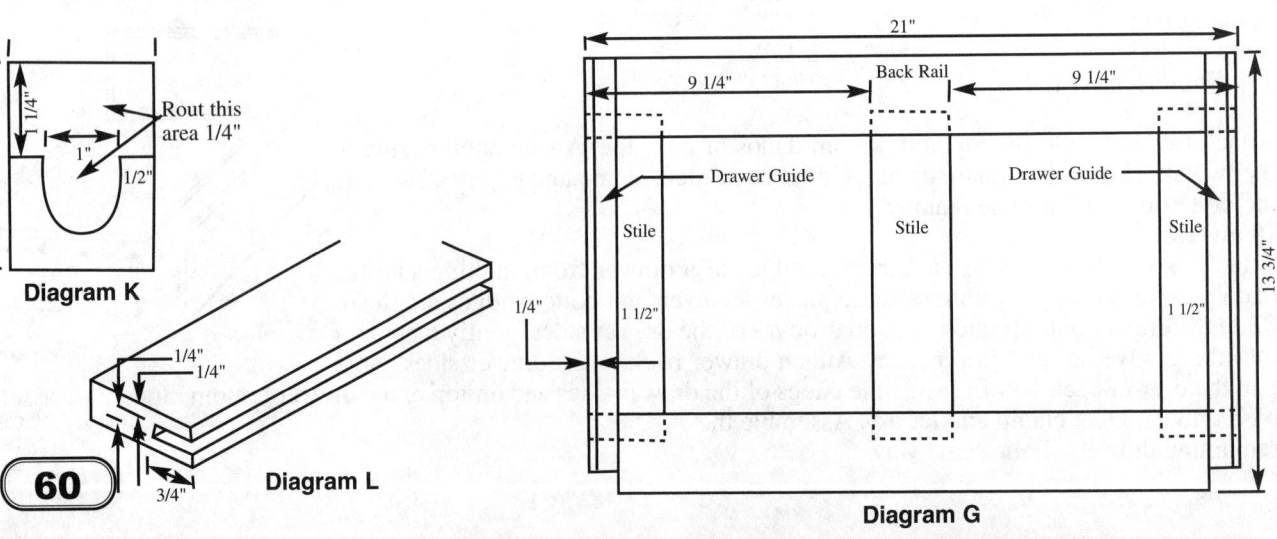

Furniture

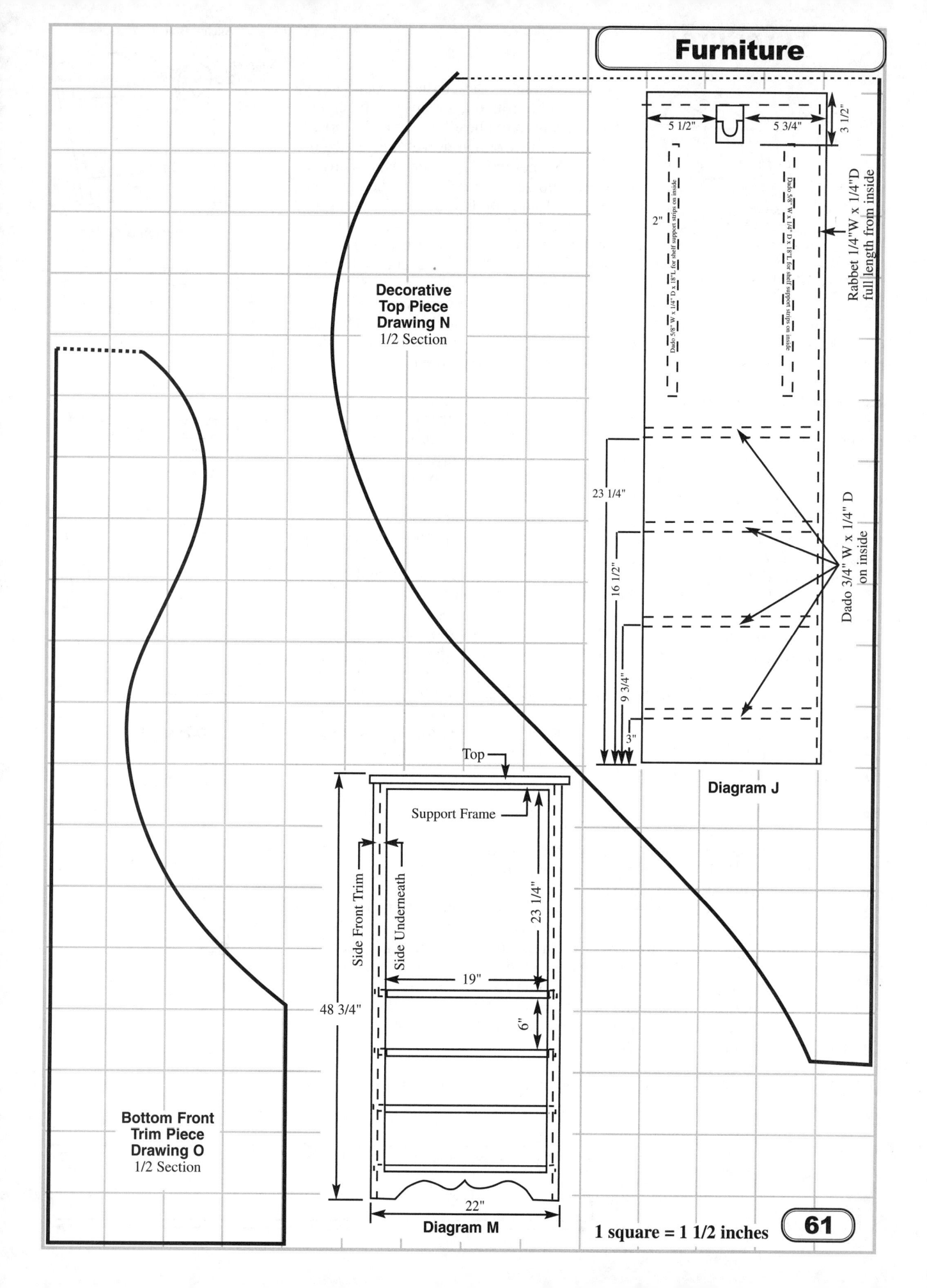

Decorative Top Piece
Drawing N
1/2 Section

5 1/2" 5 3/4" 3 1/2"

2"

Dado 5/8" W x 1/4" D x 18"L for shelf support strips on inside

Dado 5/8" W x 1/4" D x 18"L for shelf support strips on inside

Rabbet 1/4"W x 1/4"D full length from inside

23 1/4"

16 1/2"

9 3/4"

3"

Dado 3/4" W x 1/4" D on inside

Diagram J

Top

Support Frame

Side Front Trim

Side Underneath

23 1/4"

19"

6"

48 3/4"

22"

Bottom Front Trim Piece
Drawing O
1/2 Section

Diagram M

1 square = 1 1/2 inches

61

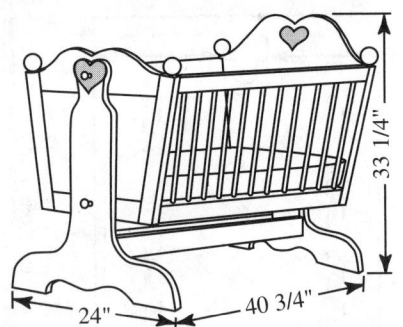

Furniture

Note: To enable the cradle to rock gently and smoothly rout out and insert a precision ball bearing in the headboard and footboard and insert the wooden dowel into the bearing. This method is better than using a wooden dowel inserted into a hole in the headboard and footboard. See Drawing Q. A precision ball may be purchased from a local hardware store. A bearing of no more than 1/2" in depth, with a center hole of 5/8" is recommended. Then use 5/8" wooden dowels for the support rods with decorative caps attached to the ends. A 3/8" dowel should be used for the locking peg. The size of the bearing you choose will determine the size of holes you rout out and drill per Drawings R, S, and T. The centers of these holes are marked.

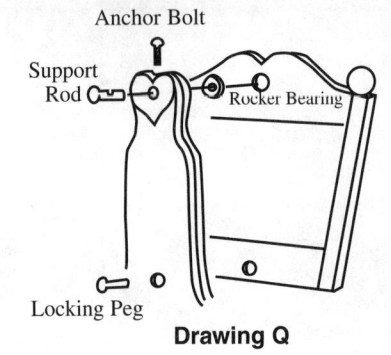

Headboard and Footboard

Note: Before you begin assembly of this section, put the pieces together without gluing or nailing to check fit. Trim as necessary. Also, be sure all mill work is done, particularly routing out the top rail for the rocker bearing and drilling the hole in the footboard bottom rail for the locking peg. See Drawing R. The rocker bearing should fit very snugly into the top rail.

Pieces Needed: One bottom rail; one panel; two stiles; and one top rail. Please double-check the Bill of Materials to be sure you have the proper pieces before you begin assembly! See Drawing R for assembly.

1) Attach the top and bottom rails to one stile, making sure the top and bottom edges are flush. Also be sure the routed side of the top rail (for rocker bearing) faces the opposite direction as the stop dado on the stiles. The routed side of the top rail will be toward the outside of the cradle and the stop dado on the stiles will be toward the inside to accommodate the sides.
2) Slide the panel into the dado grooves in the rails, tapping it gently into place in the stile. Do not glue the panel. Let it "float," allowing for expansion and contraction with humidity changes. Trim panel if necessary.
3) Attach the opposite stile to the top and bottom rails making sure the outside edges are flush while sliding the panel into the dado groove in the stile.
4) Glue and clamp assembly, then let dry.

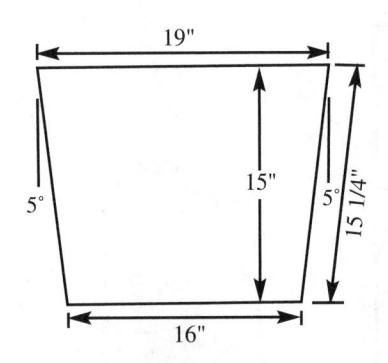

Sides

Pieces needed: Four bottom/top rails; and twenty-two spindles.

Note: For correct assembly, it is suggested that 2 or 3 spacers be cut from 1 x 2 boards, 15 3/4" long to be used as gauges to insure correct overall dimensions. See Drawing Y for spacing.

1) Glue and insert eleven spindles in the holes in one of the rails, tapping them firmly into place.
2) After putting glue on the top edges of the spindles, beginning at one end begin to tap another rail onto the spindles. Once the top rail on all the spindles is started, firmly tap it into place. Use the 15 3/4" spacers as a gauge for the distance between the top and bottom rail. (Overall height of the finished side assembly, including top and bottom rails should be 18 3/4".)
3) Using spacers, clamp and let dry.
4) Assemble the other side in the same way.
5) After side assemblies are dry, bevel top and bottom edges at 5 degrees per Drawing V.

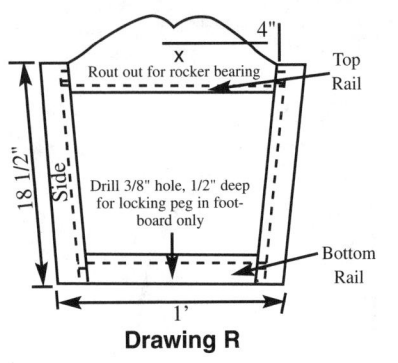

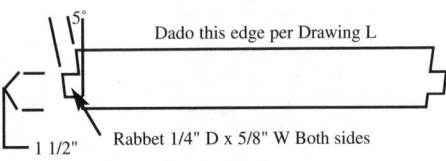

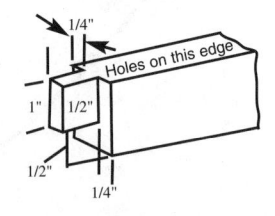

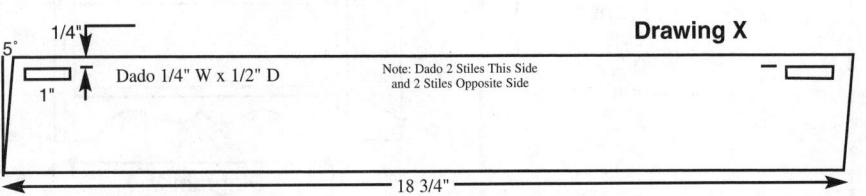

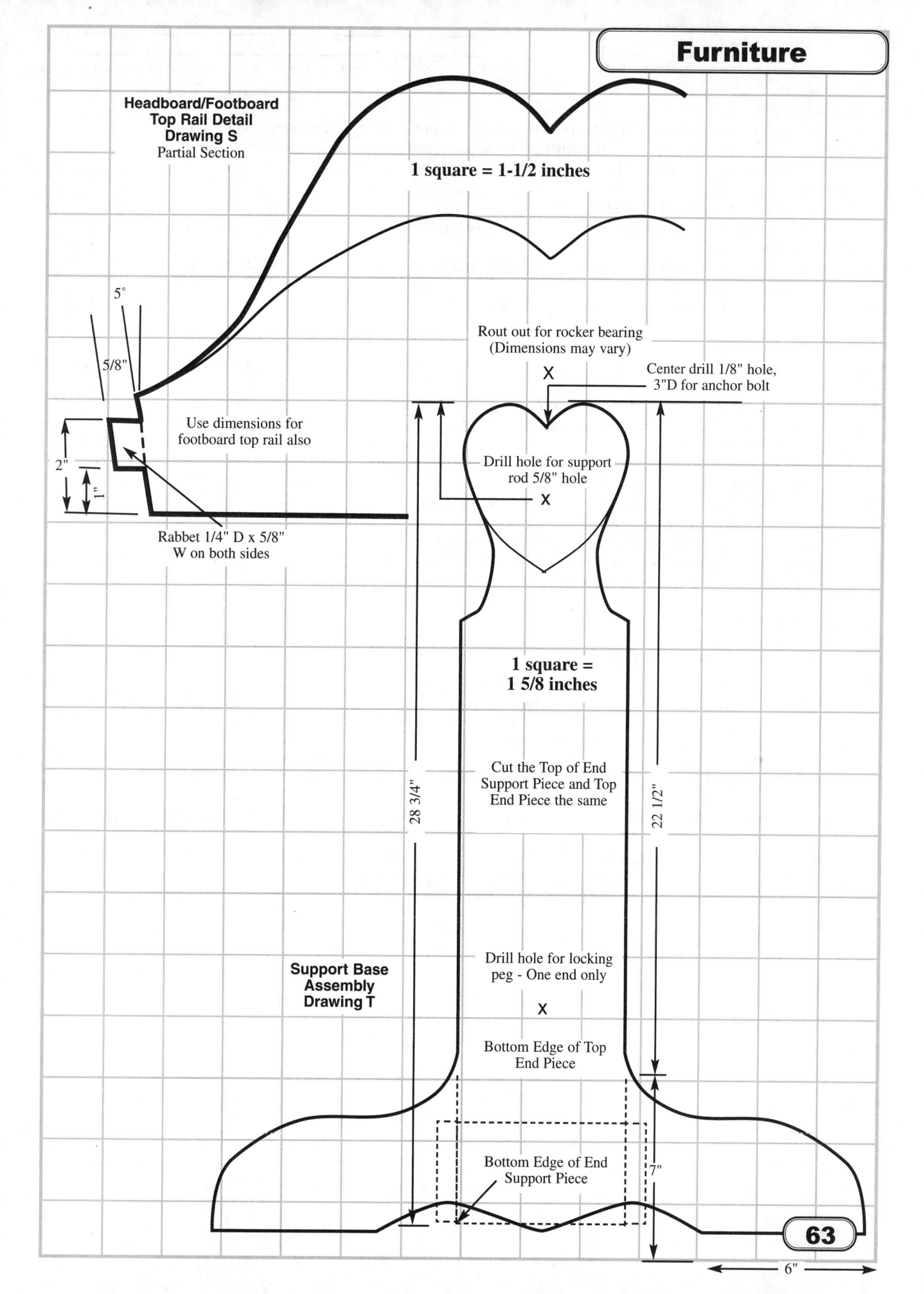

**Headboard/Footboard Top Rail Detail
Drawing S**
Partial Section

1 square = 1-1/2 inches

5°

5/8"

2"

1"

Use dimensions for footboard top rail also

Rabbet 1/4" D x 5/8" W on both sides

Rout out for rocker bearing (Dimensions may vary)

Center drill 1/8" hole, 3"D for anchor bolt

X

Drill hole for support rod 5/8" hole

X

1 square = 1 5/8 inches

Cut the Top of End Support Piece and Top End Piece the same

**Support Base Assembly
Drawing T**

28 3/4"

22 1/2"

Drill hole for locking peg - One end only

X

Bottom Edge of Top End Piece

Bottom Edge of End Support Piece

7"

6"

Furniture

63

Furniture

Drawing Y
| 3 1/2" | 3" | 3" | 3" | 3" | 3" | 3" | 3" | 3" | 3" | 3 1/2" |
Drill 1/2" hole 3/4"

Cradle Assembly
Pieces needed: Footboard assembly; headboard assembly; and two side assemblies, cradle floor.
1) Lay the headboard assembly on a flat surface. Glue and gently tap one side assembly into the dado of the headboard stile. Make sure the beveled edges of the side assembly are flush with the edges of the stile.
2) Do the same thing with other side assembly.
3) Glue the other ends of the side assemblies and gently tap the footboard assembly and the side assemblies together.
4) Insert floor of cradle into the assembly from the top and secure by nailing or screwing to headboard, footboard and sides.
5) Clamp entire cradle assembly together and let dry.

Drawing Z — 5°, 18 3/4", 15 3/4"

Support Base
Pieces needed: Two bottom end-pieces; two end-piece supports; two horizontal supports; and two top end-pieces.
Note: The end-piece is designed to be built from two pieces: top and bottom, with end-piece support attached to the inside (see Drawing T). Using this construction, cut the top and bottom end-pieces from 1 x 8 material. If the woodworker desires, these two pieces can be combined and cut as one piece from plywood. Also drill holes per Drawing T.
1) Glue and screw together one top end-piece and one end-piece support, making sure top edges are flush.
2) Glue and screw one bottom end-piece to the above assembly.
3) Assemble the opposite end-piece in the same way.
4) Clamp both end-piece assemblies together by gluing and screwing the horizontal supports to the lower edges of the end-piece supports. Also screw through the bottom end-piece into the edges of the horizontal supports, drilling smaller pilot holes first so wood does not split.

Drawing AA — 5°, 18"

Final Assembly
1) Before beginning the final assembly, do any final sanding and apply stain, finish or decorative painting to the cradle and support-base assemblies.
2) Place cradle assembly on floor beside the support-base assembly.
3) Tap the 5/8" cradle support rods into the holes in the support end-pieces until they are flush with the inside edges. Make sure the hole in the side of the support rod is toward the outside and faces upward to line up with the anchor-bolt-hole in the top of the end support.
4) Instead of trying to support the cradle between the support base end-pieces, tilt the support base sideways toward, and around the cradle. This will line up the holes inserted into the support rods with the holes in the rocker bearings. Gently tap the rods into the bearings.
5) Insert the anchor bolts from the top of the end-pieces into the support rods to secure them. The holes in the top of the end-pieces should be countersunk.
6) Turn the cradle upright and insert the 3/8" locking peg through the support base into the hole in the footboard bottom rail to keep cradle from rocking. Remove this peg to enable the cradle to rock.
7) Attach the decorative wooden balls to the top corners.

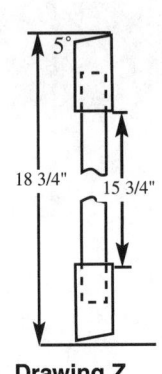

TV/VCR Stand

Furniture

Item#	Qty	Description	Size	Material
1	3	Drawer fronts	3/4" x 5 1/4" x 22 3/4"	White pine
2	6	Drawer sides	3/4" x 5 1/4" x 17 3/8"	White pine
3	3	Drawer dividers	3/4" x 5 1/4" x 20 1/4"	White pine
4	3	Drawer back	3/4" x 5 1/4" 20 1/4"	White pine
5	3	Drawer bottom	1/4" x 16" x 20 5/16"	Almacega
6	2	Side panels	3/4" x 19" x 28"	White pine
7	2	Front center brace	3/4" x 3" x 23"	White pine
8	3	Back center brace	3/4" x 3" x 23"	White pine
9	6	Side panel brace	3/4" x 1 1/2" x 13"	White pine
10	2	Top side panel brace	3/4" x 1 1/4" x 18 1/4"	White pine
11	1	Front bottom brace	3/4" x 3 3/16" x 23"	White pine
12	1	Front top brace	3/4" x 1 1/4" x 23"	White pine
13	1	Top center brace	3/4" x 4" x 21 1/2"	White pine
14	1	Shelf	3/4" x 20" x 24 1/2"	White pine
15	1	Top	3/4" x 20 1/4" x 27"	White pine
16	1	Back	1/4" x 24" x 28 1/2"	Almacega
17	4	Top door guides	3/4" x 2" x 12 1/8"	White pine
18	4	Side door guides	3/4" x 2" x 18 5/8"	White pine
19	2	Door panels	1/4" x 8 3/4" x 15 1/8"	Almacega
20	1	Crown mold (6' approx)	1 1/4" (height)	White pine
21	3	Sets of drawer slides	18" (side mount)	Your choice
22	2	Sets of double caster	——	Your choice
23	2	Brass door pulls	optional	Your choice
24	2	Door catches	(not magnetic)	Your choice

TV/VCR Front diagram

This project will be assembled in three phases. Phase One consists of Items 6 thru 16 and comprises the basic frame structure. Phase Two consists of Items 1 thru 5 and makes up the drawers. In Phase Three, the front doors will be assembled and installed.

You will need to use #8 x 1", #8 x 1 1/2", and #8 x 2" wood screws, 1 1/2" finishing nails, and wood glue for this cabinet.

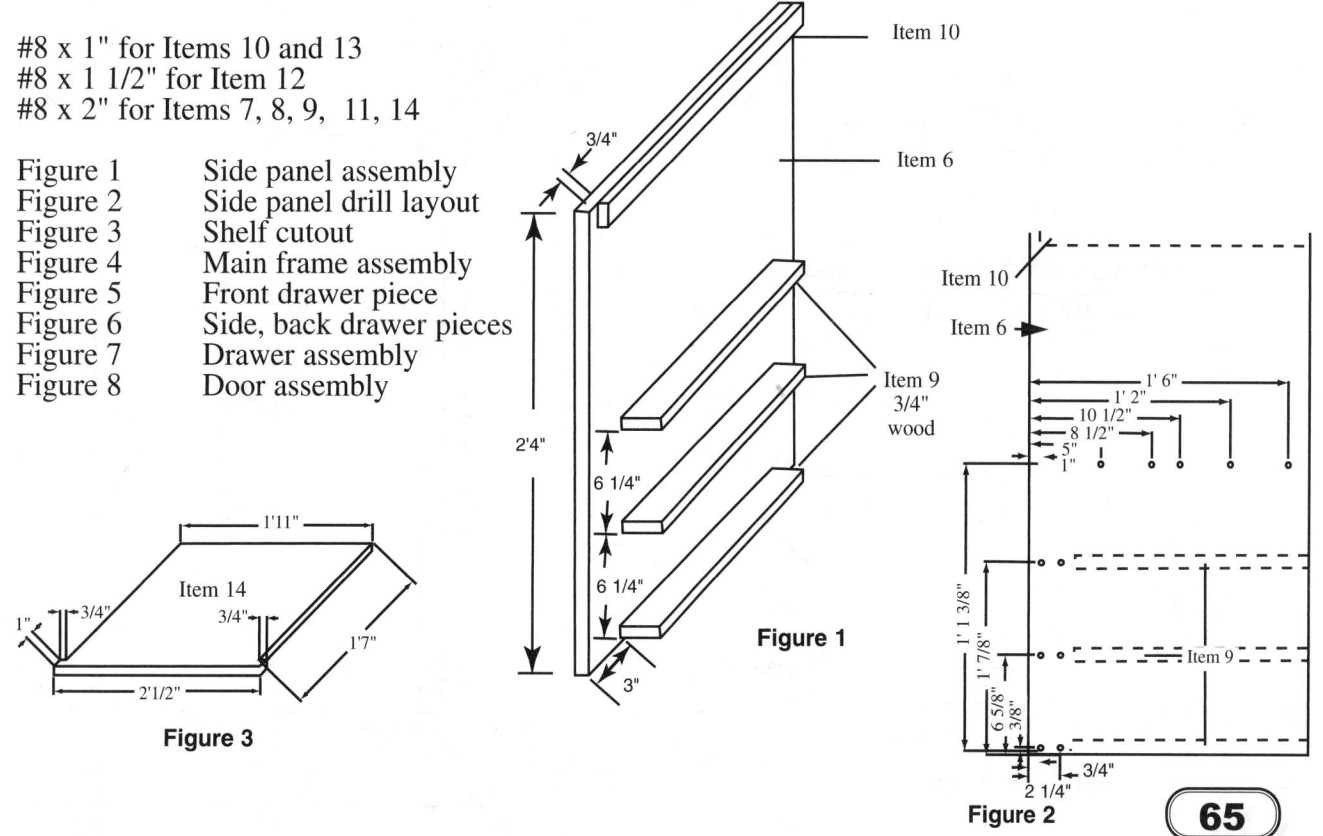

#8 x 1" for Items 10 and 13
#8 x 1 1/2" for Item 12
#8 x 2" for Items 7, 8, 9, 11, 14

Figure 1	Side panel assembly
Figure 2	Side panel drill layout
Figure 3	Shelf cutout
Figure 4	Main frame assembly
Figure 5	Front drawer piece
Figure 6	Side, back drawer pieces
Figure 7	Drawer assembly
Figure 8	Door assembly

Figure 1

Figure 3

Figure 2

65

Furniture

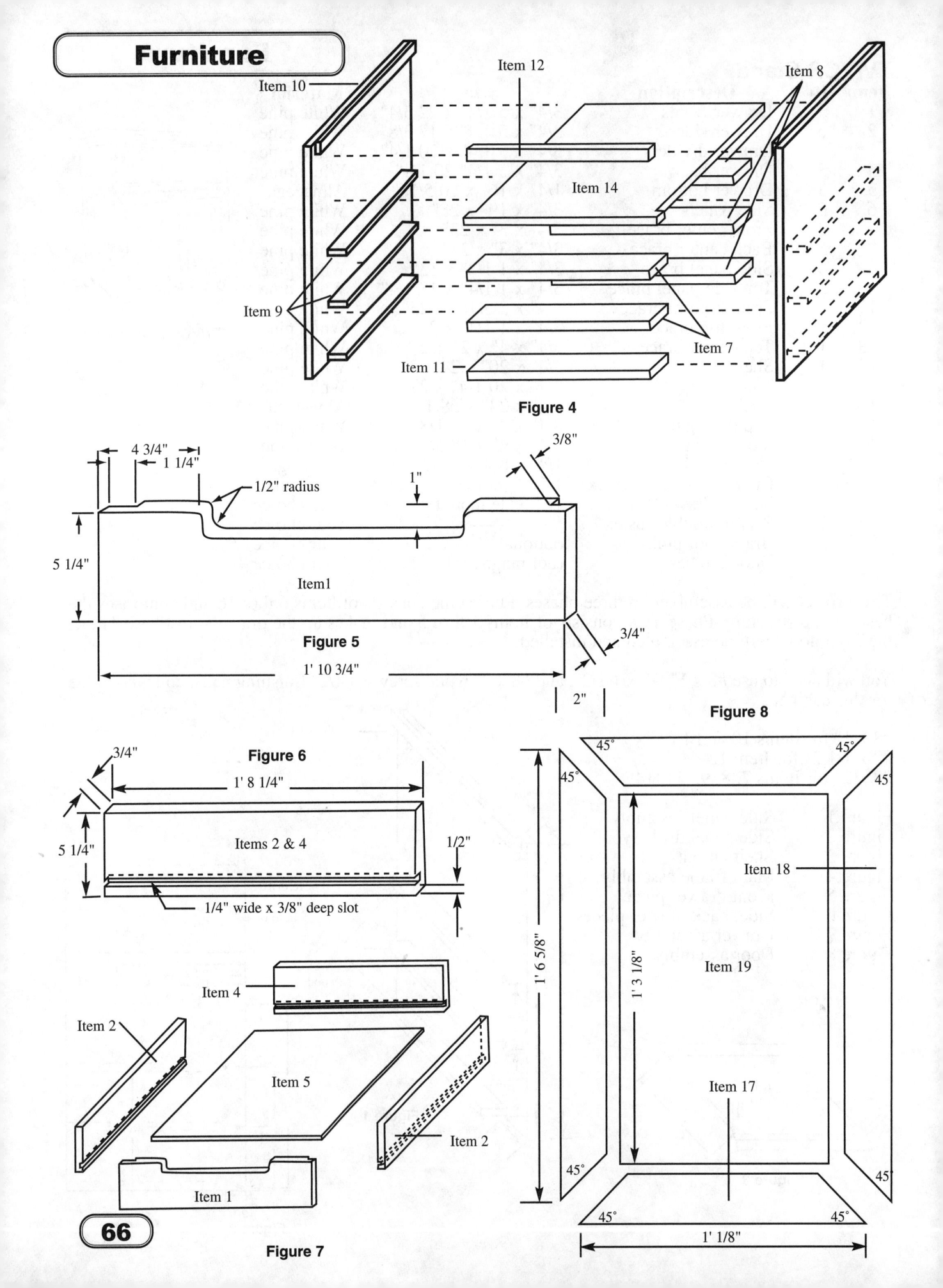

Figure 4

Item 10, Item 12, Item 8, Item 9, Item 14, Item 7, Item 11

Figure 5

Item 1
- 4 3/4"
- 1 1/4"
- 1/2" radius
- 1"
- 3/8"
- 5 1/4"
- 3/4"
- 2"
- 1' 10 3/4"

Figure 6

Items 2 & 4
- 3/4"
- 1' 8 1/4"
- 5 1/4"
- 1/2"
- 1/4" wide x 3/8" deep slot

Figure 7

Item 4, Item 2, Item 5, Item 2, Item 1

Figure 8

Item 18, Item 19, Item 17
- 45° (all corners)
- 1' 6 5/8"
- 1' 3 1/8"
- 1' 1/8"

66

CHAPTER SIX
Garden

Grandpa Bunny

Cut each pattern from 3/8" exterior grade plywood. Cut a stake from 1" x 2" stock. Pre-drill the pattern and the stake where indicated for insertion of 1", #8 or #10 screws. Sand well. Base coat the cut-out pattern. Trace the lines onto the pattern using graphite or carbon paper. Paint with acrylic paints. Attach the bird's wing and Grandpa's arm using yellow wood glue. Apply several coats of outdoor polyurethane. Insert the stake into the ground, then attach the pattern with screws.

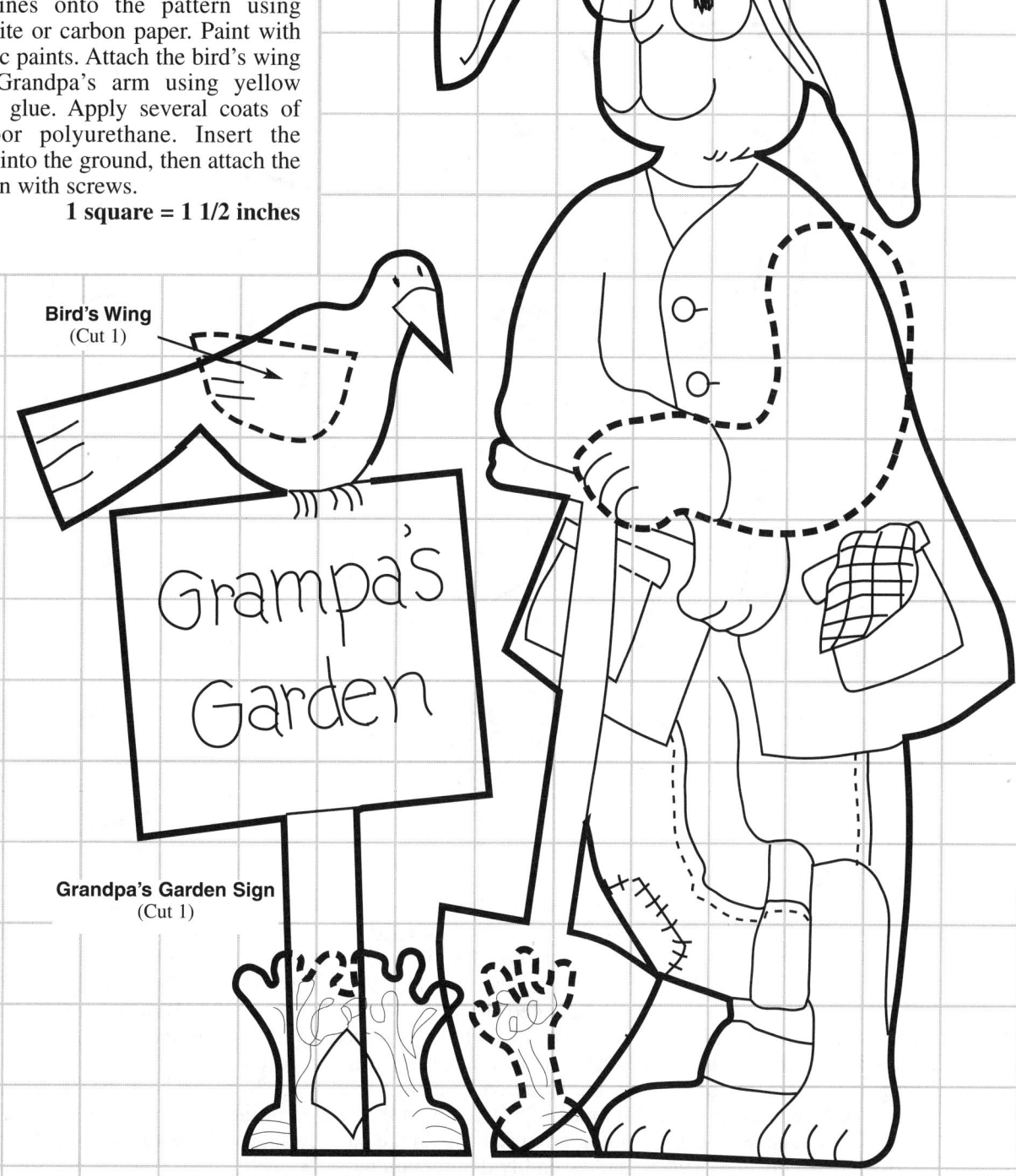

1 square = 1 1/2 inches

Grandpa Bunny
(Cut 1)

Bird's Wing
(Cut 1)

Grampa's Garden

Grandpa's Garden Sign
(Cut 1)

67

Garden

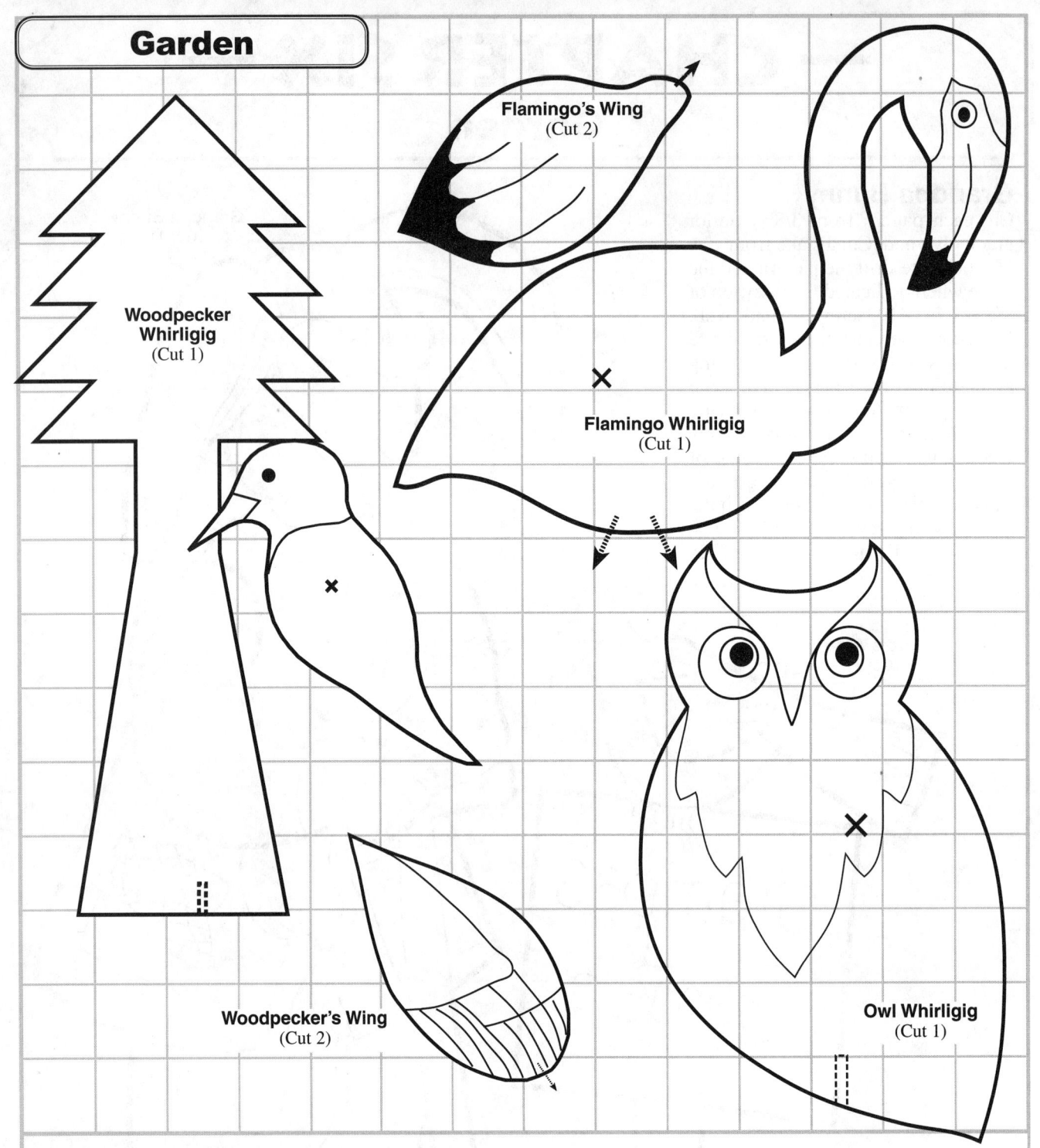

Woodpecker Whirligig (Cut 1)

Flamingo's Wing (Cut 2)

Flamingo Whirligig (Cut 1)

Woodpecker's Wing (Cut 2)

Owl Whirligig (Cut 1)

Whirligig Instructions

Use outdoor grade plywood, 3/4" wood for the whirligig body or central piece, block and blade base. Use 1/8" wood for blades. Cut two, 3" x 3/4" blade bases from 1/4" wood. Cut a 1/8" kerf, 7/8" long at opposite 45° angles in the end of each blade base. Drill a 3/16" hole through the center of both blade bases and both blocks. (Cut two blocks and four blades for each whirligig. Arrow on blade indicates which end goes into block.) Attach a blade base to each side of whirligig as indicated by an X. Insert a 3/16" x 3" galvanized machine screw through the assembly and blade bases. Assemble blade base with metal washers onto the screw in the following order: metal washer, block, metal washer. Attach a self-locking nut to the end of the screw to hold the assembly together. Insert the blades into the blade bases using wood glue. To insure that the blades will be secure, attach the blade base using small brads. Drill a hole at the bottom of the pattern for insertion of a rod or dowel. Sand and paint. Seal using outdoor polyurethane. Some patterns may require additional instructions.
  See blade and block pattern and assembly diagram on page 53.

All whirligigs: 1 square = 1 1/2 inches

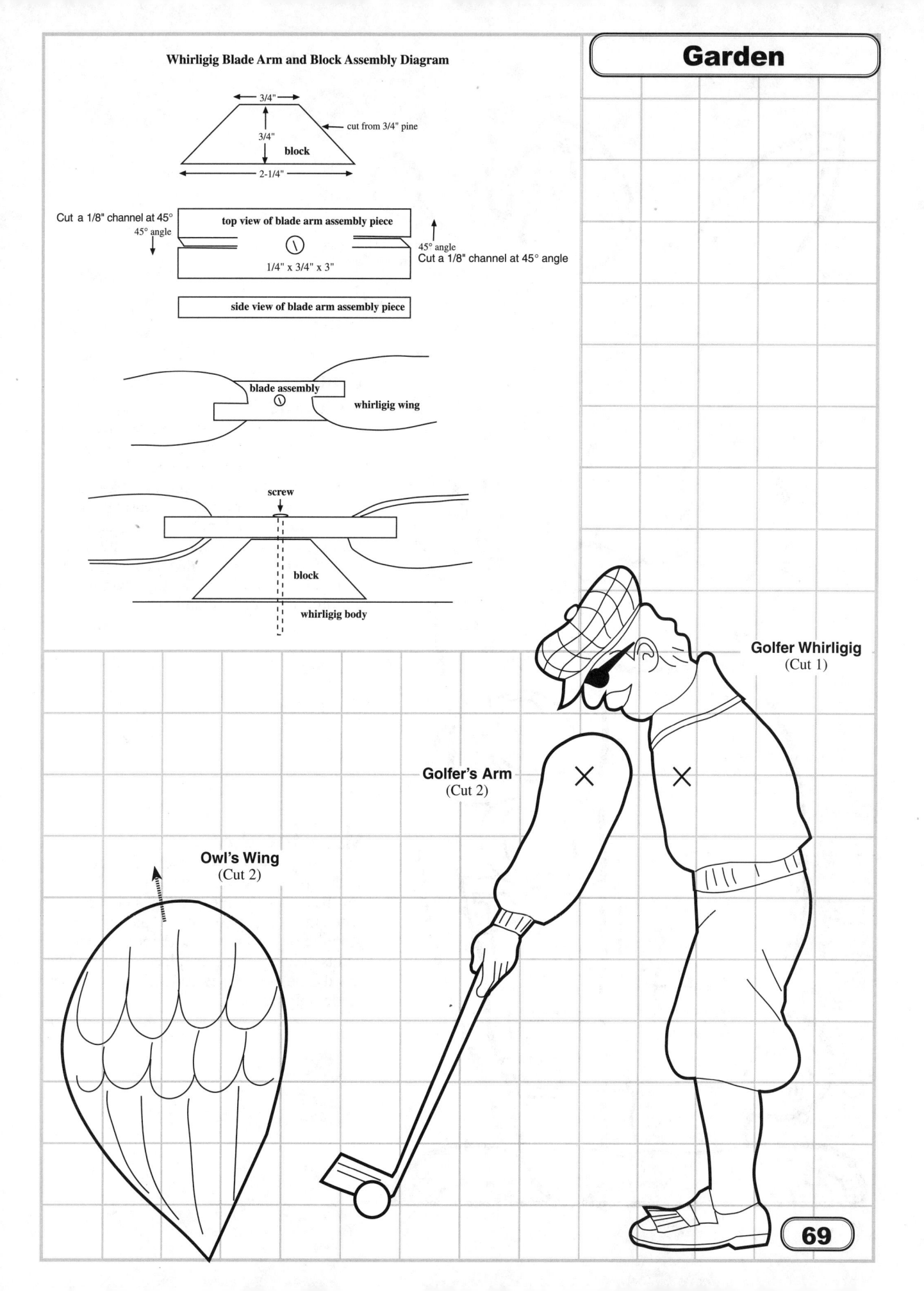

Garden

Whirligig Blade Arm and Block Assembly Diagram

- 3/4"
- 3/4"
- cut from 3/4" pine
- block
- 2-1/4"

Cut a 1/8" channel at 45°
45° angle

top view of blade arm assembly piece
1/4" x 3/4" x 3"

45° angle
Cut a 1/8" channel at 45° angle

side view of blade arm assembly piece

blade assembly
whirligig wing

screw
block
whirligig body

Golfer Whirligig (Cut 1)

Golfer's Arm (Cut 2)

Owl's Wing (Cut 2)

69

Garden

Grandpa Bunny Garden Welcome
Cut bunny from 3/4" stock. Cut carrot from 1/2" wood. Cut letters and hands from 1/4" stock. Sand and basecoat the pieces. Transfer the lines onto the dry, basecoated pattern using graphite or carbon paper. Paint with acrylic paints. Glue carrot to bunny using yellow wood glue and secure with finishing nails. Glue hands to carrot with yellow wood glue. Apply several coats of outdoor-grade polyurethane.

Actual Size

Mary, the Bird Lady
Cut Mary from 3/4" stock. Cut pockets, birds, and sunflower from 1/4" stock. Sand and basecoat the pieces. Transfer the lines onto the dry, basecoated pattern using graphite or carbon paper. Paint with acrylic paints. Glue pieces in place with yellow wood glue. Apply several coats of outdoor-grade polyurethane.

Actual Size

Garden

Sunflower
(Cut 1)

Pocket
(Cut 1)

Mary, the Bird Lady
(Cut 1)

Pocket
(Cut 1)

71

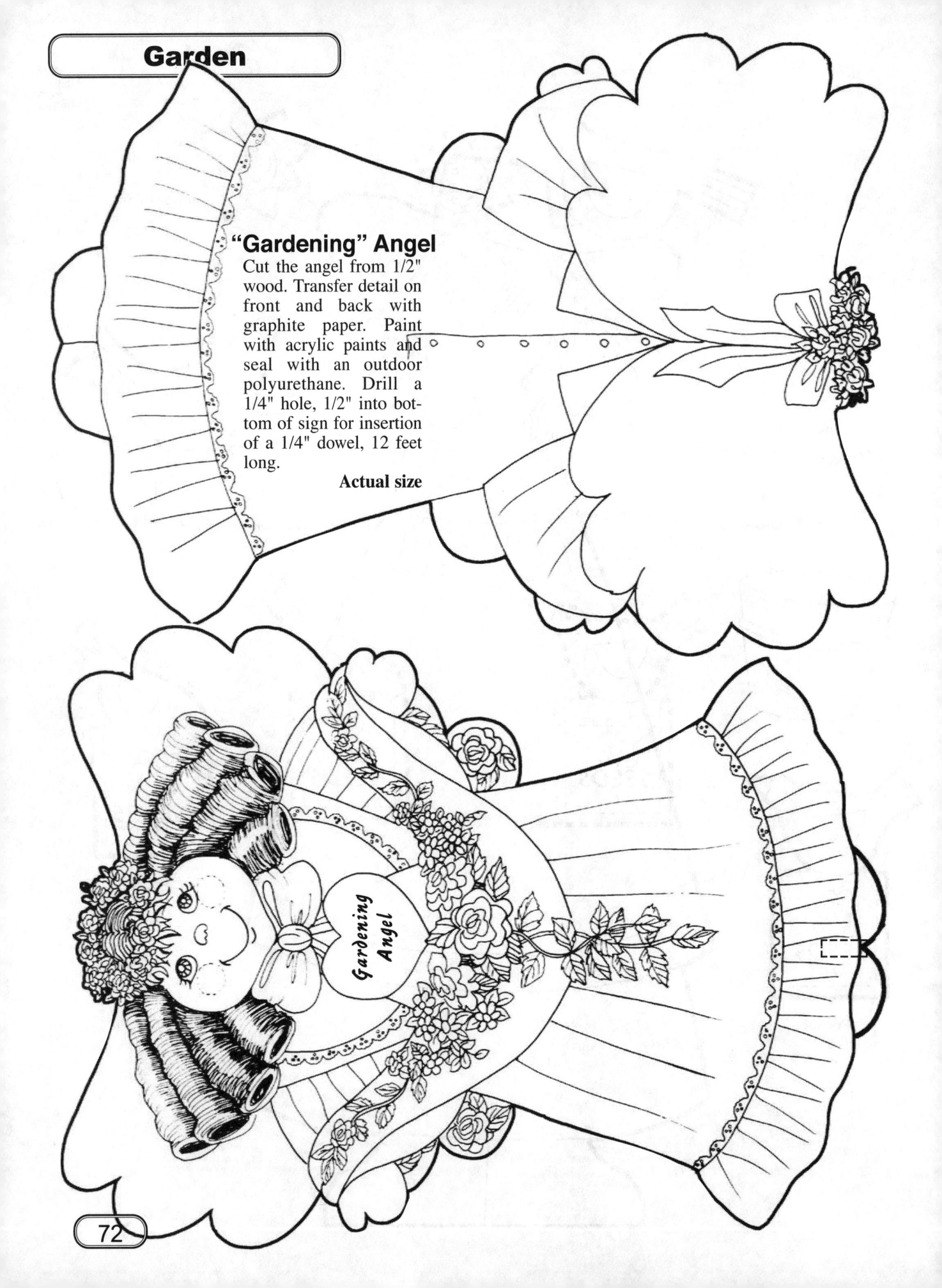

Garden

"Gardening" Angel

Cut the angel from 1/2" wood. Transfer detail on front and back with graphite paper. Paint with acrylic paints and seal with an outdoor polyurethane. Drill a 1/4" hole, 1/2" into bottom of sign for insertion of a 1/4" dowel, 12 feet long.

Actual size

Garden

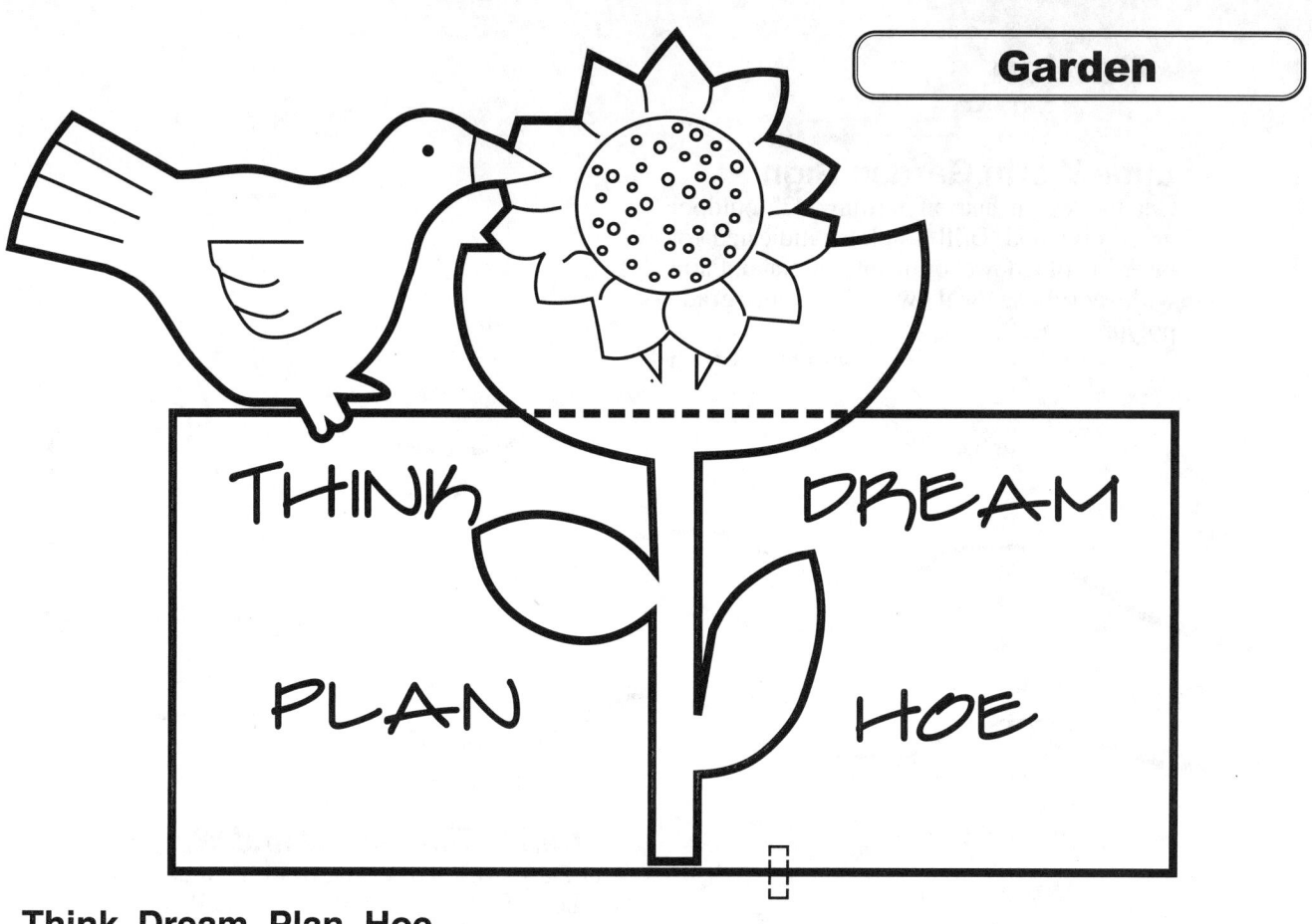

Think, Dream, Plan, Hoe Garden Sign

Cut the sign back from 1/2" wood. Cut the flower and bird from 1/4" wood. Drill a hole in the bottom of the sign for insertion of a metal rod. Glue the flower and bird onto the back with waterproof glue. Paint with acrylic paints and seal with an outdoor polyurethane.

Actual size

No Old Crows Garden Sign

Cut the sign back from 1/2" wood. Cut 4 flowers from 1/4" wood. Drill 4 holes in the bottom of the sign for insertion of wire on which the flowers will be hung. Paint with acrylic paints and seal with an outdoor polyurethane. Drill a 1/4" hole, 1/2" into bottom of sign for insertion of a 1/4" dowel, 3 feet long.

Actual size

NO OLD CROWS ALLOWED

73

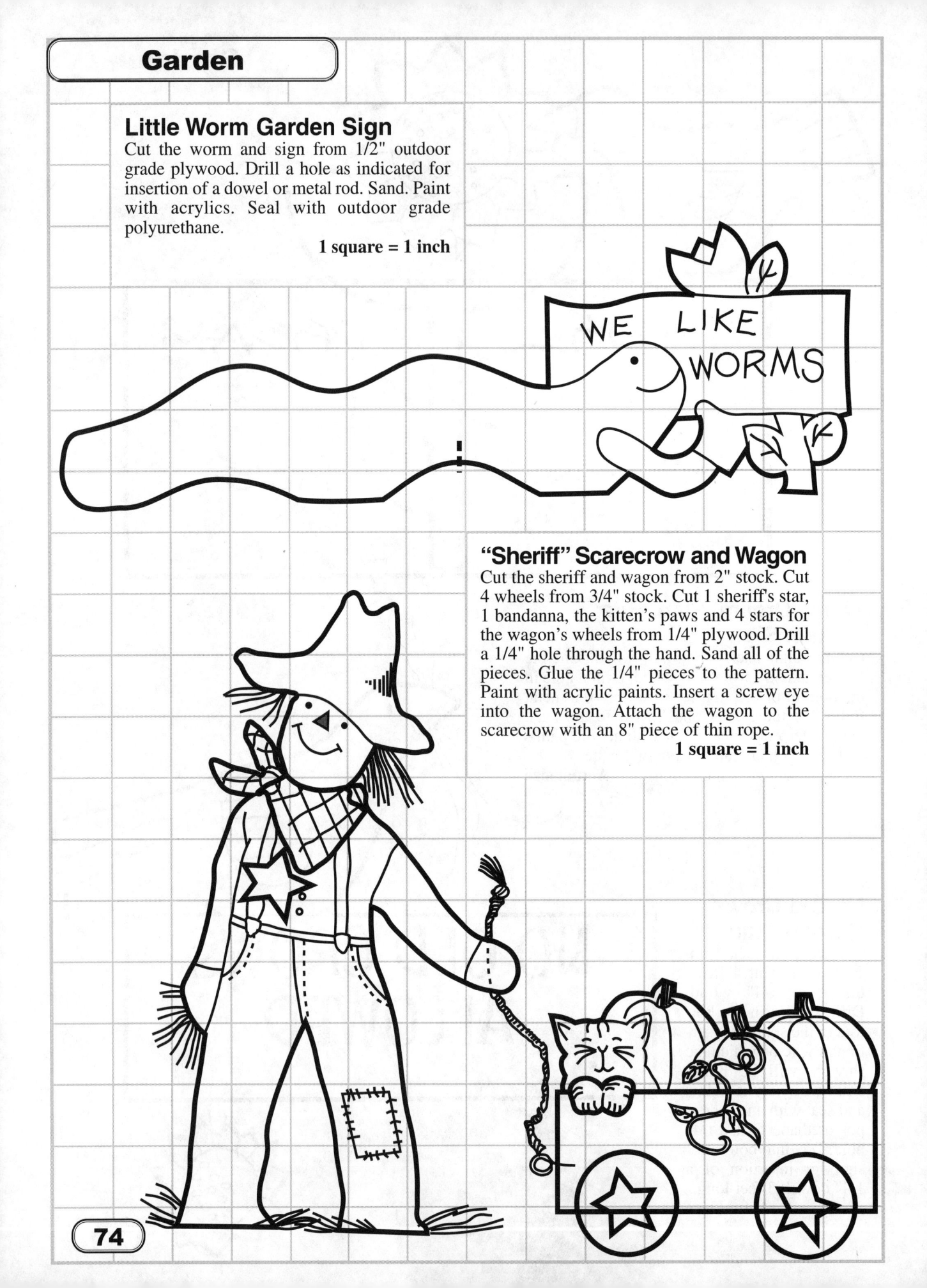

Garden

Little Worm Garden Sign

Cut the worm and sign from 1/2" outdoor grade plywood. Drill a hole as indicated for insertion of a dowel or metal rod. Sand. Paint with acrylics. Seal with outdoor grade polyurethane.

1 square = 1 inch

"Sheriff" Scarecrow and Wagon

Cut the sheriff and wagon from 2" stock. Cut 4 wheels from 3/4" stock. Cut 1 sheriff's star, 1 bandanna, the kitten's paws and 4 stars for the wagon's wheels from 1/4" plywood. Drill a 1/4" hole through the hand. Sand all of the pieces. Glue the 1/4" pieces to the pattern. Paint with acrylic paints. Insert a screw eye into the wagon. Attach the wagon to the scarecrow with an 8" piece of thin rope.

1 square = 1 inch

— CHAPTER SEVEN —
Holiday/Seasonal

Santa and Sleigh
(Cut 1)

Reindeer
(Cut 1)

Moon
(Cut 1)

Star
(Cut 1)

Star
(Cut 1)

Base
(Cut 1)

...and to all a good night.

"And to All a Good Night" Decoration
Cut the base from 2" wood. Cut Santa and sleigh, the reindeer, stars and moon from 3/4" wood. Drill small holes as indicated for insertion of 19 gauge wire. Sand all of the pieces, then paint with acrylic paints. Seal with a spray or brush on varnish. Use hot glue to attach the wire into the drilled holes. Glue small greenery to the reindeer and into santa's bag. Glitter can also be sprinkled over the tops of the buildings and on the stars for added effect.

1 square = 1 inch

Holiday/Seasonal

Magi #1

Magi #2

Camel

Magi #3

Mary

Baby Jesus

Joseph

Diagram #1

Diagram #2

Diagram #3

76

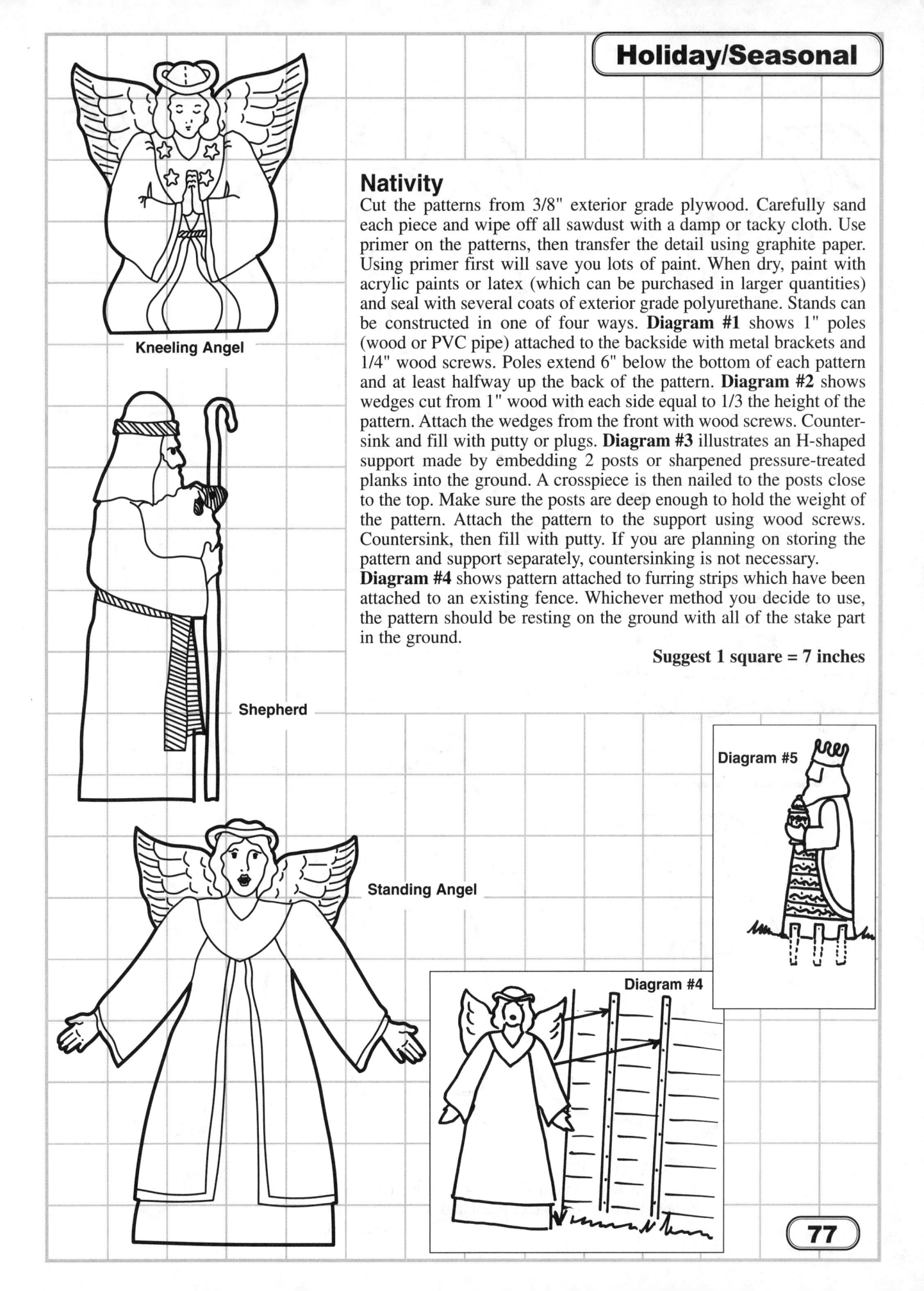

Holiday/Seasonal

Kneeling Angel

Shepherd

Nativity

Cut the patterns from 3/8" exterior grade plywood. Carefully sand each piece and wipe off all sawdust with a damp or tacky cloth. Use primer on the patterns, then transfer the detail using graphite paper. Using primer first will save you lots of paint. When dry, paint with acrylic paints or latex (which can be purchased in larger quantities) and seal with several coats of exterior grade polyurethane. Stands can be constructed in one of four ways. **Diagram #1** shows 1" poles (wood or PVC pipe) attached to the backside with metal brackets and 1/4" wood screws. Poles extend 6" below the bottom of each pattern and at least halfway up the back of the pattern. **Diagram #2** shows wedges cut from 1" wood with each side equal to 1/3 the height of the pattern. Attach the wedges from the front with wood screws. Countersink and fill with putty or plugs. **Diagram #3** illustrates an H-shaped support made by embedding 2 posts or sharpened pressure-treated planks into the ground. A crosspiece is then nailed to the posts close to the top. Make sure the posts are deep enough to hold the weight of the pattern. Attach the pattern to the support using wood screws. Countersink, then fill with putty. If you are planning on storing the pattern and support separately, countersinking is not necessary.

Diagram #4 shows pattern attached to furring strips which have been attached to an existing fence. Whichever method you decide to use, the pattern should be resting on the ground with all of the stake part in the ground.

Suggest 1 square = 7 inches

Standing Angel

Diagram #5

Diagram #4

Holiday/Seasonal

PEACE

NOEL

HOME IS WHERE THE ♥ IS

Ornaments
Cut each ornament from 1/4" wood. Drill a 1/8" hole for hanging. Sand. Paint and seal with acrylics.
Actual Size

Holiday/Seasonal

NOEL

Some bunny loves Rachel

NOEL

Let it Snow

79

Holiday/Seasonal

Arm
(Cut 2)

Drill Here

Wing
(Cut 2)

Drill Here

Little Angel Candy Holder
Cut the cute little angel from 3/4" wood. Cut 2 arms from 1/2" wood. Cut 2 wings and 1 star from 1/4" wood. Cut a base 4 3/4" x 1 3/4" from 1/2" wood. Drill a 1/4" hole through one hand. Sand all of the pieces well. Glue the arms and wings to the body. Insert a 7" long 1/4" diameter dowel into the hand. Glue the star to the dowel and angel's dress. Paint with acrylics. Glue the angel to the base. Spray with acrylic sealer.

Actual Size

Holiday Welcome Sign (starts on next page)
Cut the pieces from 1/2" wood. Separate cuts for a 3-D effect can be cut from 1/4" wood. For example, the different pieces of the house can be layered on top of each other. Each layered item should be thinner than the layer below it. Lightly sand the pieces and then paint with acrylic paints and seal with a brush or spray on varnish. Drill holes in the welcome sign for screw eyes and into each holiday pattern for placement of hooks. Be sure the hooks are lining up to the screw eyes in the welcome sign. Attach the welcome sign to the upper part of the house where indicated with wood glue and reinforce from the back with wood screws. Attach a sawtooth hanger to the back.

1 square = 1 inch

Holiday/Seasonal

Santa Bear Shelf Sitter Diagram

Santa Bear Shelf Sitter

Cut the bear and his legs from 1" wood. Cut the bear's snout and the bow from 1/4" wood. Sand the pieces well. Glue the pieces to the body. Paint and seal with acrylics.

Actual Size

Santa Bear Leg (Cut 2)

Glue Leg Here

Santa Bear's Bow (Cut 1)

Santa Bear's Nose (Cut 1)

Holiday Welcome Sign
Instructions on page 80

House Base (Cut 1)

Gable (Cut 1)

Attach Welcome Sign here

Porch Roof (Cut 1)

Welcome Sign (Cut 1)

WELCOME

81

Holiday/Seasonal

Holiday Welcome Sign (Continued)

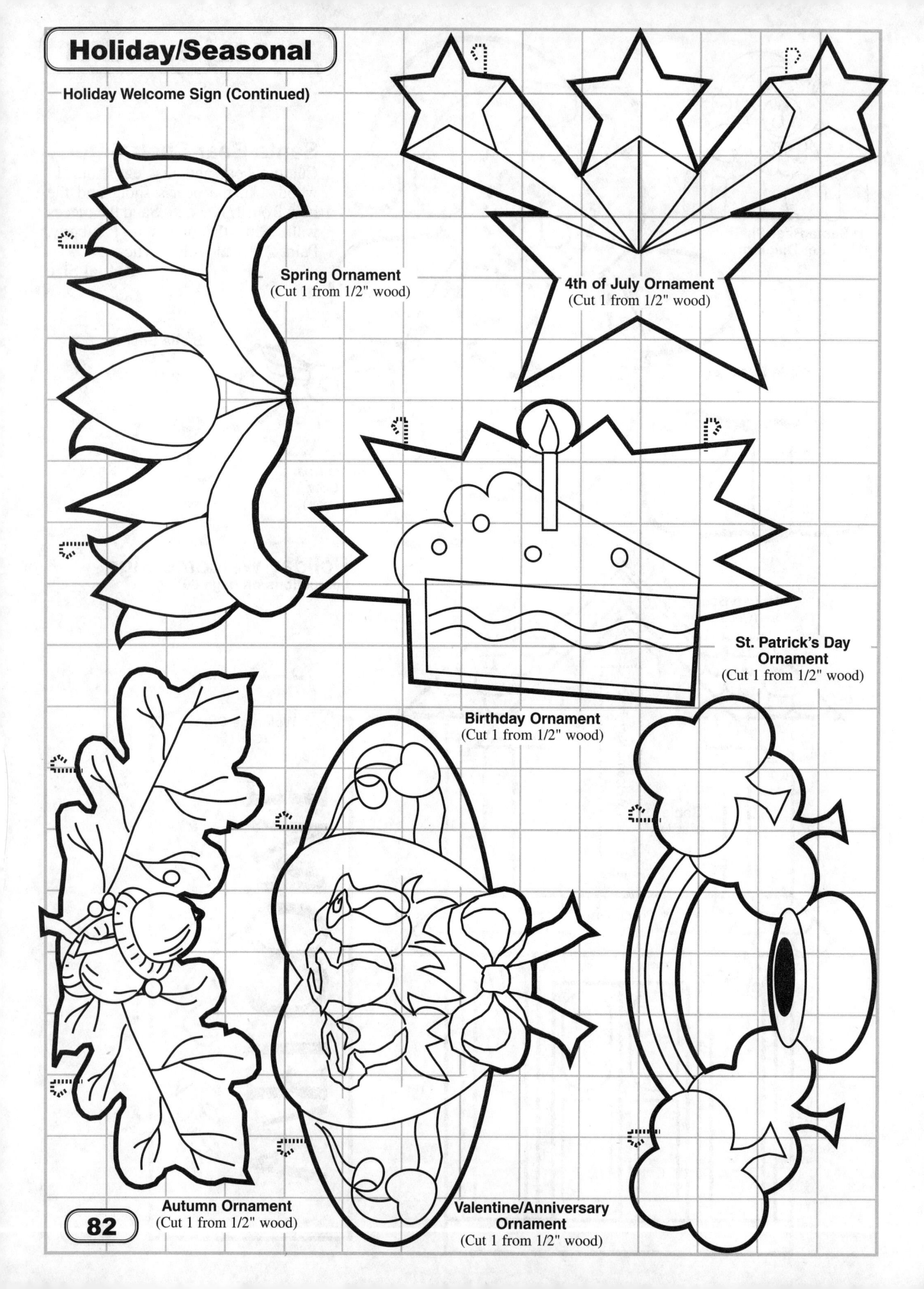

Spring Ornament
(Cut 1 from 1/2" wood)

4th of July Ornament
(Cut 1 from 1/2" wood)

St. Patrick's Day Ornament
(Cut 1 from 1/2" wood)

Birthday Ornament
(Cut 1 from 1/2" wood)

Autumn Ornament
(Cut 1 from 1/2" wood)

Valentine/Anniversary Ornament
(Cut 1 from 1/2" wood)

82

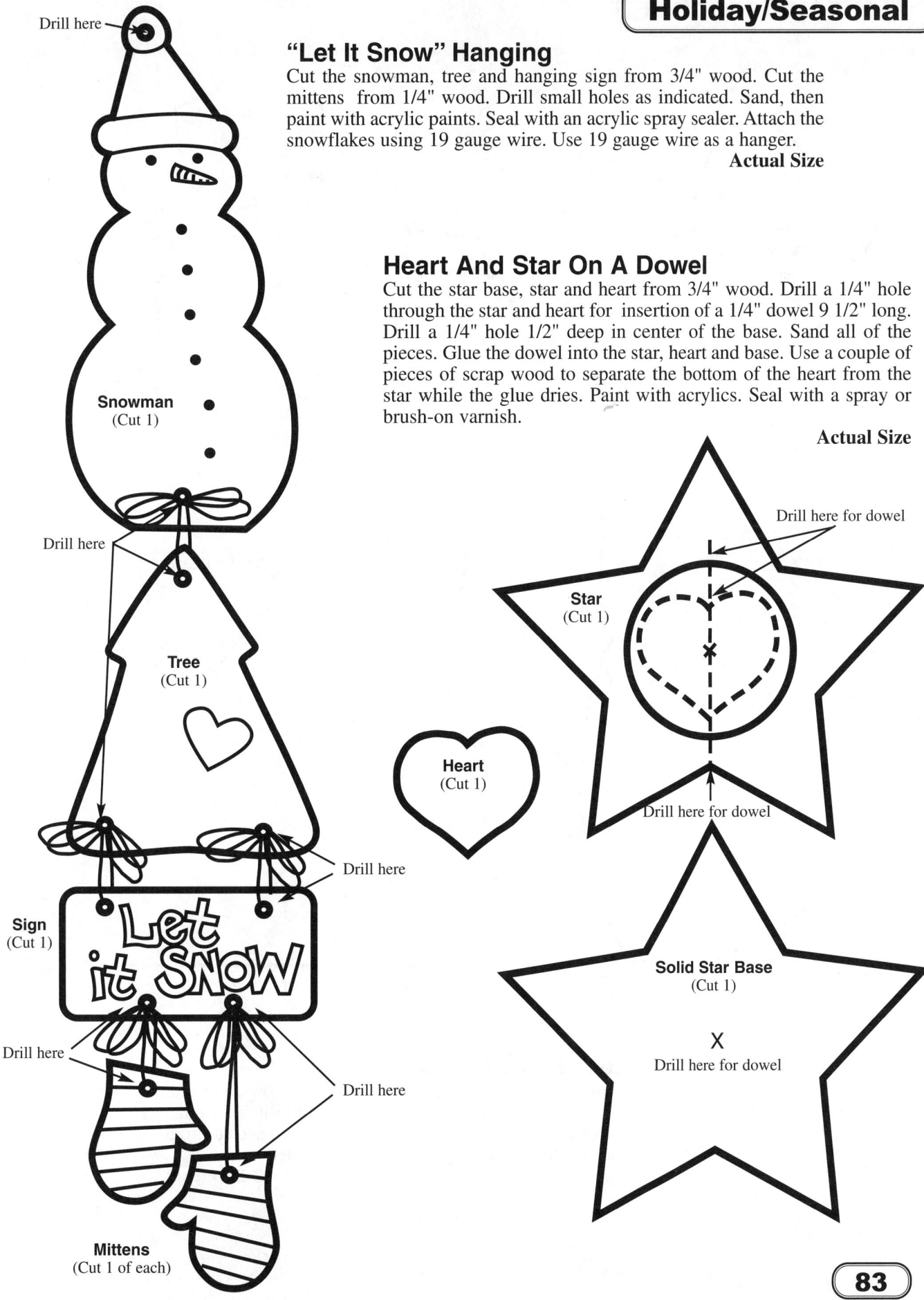

Holiday/Seasonal

"Let It Snow" Hanging

Cut the snowman, tree and hanging sign from 3/4" wood. Cut the mittens from 1/4" wood. Drill small holes as indicated. Sand, then paint with acrylic paints. Seal with an acrylic spray sealer. Attach the snowflakes using 19 gauge wire. Use 19 gauge wire as a hanger.

Actual Size

Drill here

Snowman (Cut 1)

Drill here

Tree (Cut 1)

Drill here

Sign (Cut 1)

Drill here

Drill here

Mittens (Cut 1 of each)

Heart And Star On A Dowel

Cut the star base, star and heart from 3/4" wood. Drill a 1/4" hole through the star and heart for insertion of a 1/4" dowel 9 1/2" long. Drill a 1/4" hole 1/2" deep in center of the base. Sand all of the pieces. Glue the dowel into the star, heart and base. Use a couple of pieces of scrap wood to separate the bottom of the heart from the star while the glue dries. Paint with acrylics. Seal with a spray or brush-on varnish.

Actual Size

Drill here for dowel

Star (Cut 1)

Drill here for dowel

Heart (Cut 1)

Solid Star Base (Cut 1)

X
Drill here for dowel

Holiday/Seasonal

Frosty And Freeza Snow People
Cut this cute couple actual size from 2" wood for festive table toppers. Sand, paint with acrylics and coat with acrylic spray or brush-on varnish. To use the snow people as lawn decorations, enlarge this pattern (as directed) and cut from 1/2" plywood. Paint and seal with exterior grade paints and sealer.

1 square = 2 1/2 inches

84

Holiday/Seasonal

Little Snowmen Linkables
Cut these adorable little snowmen from 1/2" wood. Paint the clothing in bright, primary colors. Seal with an acrylic sealer. They will form a zig-zag line when linked together.

Actual Size

85

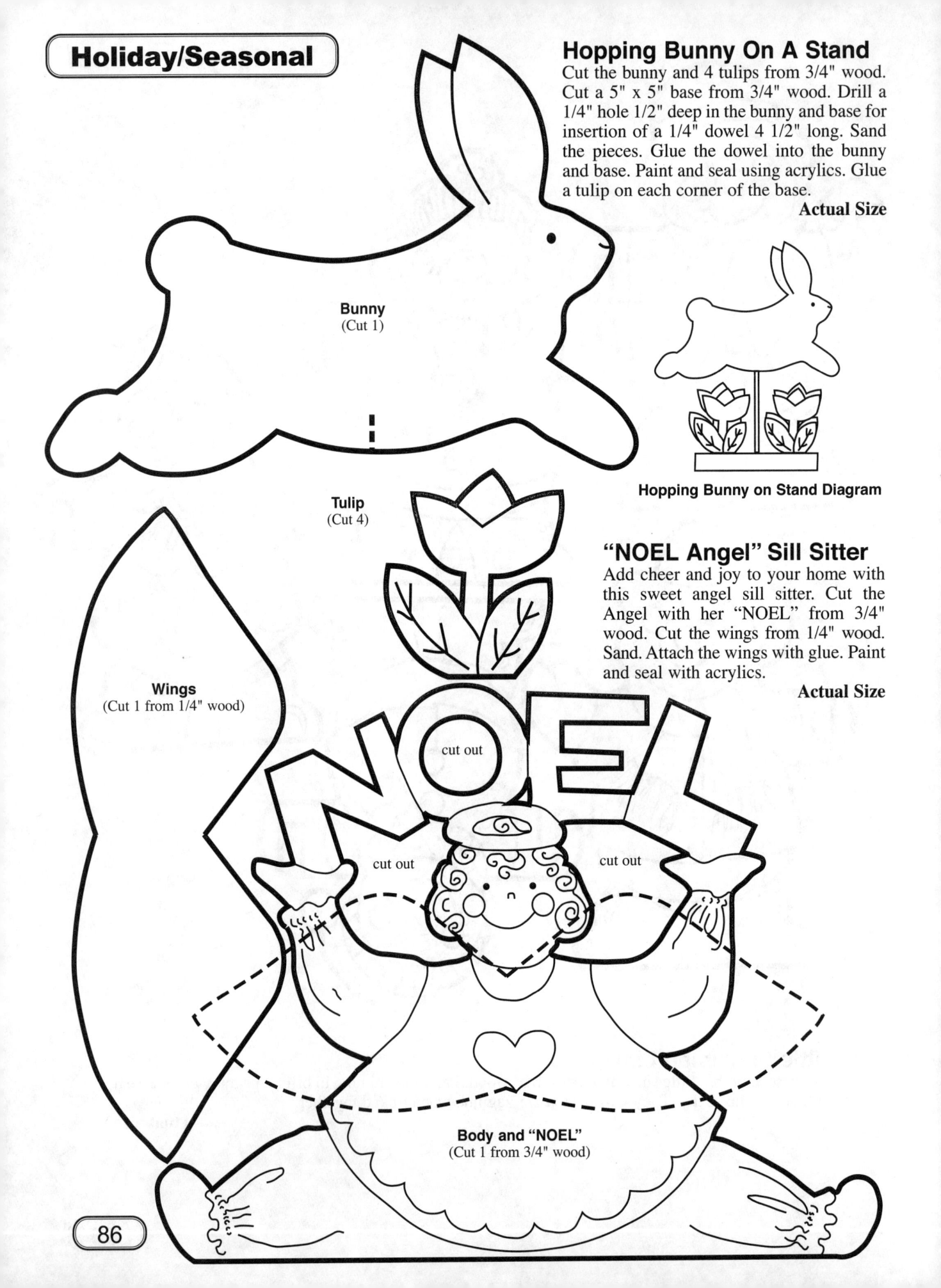

Holiday/Seasonal

Hopping Bunny On A Stand

Cut the bunny and 4 tulips from 3/4" wood. Cut a 5" x 5" base from 3/4" wood. Drill a 1/4" hole 1/2" deep in the bunny and base for insertion of a 1/4" dowel 4 1/2" long. Sand the pieces. Glue the dowel into the bunny and base. Paint and seal using acrylics. Glue a tulip on each corner of the base.

Actual Size

Bunny
(Cut 1)

Hopping Bunny on Stand Diagram

Tulip
(Cut 4)

"NOEL Angel" Sill Sitter

Add cheer and joy to your home with this sweet angel sill sitter. Cut the Angel with her "NOEL" from 3/4" wood. Cut the wings from 1/4" wood. Sand. Attach the wings with glue. Paint and seal with acrylics.

Actual Size

Wings
(Cut 1 from 1/4" wood)

cut out

cut out   cut out

Body and "NOEL"
(Cut 1 from 3/4" wood)

86

Christmas Cabinet

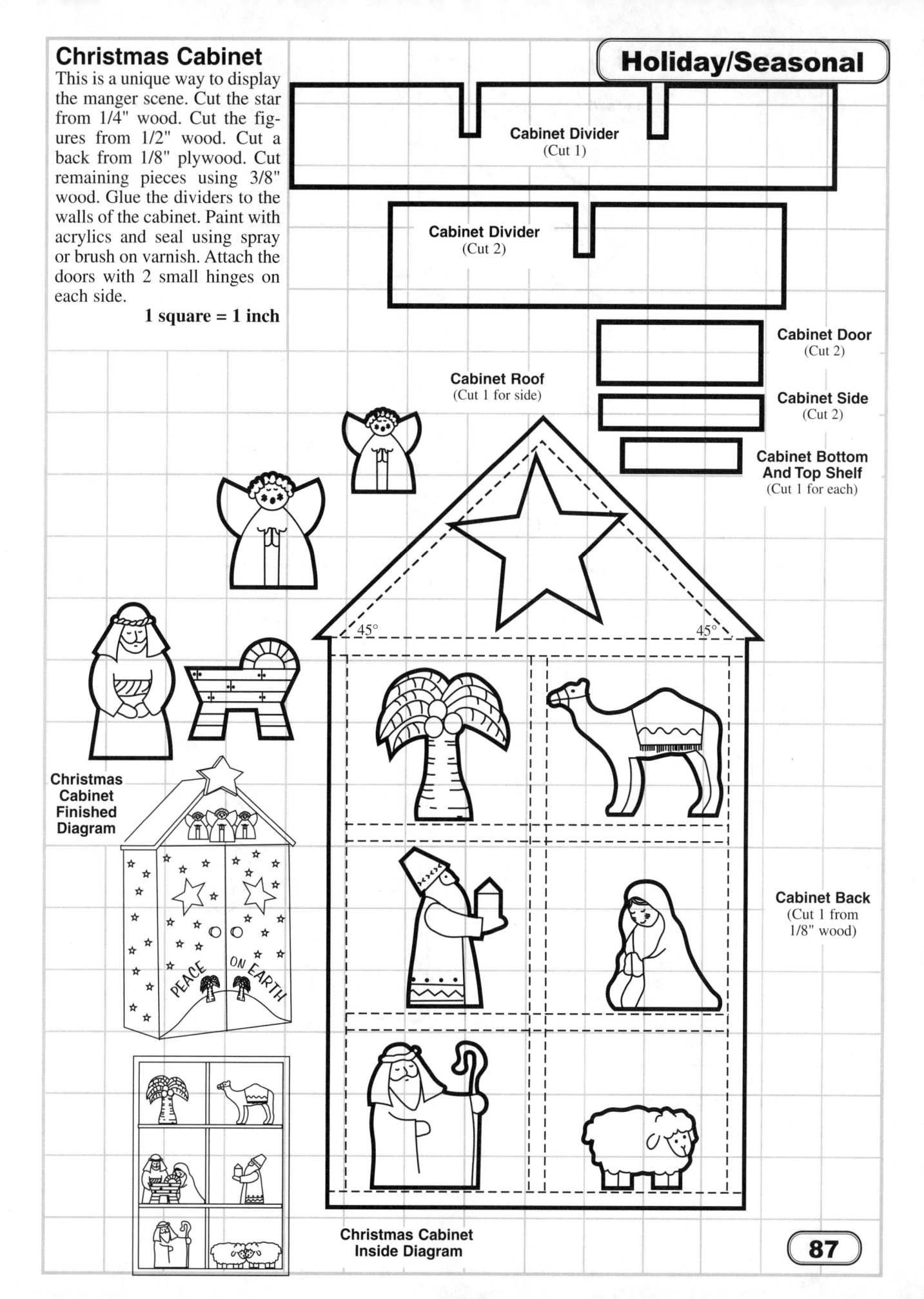

This is a unique way to display the manger scene. Cut the star from 1/4" wood. Cut the figures from 1/2" wood. Cut a back from 1/8" plywood. Cut remaining pieces using 3/8" wood. Glue the dividers to the walls of the cabinet. Paint with acrylics and seal using spray or brush on varnish. Attach the doors with 2 small hinges on each side.

1 square = 1 inch

Holiday/Seasonal

Cabinet Divider (Cut 1)

Cabinet Divider (Cut 2)

Cabinet Door (Cut 2)

Cabinet Side (Cut 2)

Cabinet Bottom And Top Shelf (Cut 1 for each)

Cabinet Roof (Cut 1 for side)

45° 45°

Cabinet Back (Cut 1 from 1/8" wood)

Christmas Cabinet Finished Diagram

Christmas Cabinet Inside Diagram

87

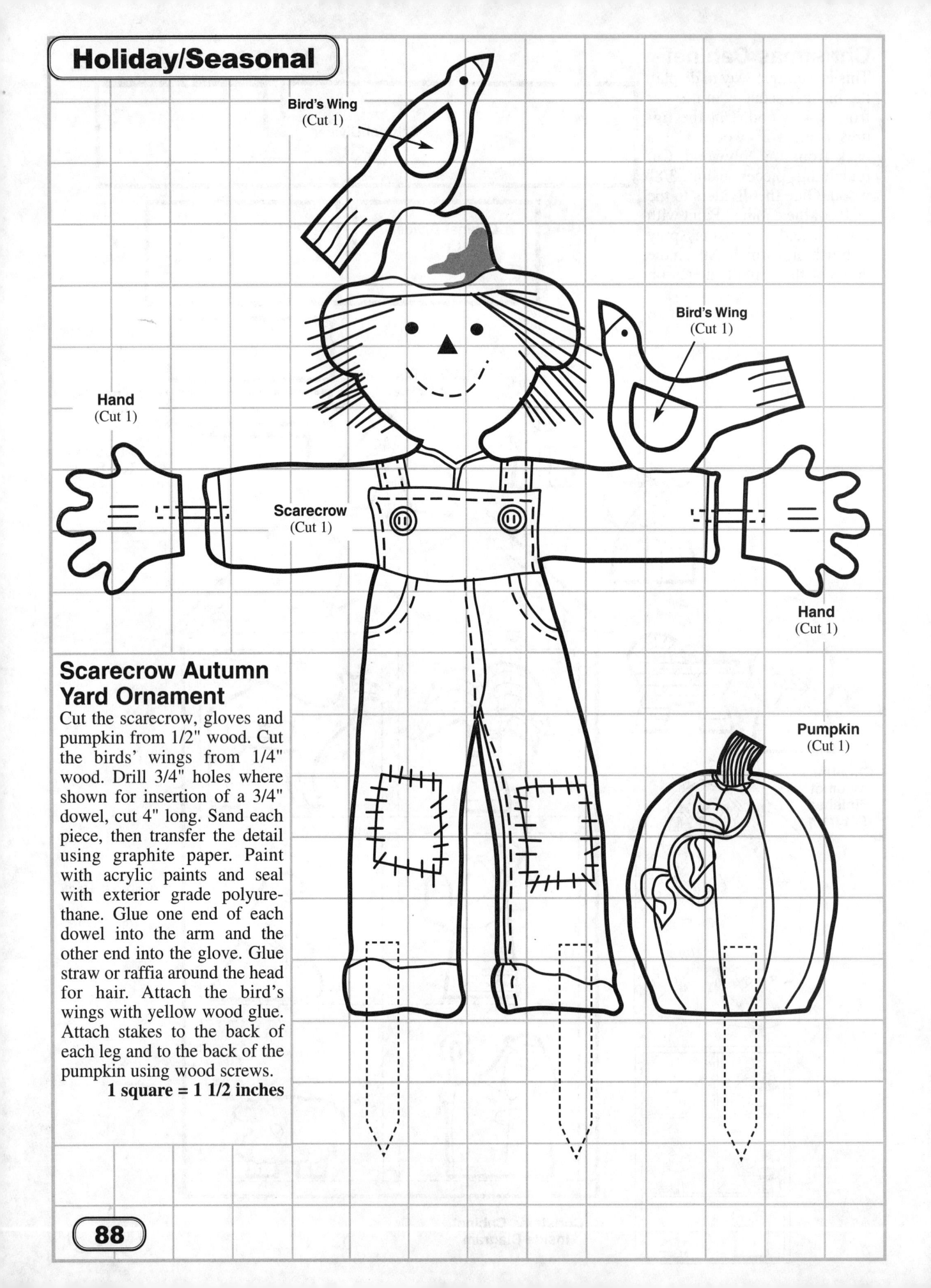

Holiday/Seasonal

Bird's Wing
(Cut 1)

Bird's Wing
(Cut 1)

Hand
(Cut 1)

Scarecrow
(Cut 1)

Hand
(Cut 1)

Pumpkin
(Cut 1)

Scarecrow Autumn Yard Ornament

Cut the scarecrow, gloves and pumpkin from 1/2" wood. Cut the birds' wings from 1/4" wood. Drill 3/4" holes where shown for insertion of a 3/4" dowel, cut 4" long. Sand each piece, then transfer the detail using graphite paper. Paint with acrylic paints and seal with exterior grade polyurethane. Glue one end of each dowel into the arm and the other end into the glove. Glue straw or raffia around the head for hair. Attach the bird's wings with yellow wood glue. Attach stakes to the back of each leg and to the back of the pumpkin using wood screws.

1 square = 1 1/2 inches

Holiday/Seasonal

Snowman Trio Ornaments

Cut each snowman from 1/4" wood. Cut the heart and star from 1/8" wood. Sand, transfer the detail with graphite paper, and paint with acrylic paints. Attach the star using yellow wood glue. Drill holes where shown for hangers. Drill a hole through the hands of the snowman with the heart and through the heart for insertion of 24 gauge wire. Seal with spray or brush on varnish. Tie small ribbon around the necks of the other two as shown. These patterns can also be cut from 1/2" wood and used as tabletop or mantel decorations. Be sure to sand bottoms flat for stability.

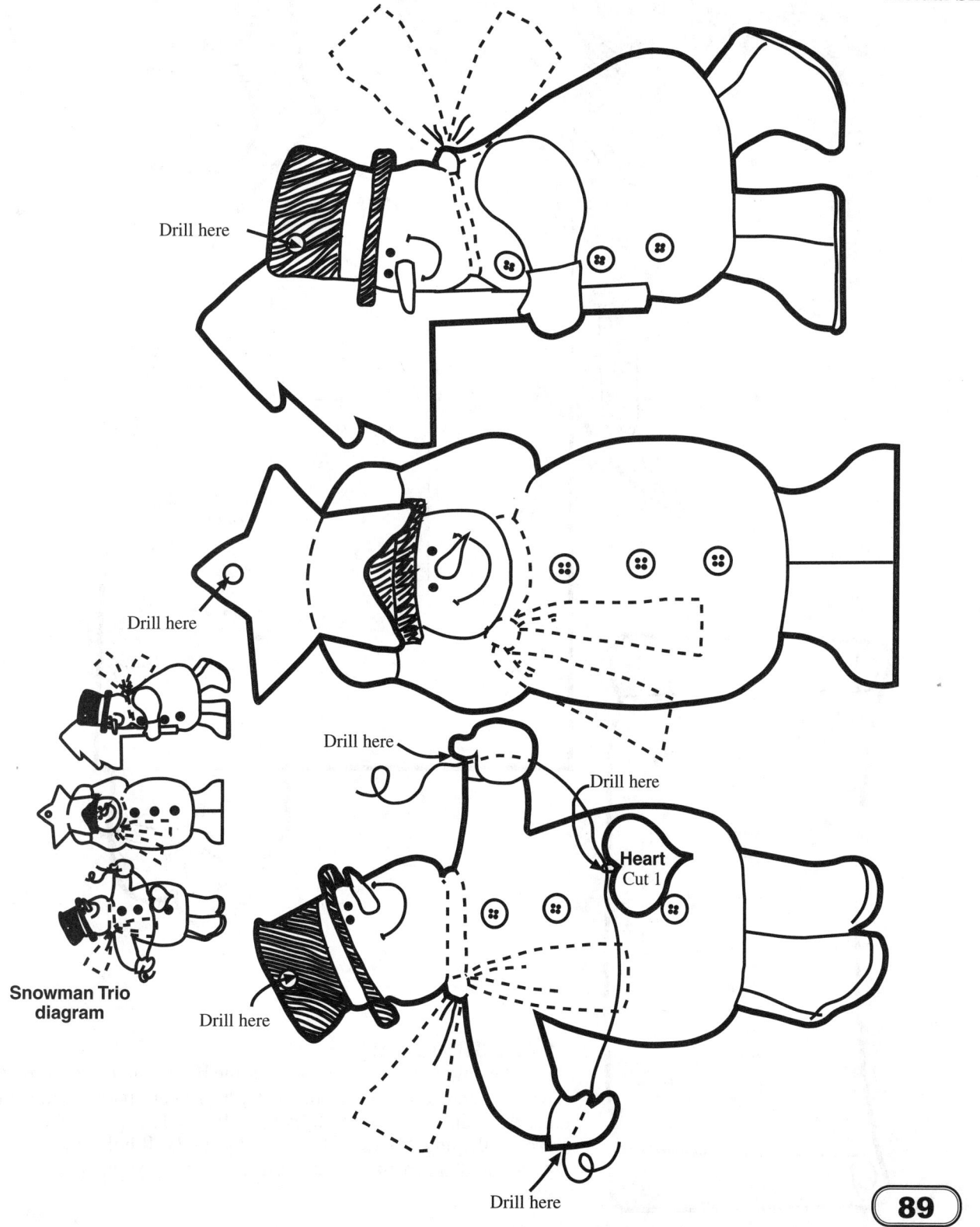

Actual Size

Drill here

Drill here

Drill here

Drill here

Drill here

Drill here

Heart Cut 1

Snowman Trio diagram

Holiday/Seasonal

Arm
(Cut 1)

Christmas Angel diagram

Banner
(Cut 1)

JOYOUS CHRISTMAS From the COLEMANS

Christmas Angel
Cut the angel from 1/2" wood. Cut the banner and arm from 1/4" wood. Sand, transfer the detail with graphite paper, paint with acrylic paints and seal with spray or brush on varnish. Attach the arm to the angel with yellow wood glue. Drill holes through the hands and the banner where shown for insertion of 24 gauge wire.

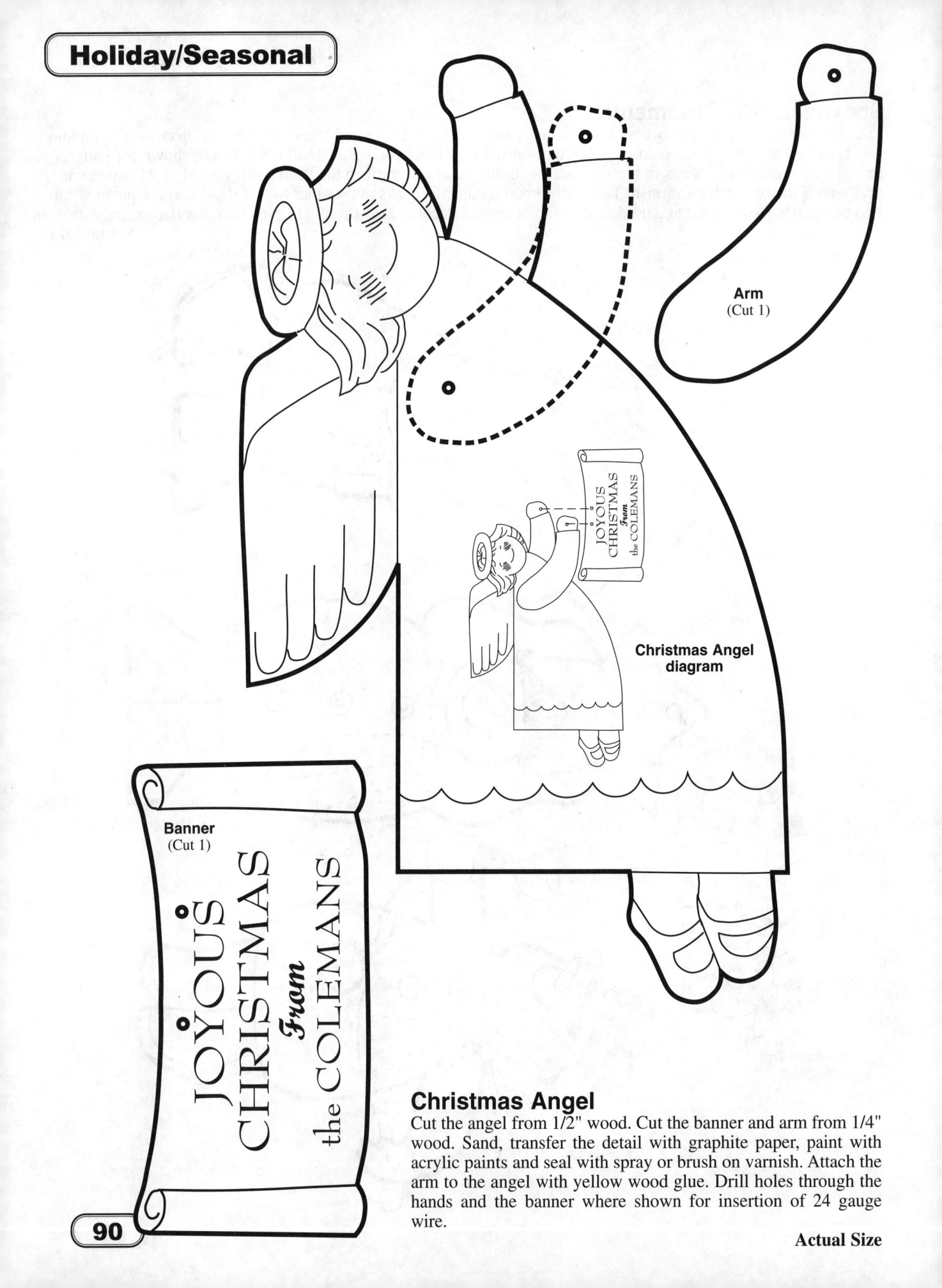

Actual Size

Holiday/Seasonal

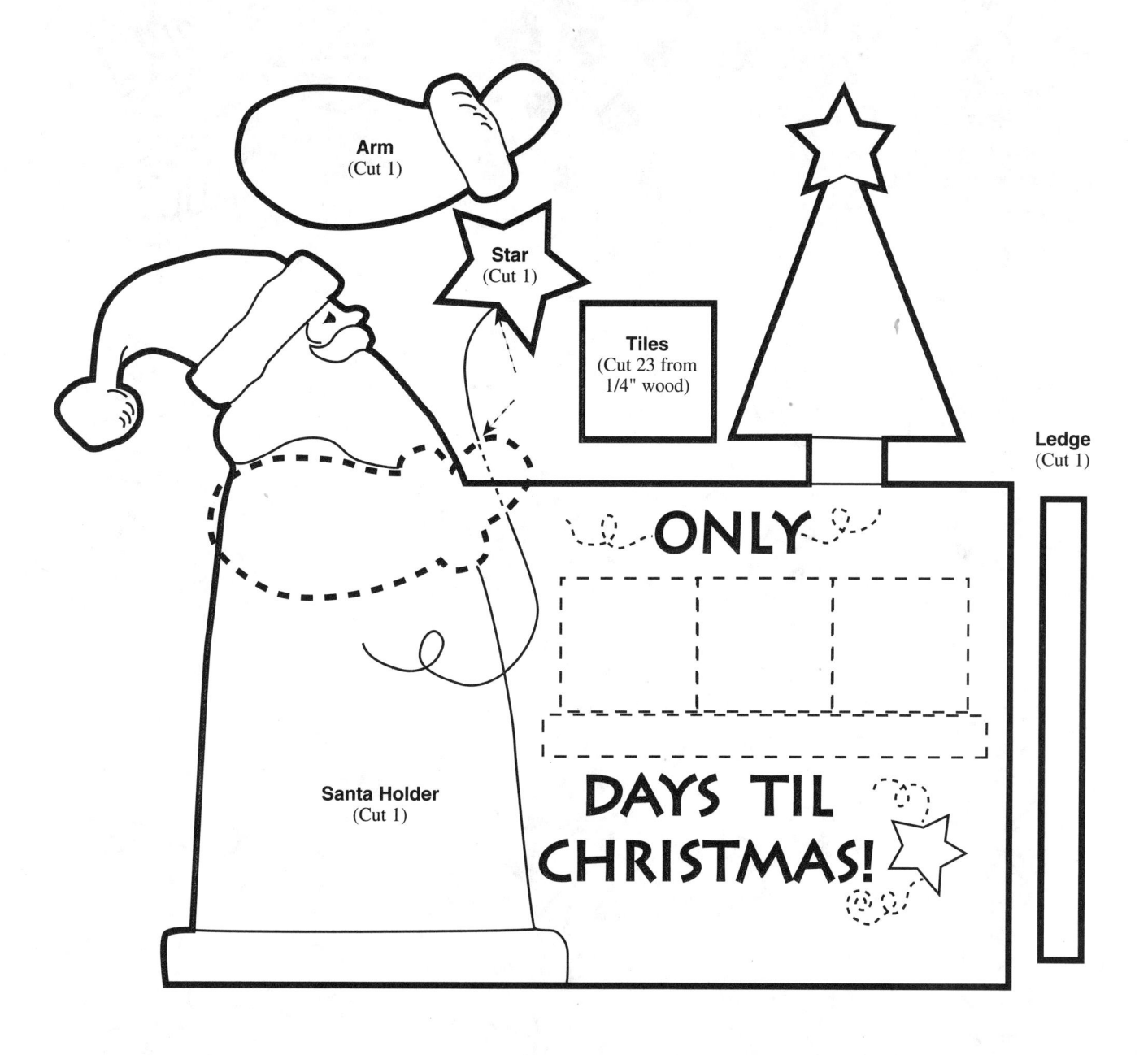

Arm (Cut 1)

Star (Cut 1)

Tiles (Cut 23 from 1/4" wood)

Ledge (Cut 1)

Santa Holder (Cut 1)

ONLY

DAYS TIL CHRISTMAS!

Christmas Countdown (for the whole year!)
Cut the pattern from 1" wood. Cut the date tiles from 1/4" wood. You will need 23 tiles, two 0's, three 1's, three 2's, two 3's and two of all the other numbers 4-9. Drill a small hole into the star and through the hand. Cut a 2 7/8" x 1/2" ledge from 1" wood. Rabbet the ledge 1/4" wide x 1/4" deep (this is where the tiles will be placed). Sand all of the pieces. Paint with acrylic paints. Seal with an acrylic spray varnish. This pattern can stand on a table or shelf or you can hang it by attaching a saw-tooth hanger to the back.

Actual Size

Holiday/Seasonal

Snowflakes

Cut several snowflakes of each pattern from 1/4" hardwood to decorate your Christmas tree. Use a very fine blade on your scroll saw. Start your cuts in the center and work your way out to the edge. Drill a small hole in the center of each dark area for insertion of the blade. The cutting may be a bit tedious but the results will be worth all the work you'll put into this project. Sand lightly. Stain the snowflakes or paint them white and sprinkle with glitter for a dazzling display.

92

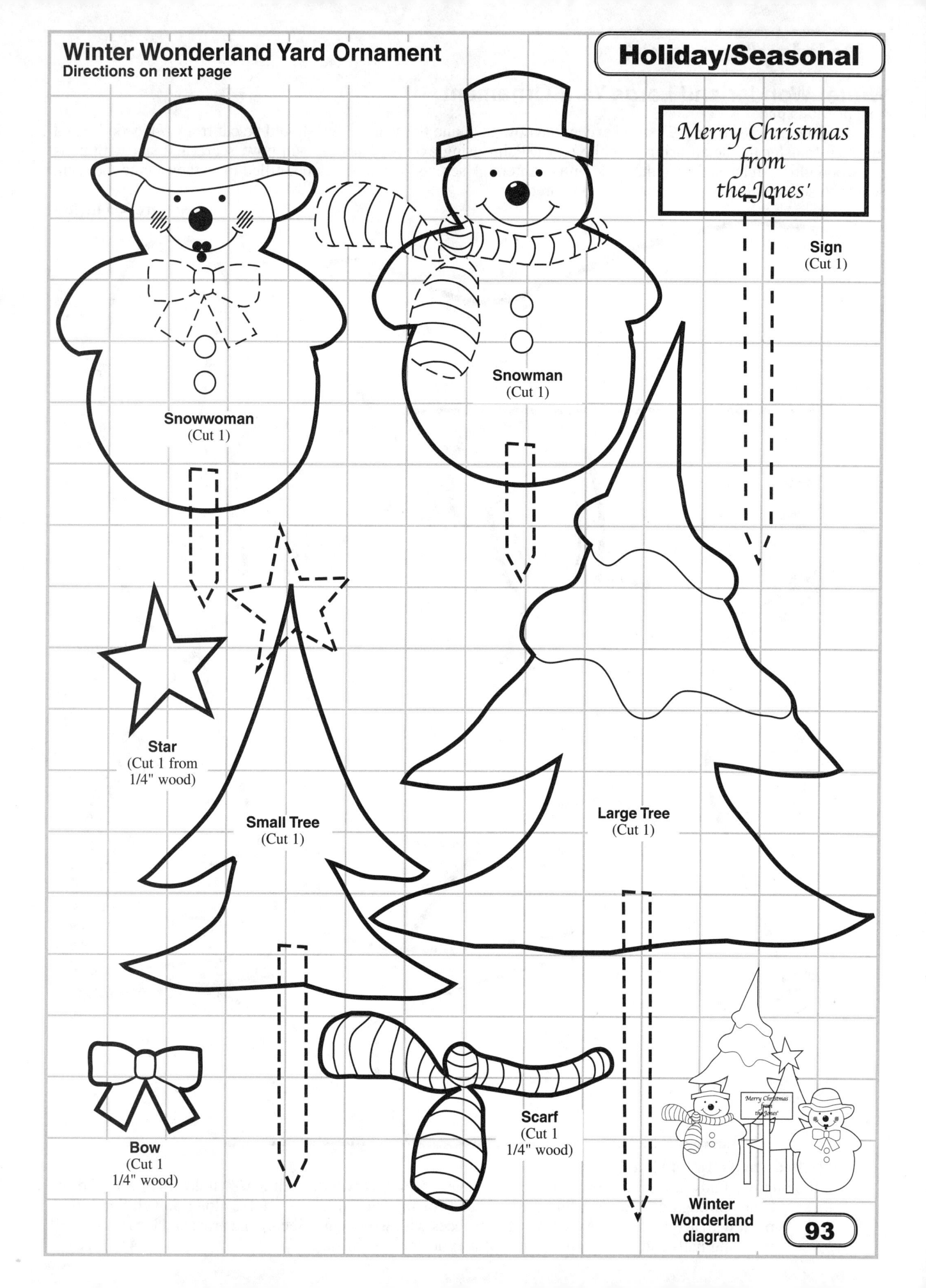

Winter Wonderland Yard Ornament
Directions on next page

Holiday/Seasonal

Merry Christmas from the Jones'

Sign (Cut 1)

Snowwoman (Cut 1)

Snowman (Cut 1)

Star (Cut 1 from 1/4" wood)

Small Tree (Cut 1)

Large Tree (Cut 1)

Bow (Cut 1 1/4" wood)

Scarf (Cut 1 1/4" wood)

Winter Wonderland diagram

93

Holiday/Seasonal

Winter Wonderland Large Yard Ornament
from previous page

Cut all of the patterns from 1/2" wood except the bow, star, and the scarf which should be cut from 1/4" wood. Sand and then transfer the detail using graphite paper. Paint using exterior latex. Attach bow, scarf, and star with nails and wood glue. Attach stakes to the back with countersink screws. The holes can be filled in so they cannot be seen. Seal with several coats of exterior grade polyurethane.

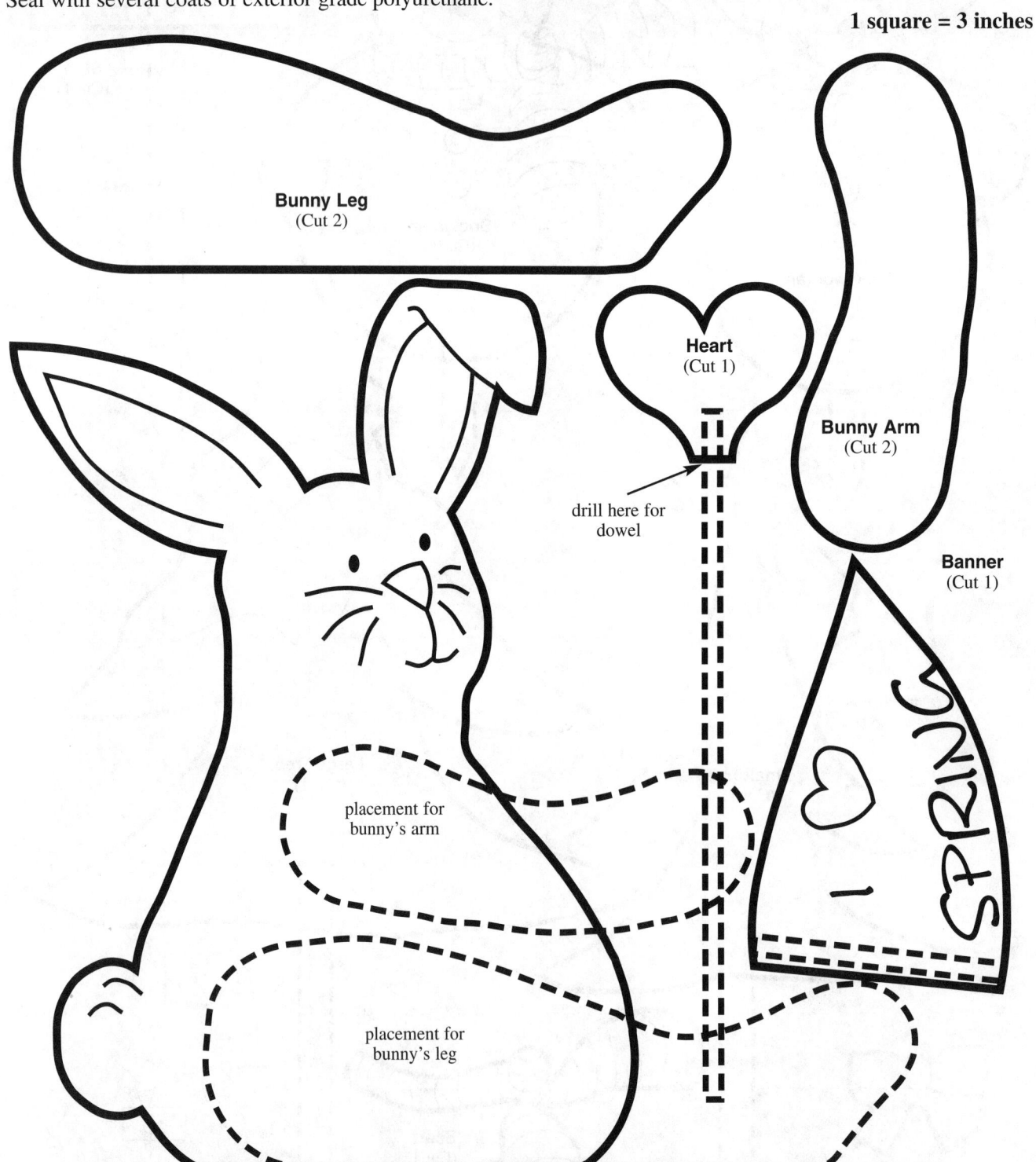

1 square = 3 inches

Bunny Leg
(Cut 2)

Heart
(Cut 1)

drill here for dowel

Bunny Arm
(Cut 2)

Banner
(Cut 1)

placement for bunny's arm

placement for bunny's leg

"I Love Spring" Bunny

Cut the bunny's body, 2 legs, 2 arms, 1 flag and 1 heart from 3/4" wood. Drill a 1/8" hole 1/4" deep into the heart, through the flag and through the hand for insertion of a 1/8", 4 1/2" long dowel. Sand, then paint with acrylic paints. Attach all of the pieces with wood glue. Secure the arms and legs with small finishing nails and glue. Apply a coat of acrylic spray varnish.

Actual Size

Holiday/Seasonal

Hat Brim
(Cut 1)

placement for hat brim

Carrot Nose
(Cut 1)

Scarf Front Piece
(Cut 1)

placement for scarf front piece

Snowman
(Cut 1)

Snowman Lawn Decoration
Cut the snowman's body from 1" exterior grade wood. Cut the snowman's nose, broom and two stakes from 1/2" wood. Cut the hat brim and scarf from 1/4" wood. Sand and basecoat. Transfer the detail with graphite paper. Paint with acrylic paints. Lightly sand the areas where the additional pieces will be attached. Attach the snowman's nose, hat brim, scarves and broom with all-weather glue and small nails. Attach the small stakes to the back with wood screws. Seal with several coats of exterior grade polyurethane. This pattern can also be cut actual size from 1/2" wood for a table top or mantel.

1 square = 3 inches

95

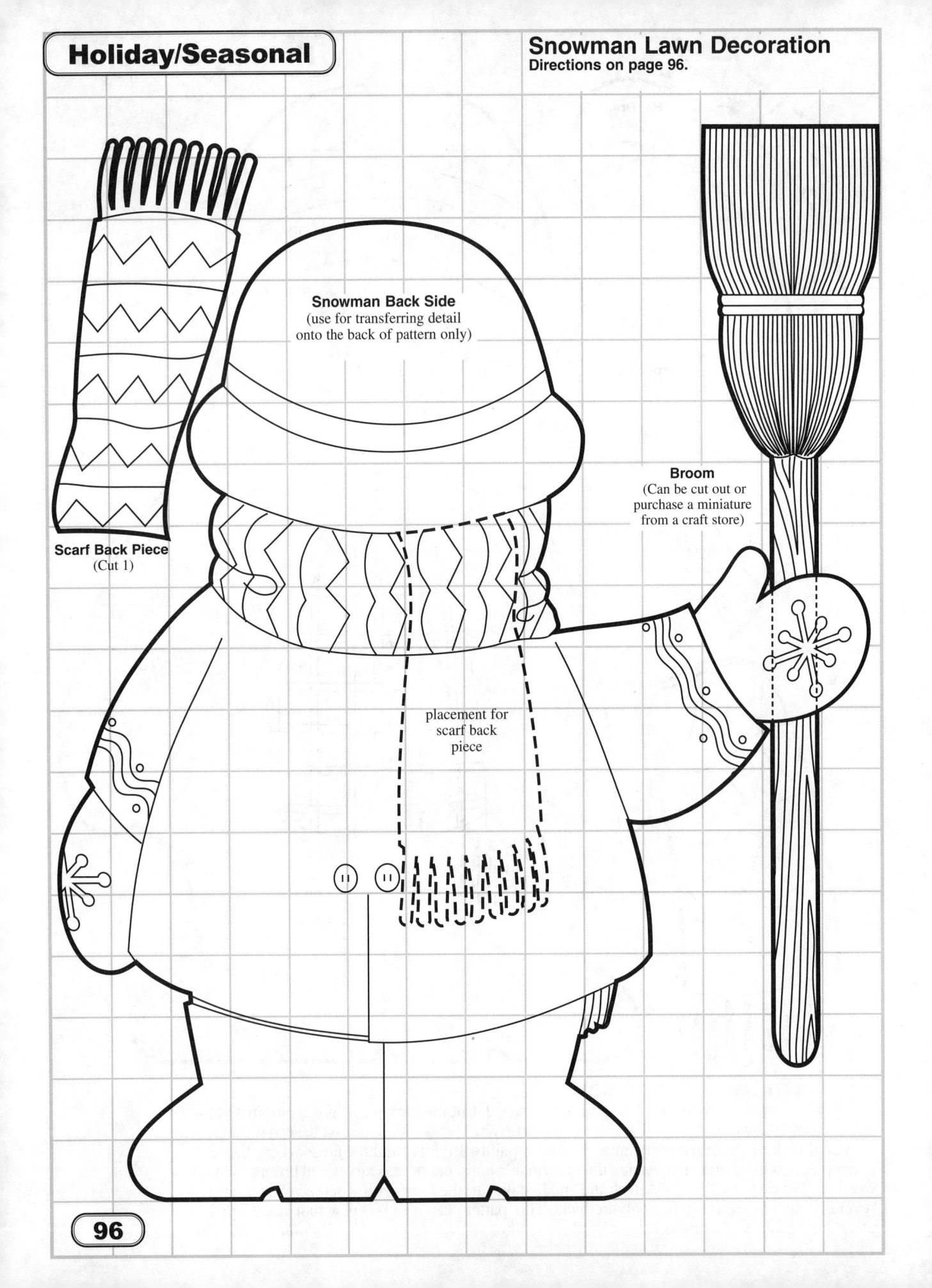

Holiday/Seasonal

Snowman Lawn Decoration
Directions on page 96.

Snowman Back Side
(use for transferring detail onto the back of pattern only)

Scarf Back Piece
(Cut 1)

Broom
(Can be cut out or purchase a miniature from a craft store)

placement for scarf back piece

— CHAPTER EIGHT —
Household Helpers

Country Seed Plaque
(Cut 1)

Bird
(Cut 1)

Bird's Wing
(Cut 1)

Drill here

Drill here

Drill here

Country Seed Plaque And Key Holder

Cut the plaque from 1/2" wood. Cut the watermelon, sunflower, bird and wing from 1/4" wood and drill a small hole at the top of each. Sand well. Paint and seal using acrylics. Insert a large cup hook at each "X" on the plaque. Insert raffia through each hole in the watermelon, sunflower and bird, then make a bow and hang from the cup hooks. Also hang keys onto the cup hooks.

Actual Size

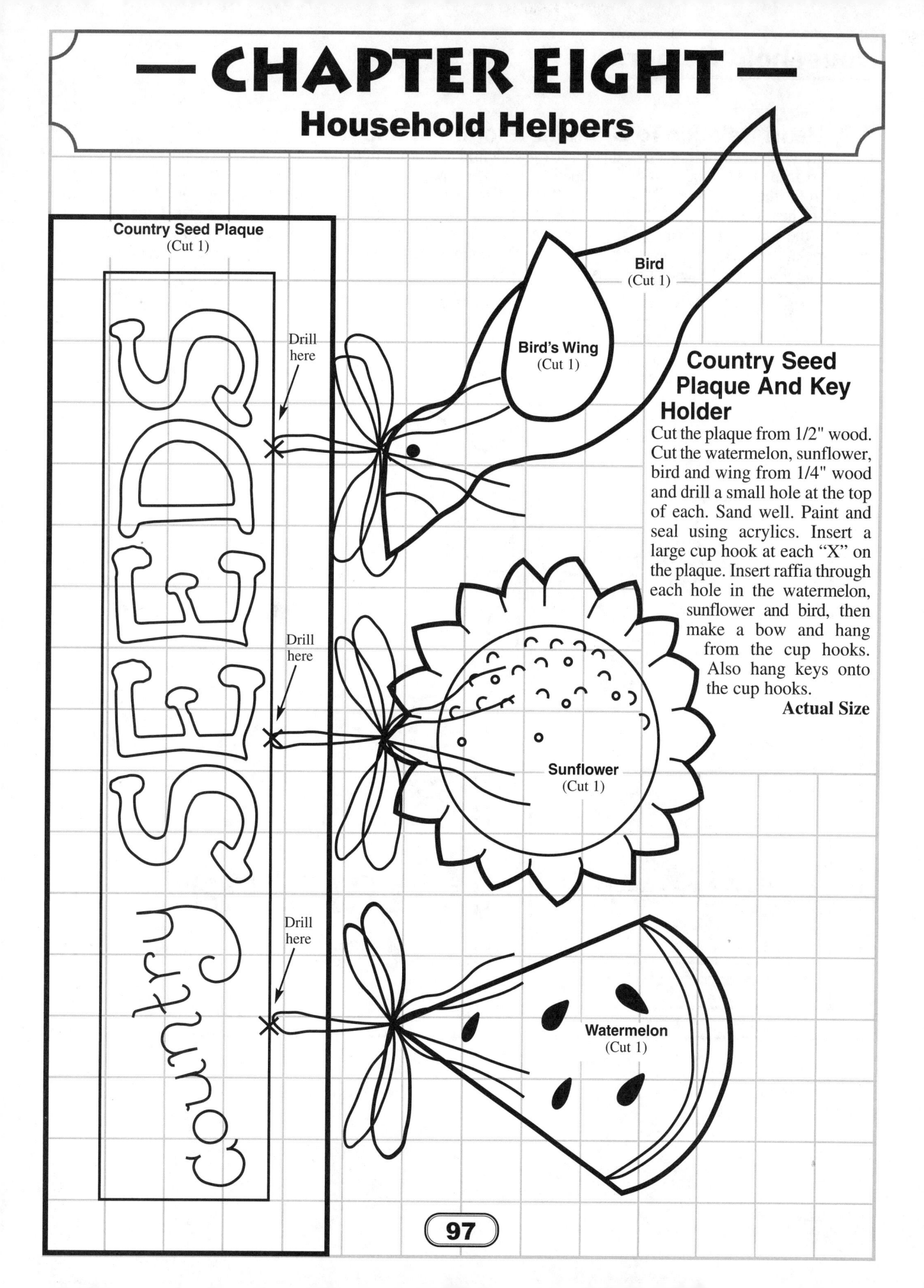

Sunflower
(Cut 1)

Watermelon
(Cut 1)

Household Helpers

"My Heart Belongs To Gramma" Picture Frame

Every grandma needs a frame like this for her grandchild's photo. Cut the frame from 1/2" wood. Cut the word and heart from 1/8" wood. Cut out the opening for the photo. Cut a 3 1/8" x 3 3/4" back from 1/8" wood. Cut the stand for the back from 1/2" wood. Cut 2 strips from 1/4" wood, 1/4" x 3 3/4" and 1 strip 1/4" x 2 5/8 ". Cut a piece of heavy plastic 2 3/4" x 3 1/2" to use as a dust cover for the photo. Sand the cut pieces. Glue the 1/4" strips to the back of the frame as shown by the dotted line. Glue the 1/8" back to the strips. Find the center of the frame at the back; glue the stand in this area. Paint the pieces. Glue "MY Heart" to the front. Seal the frame with an acrylic spray sealer.

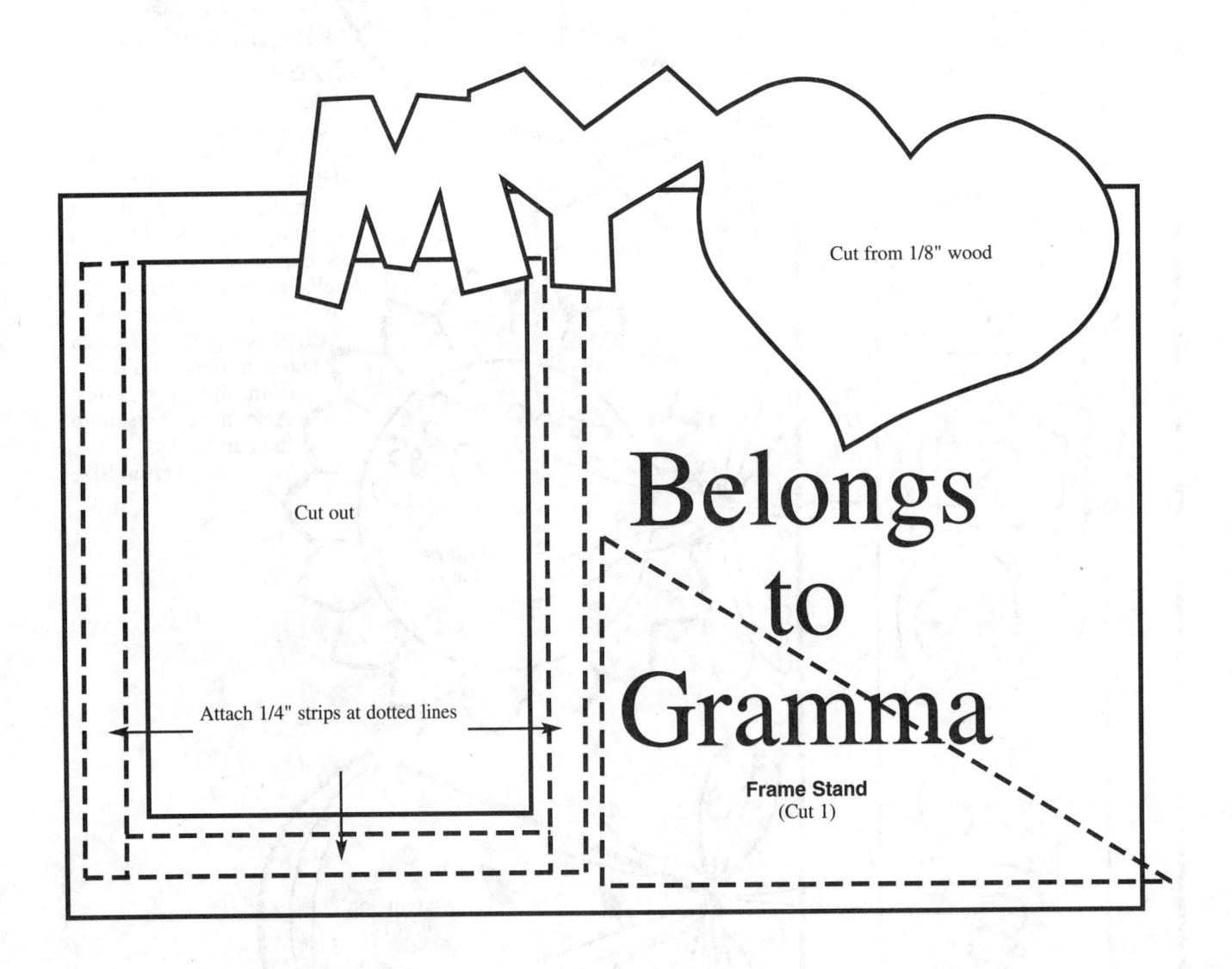

Actual Size

Cut from 1/8" wood

Cut out

Attach 1/4" strips at dotted lines

Belongs to Gramma

Frame Stand
(Cut 1)

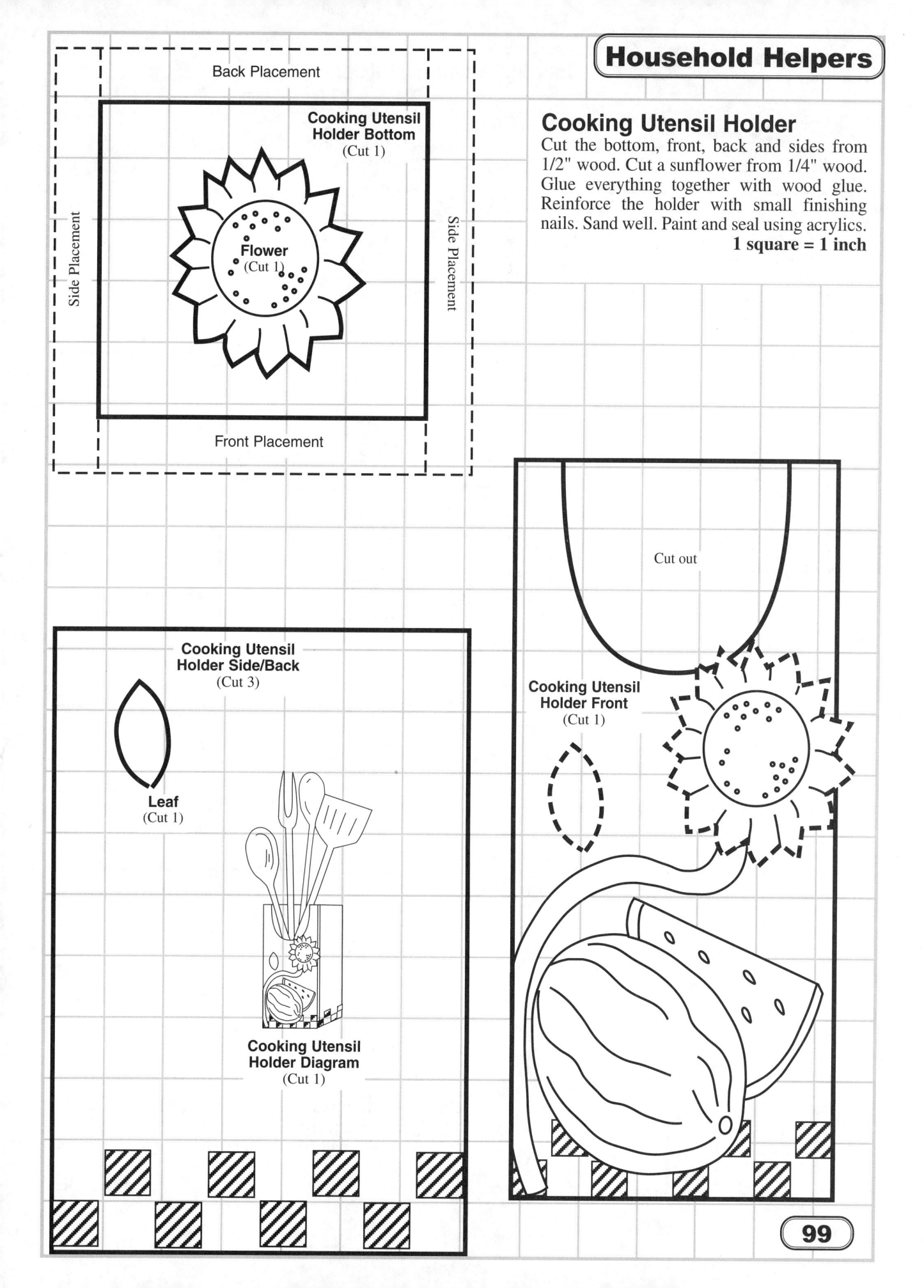

Household Helpers

Cooking Utensil Holder

Cut the bottom, front, back and sides from 1/2" wood. Cut a sunflower from 1/4" wood. Glue everything together with wood glue. Reinforce the holder with small finishing nails. Sand well. Paint and seal using acrylics.

1 square = 1 inch

Back Placement

Cooking Utensil Holder Bottom (Cut 1)

Side Placement

Flower (Cut 1)

Side Placement

Front Placement

Cooking Utensil Holder Side/Back (Cut 3)

Leaf (Cut 1)

Cooking Utensil Holder Diagram (Cut 1)

Cut out

Cooking Utensil Holder Front (Cut 1)

Household Helpers

Cow Notepaper Holder

Cow Back (Cut 1)

holder placement

Cow Front (Cut 1)

Animal Note Holder Diagram

Cow's Head (Cut 1)

Notepaper Holder Side (Cut 2 for each holder)

Lamb's Head (Cut 1)

Lamb Front/Back (Cut 1)

holder placement

Lamb Notepaper Holder

Note Paper Holder Instructions

Cut all pieces from 3/8" plywood. Assemble with glue and small brads. Paint with acrylic paints and seal using an acrylic sealer.

Actual Size

100

Household Helpers

Moose Notepaper Holder

Moose Front/Back
(Cut 1)

Holder placement

Moose's Head
(Cut 1)

Notepaper Holder Bottom
(Cut 1 for each holder)

Flower
(Cut 1)

Sugar Packet Caddy End
(Cut 2)

Glue Side Here

Glue Side Here

Glue Bottom Here

Sugar Packet Caddy Diagram

Sugar Packet Caddy Bottom
(Cut 1)

Sugar Packet Caddy Side
(Cut 2)

Leaf
(Cut 1)

Sugar Packet Caddy

Cut all of the pieces from 1/4" wood. Sand all of the pieces. Glue the flower and leaf to the sides. Glue the side and bottom slats to the watermelon ends. Paint and seal with acrylics.

Actual Size

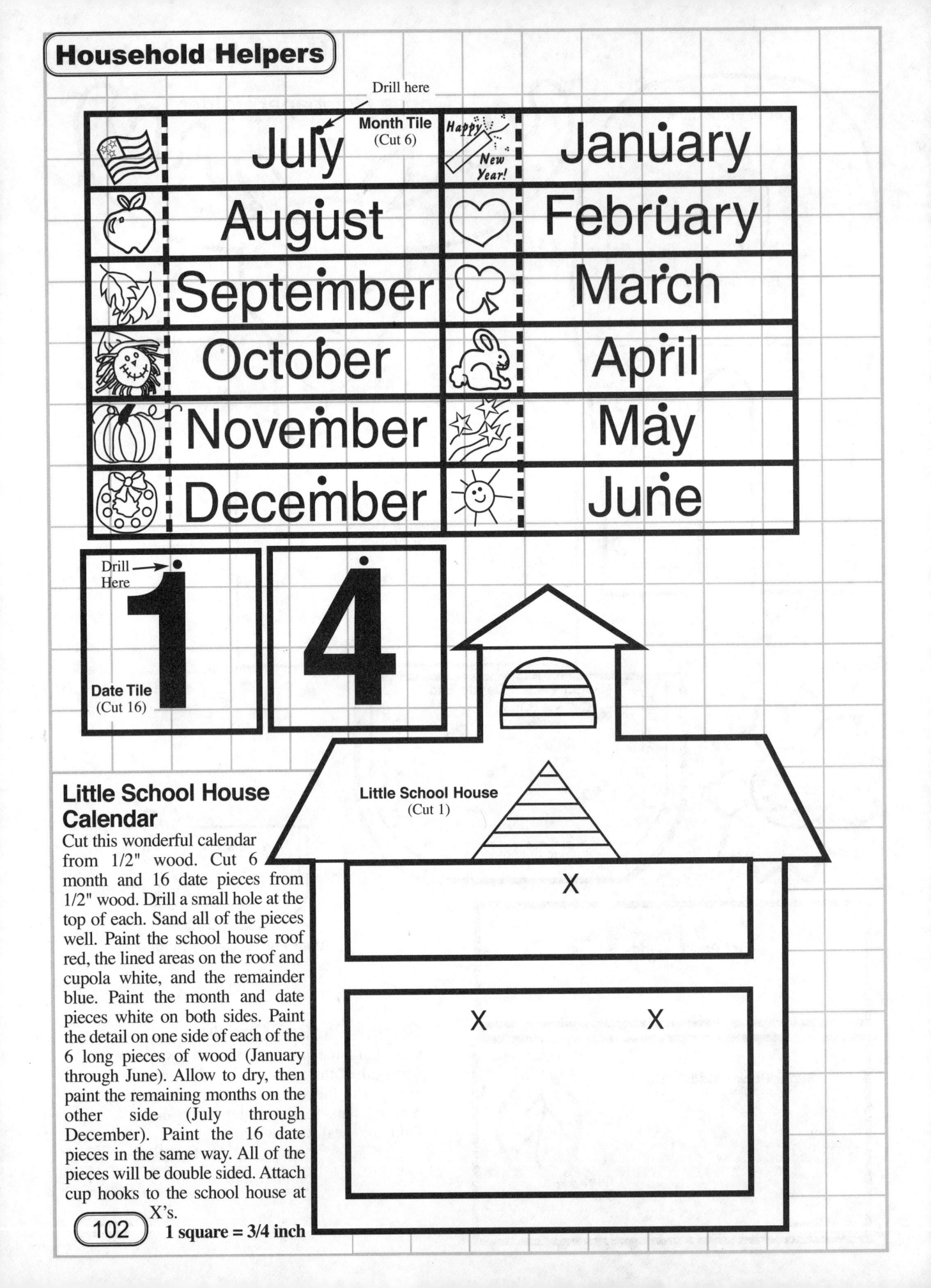

Household Helpers

Drill here

Month Tile (Cut 6)

July | January
August | February
September | March
October | April
November | May
December | June

Drill Here

Date Tile (Cut 16)

1 4

Little School House (Cut 1)

Little School House Calendar

Cut this wonderful calendar from 1/2" wood. Cut 6 month and 16 date pieces from 1/2" wood. Drill a small hole at the top of each. Sand all of the pieces well. Paint the school house roof red, the lined areas on the roof and cupola white, and the remainder blue. Paint the month and date pieces white on both sides. Paint the detail on one side of each of the 6 long pieces of wood (January through June). Allow to dry, then paint the remaining months on the other side (July through December). Paint the 16 date pieces in the same way. All of the pieces will be double sided. Attach cup hooks to the school house at X's.

1 square = 3/4 inch

Household Helpers

Potato and Onion Bin

Bill of Materials

Overall dimensions: 12" x 18" x 30"

Item#	Quantity	Detail	Description	Size	Materials
1	2	A	Side panels	3/4 x 11-1/4 x 29-1/4	White pine
2	1	C	Bottom front	3/4 x 11-1/4 x 18	White pine
3	1	B	Top front	3/4 x 11 x 18	White pine
4	1	D	Top	3/4 x 4-1/4 x 18	White pine
5	1	E	Lid	3/4 x 11 x 18	White pine
6	2	—	Front/back brace	3/4 x 1 x 16-1/2	White pine
7	2	—	Side brace	3/4 x 1 x 9-3/4	White pine
8	1	—	Floor panel	1/4 x 11-1/4 x 16-1/2	Pegboard
9	1	—	Back panel	1/4 x 17-1/2 x 27	Pegboard
10	1 pr.	—	Hinges	—	Your choice
11	1	—	Center divider	3/4 x 11-1/4 x 14	White pine

Note: All materials are optional. Please choose any type of wood or accessories you desire.

Materials and Tools Required

Skill or table saw

Jigsaw or scroll saw

Hammer

Glue

3/4" tacks

1-1/2" #8 wood screws

1" finishing nails

Screwdriver for mounting hinges and screws

Drill and 3/8" plug cutter

Your choice of stain for interior/exterior, and polyurethane for exterior

Potato & Onion Bin diagram

Household Helpers

Potato and Onion Bin Instructions

Assembly:
Cut out Items 1 through 9, using **Details A** through **E**. Sand and de-burr all edges. **Note:** Top side of Items 3, 4 and 5 are cut at a 45-degree angle. After cutting out all details, proceed with the Figure drawings to complete assembly.

Detail B (Top Front Cutout)

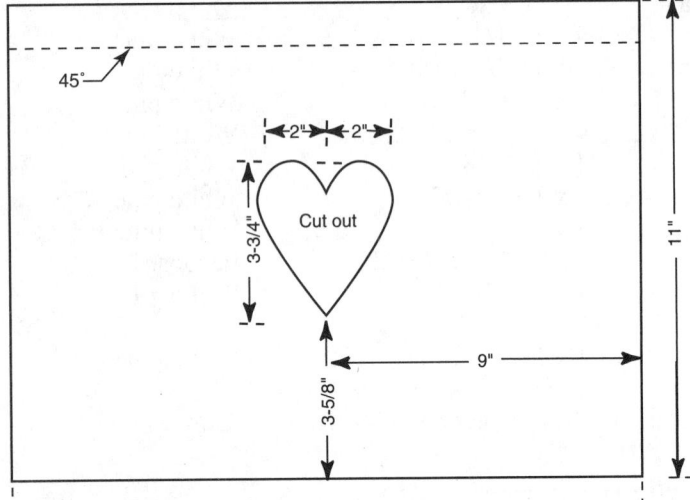

Detail C (Bottom Front Piece)

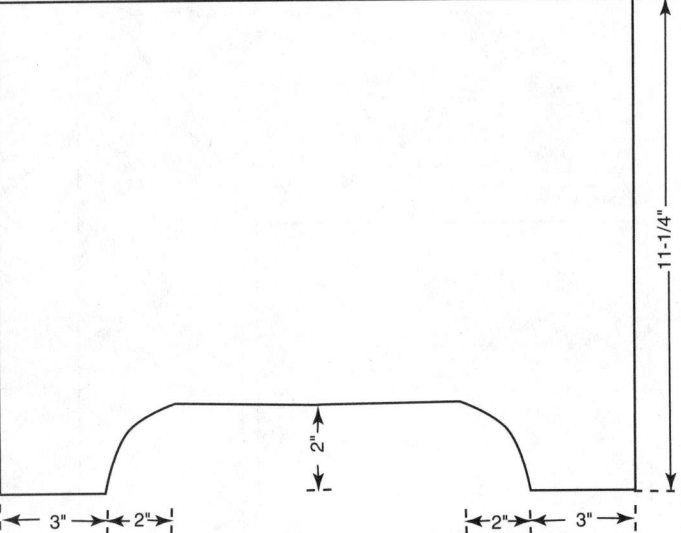

Detail A (View of Side Panels)

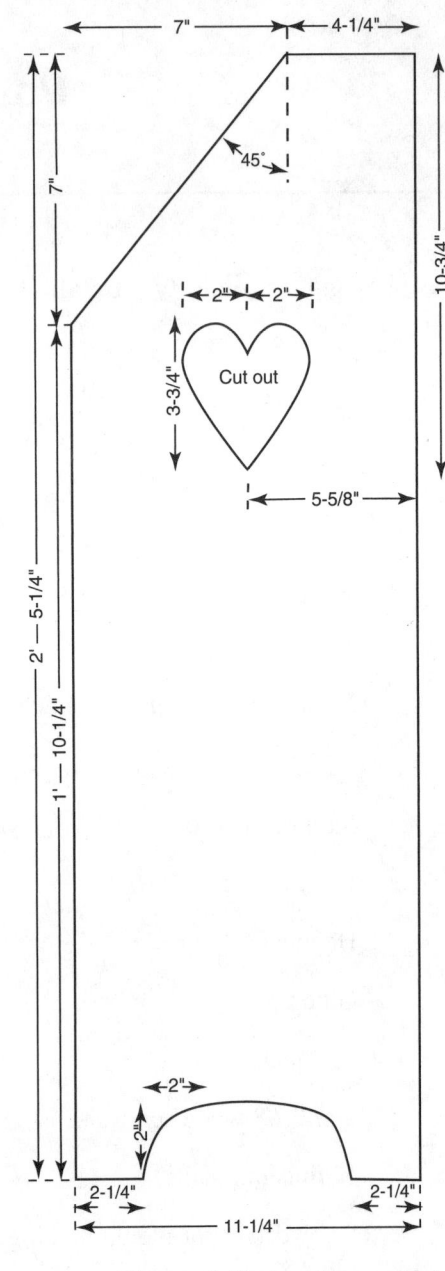

Figure 2 (Brace Assembly)

1) Using **Figure 1**, locate side braces, Item 7, 3/4 inch from front of Item 1, and 2 inches from bottom. Assemble using 1-inch finishing nails and glue. Repeat for opposite side. Next, assemble front and back brace, Item 6, to front and rear of Item 7, using 1-inch finishing nails and glue.

2) After completing Step 1, your assembly should appear as shown in Figure 2.

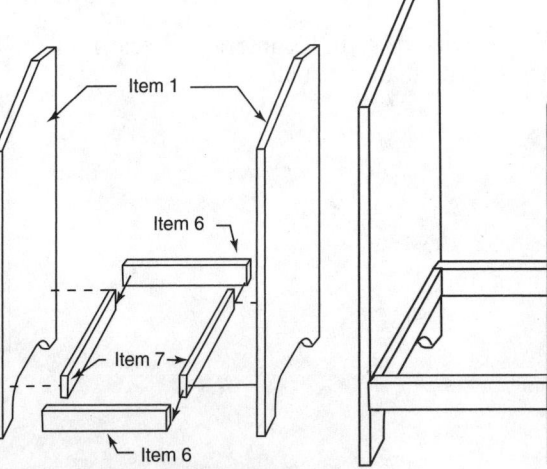

Figure 1 (Braces & Sides)

104

Household Helpers

3) To assemble Item 2 to bottom of main assembly, drill and countersink 3/8-inch holes in each side of front. Then using 1-1/2-inch long #8 wood screws, attach Item 2 to main assembly, about 3 screws on each side will do. Next, assemble Item 3 to top of Item 2 by drilling and countersinking 3/8-inch holes and attach to main assembly using 1-1/2-inch #8 wood screws. Be sure to put a layer of glue between Items 2 and 3, then clamp to form a tight bond. **Note:** Top of Item 3's 45-degree angle must match the angle on the side panels. To assemble top, Item 4, drill and countersink two holes on each side of top and attach using 1-1/2-inch #8 screws and glue.

4) Use **Figure 4** to attach Item 8, floor panel, to front, side and back braces using 3/4-inch tacks and glue. At this time if you choose to add a divider, Item 11, attach to center of floor panel (or off-center, your choice) using 1-inch finishing nails and glue. Assemble back panel, Item 9 (not shown), to back of main assembly, 1/4-inch from edge of side walls, using glue and 3/4-inch tacks.

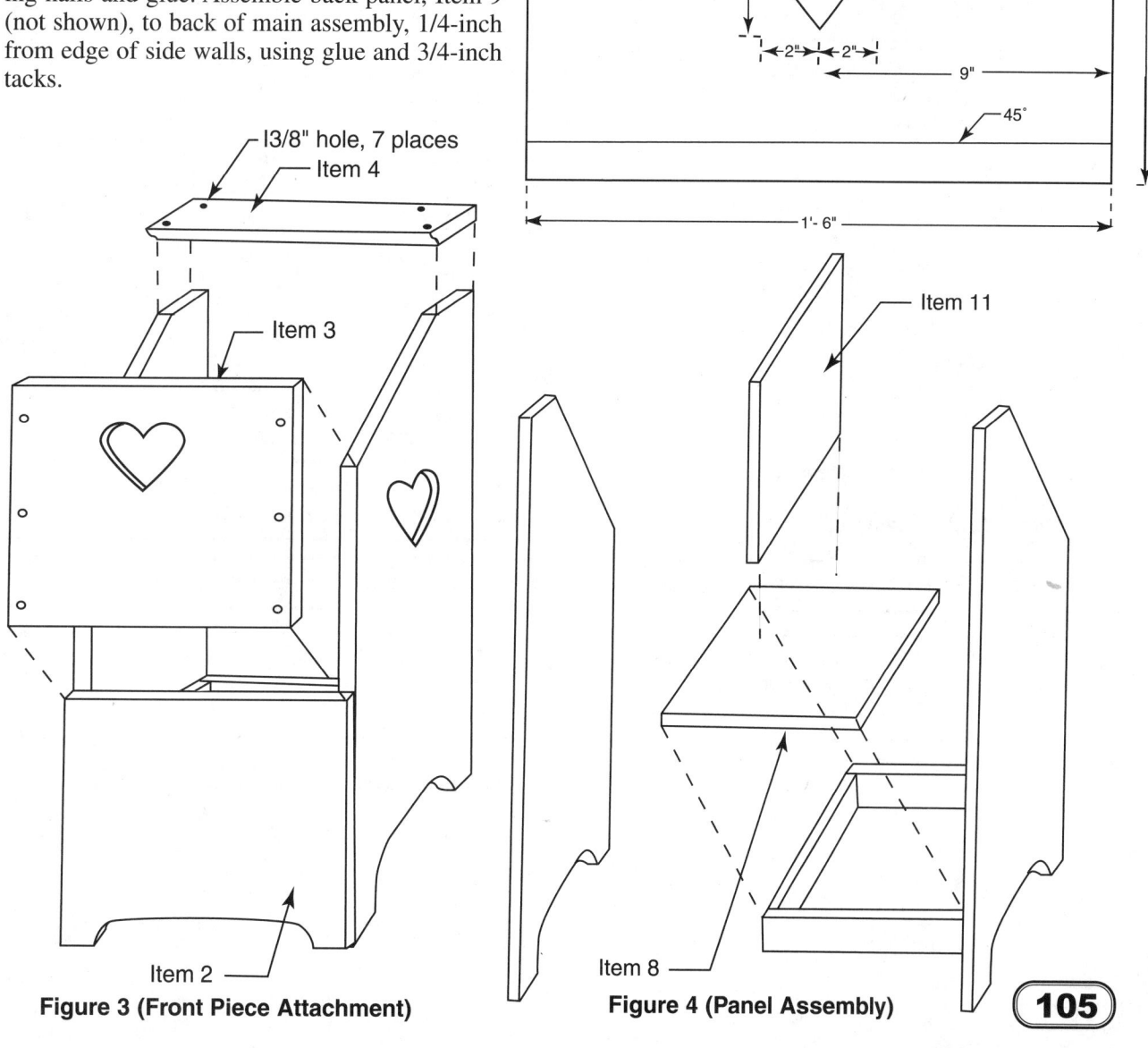

Detail D (Top Piece)

Detail E (Lid Cutout)

Figure 3 (Front Piece Attachment)

Figure 4 (Panel Assembly)

105

Household Helpers

5) To assemble lid to main assembly, locate lid, as shown in **Figure 5**. Then, sand off leading edge of Item 4 to match Item 5 lid, as shown in **Figure 6**.

6) Using **Figure 6**, attach lid to main assembly using two hinges. Using a 3/8-inch plug cutter, drill out plugs to cover all countersunk holes and glue in place. Be sure to match grain of plugs to grain of the plug location. Sand all plugs even with surface. Stain, paint designs and polyurethane at your own discretion.

7) Allow to dry and fill with your favorite veggies.

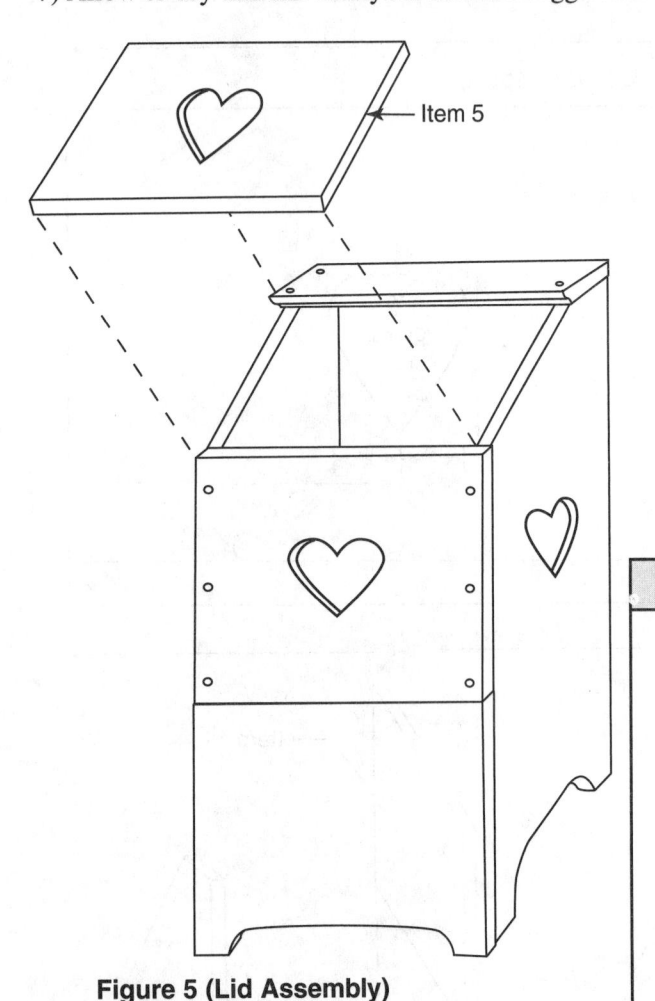

Figure 6 (Top Piece & Lid Attachment)

Figure 5 (Lid Assembly)

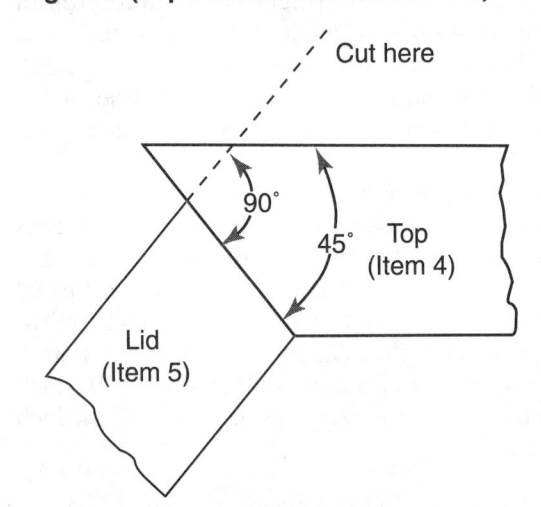

Drawings Index

Detail & Figure#	Description	Page#
Detail A	View of side panels	2
Detail B	Top front cutout	2
Detail C	Bottom front piece	2
Detail D	Top piece	3
Detail E	Lid cutout	3
Figure 1	Braces & side pieces	2
Figure 2	Brace assembly	3
Figure 3	Front piece attachment	3
Figure 4	Panel assembly	3
Figure 5	Lid assembly	4
Figure 6	Top piece & lid attachment	4

Tools Needed: Skill or table saw, jigsaw or scroll saw, hammer, glue, screwdriver, drill, plug cutter

Materials Needed: White pine, pegboard, hinges, glue, 3/4-inch tacks, 1-1/2-inch #8 wood screws, 1-inch finishing nails, stain and polyurethane

Degree of Difficulty: Simple

— CHAPTER NINE —
Lettering

ABCDEF
GHIJKL
MNOPQ
RSTUV
WXYZ
0123456789

Sherwood

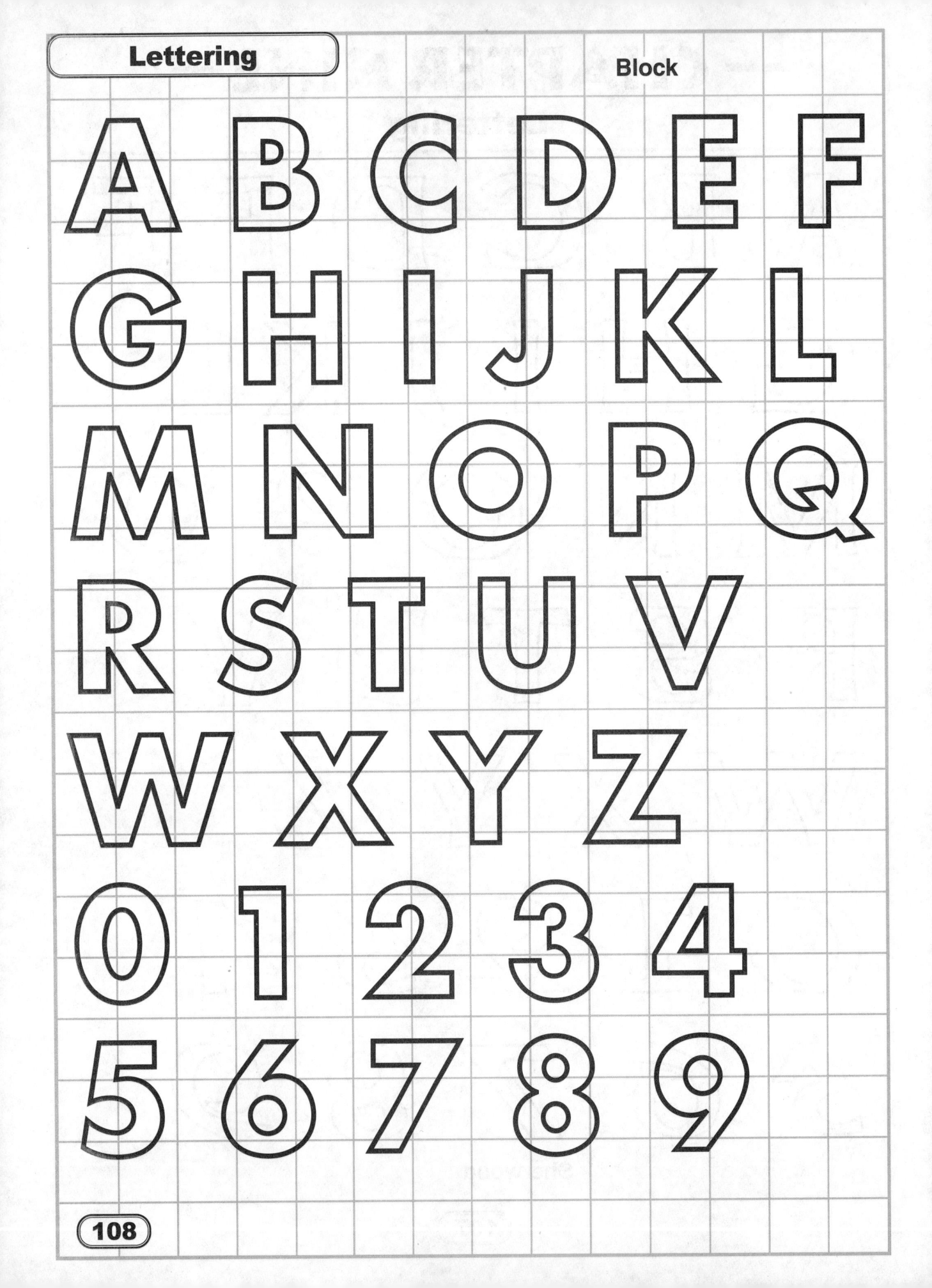

Lettering Block

ABCDEF
GHIJKL
MNOPQ
RSTUV
WXYZ
０１２３４
５６７８９

Calligraphy Lettering

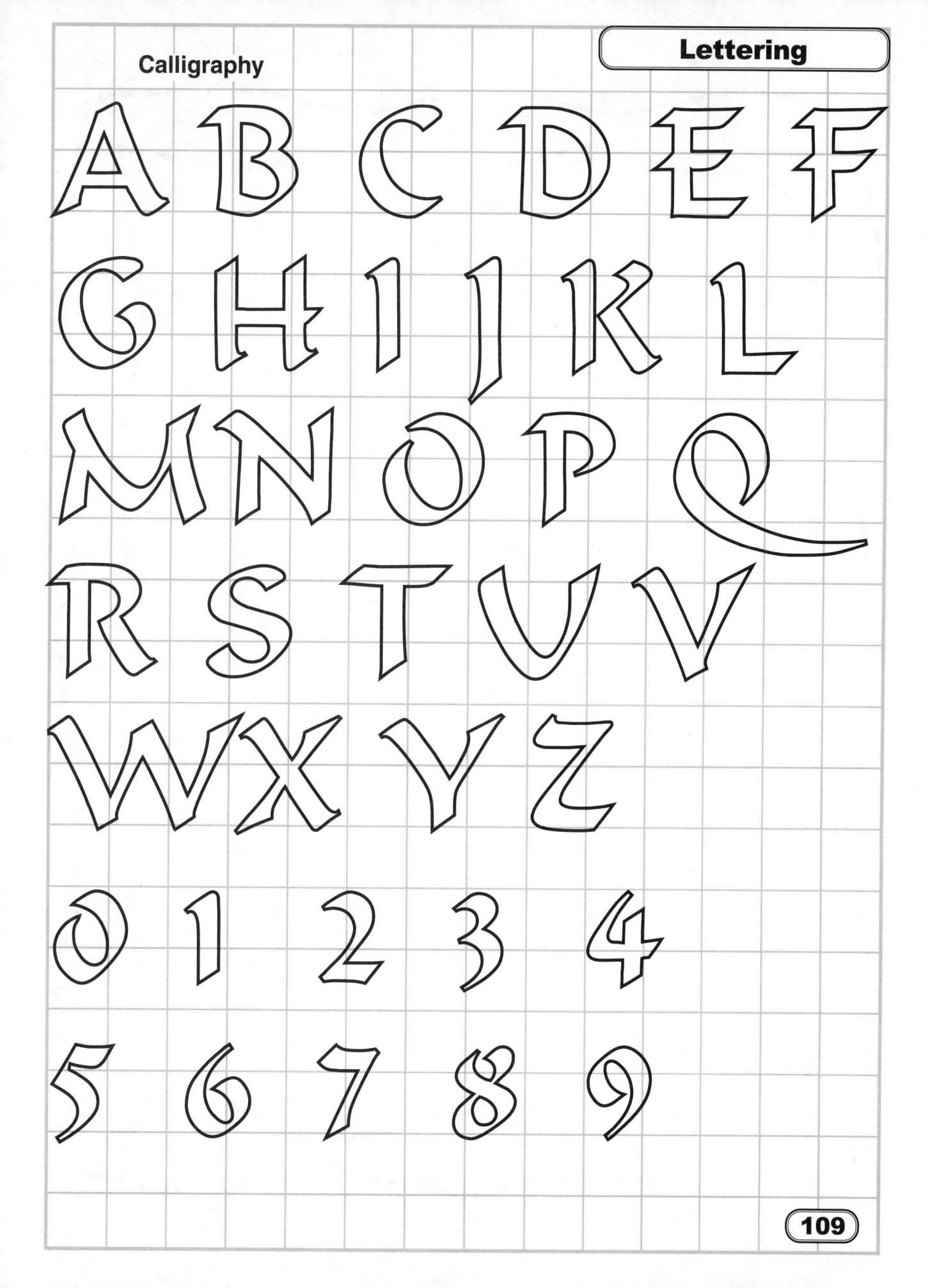

ABCDEF
GHIJKL
MNOPQ
RSTUV
WXYZ
0 1 2 3 4
5 6 7 8 9

109

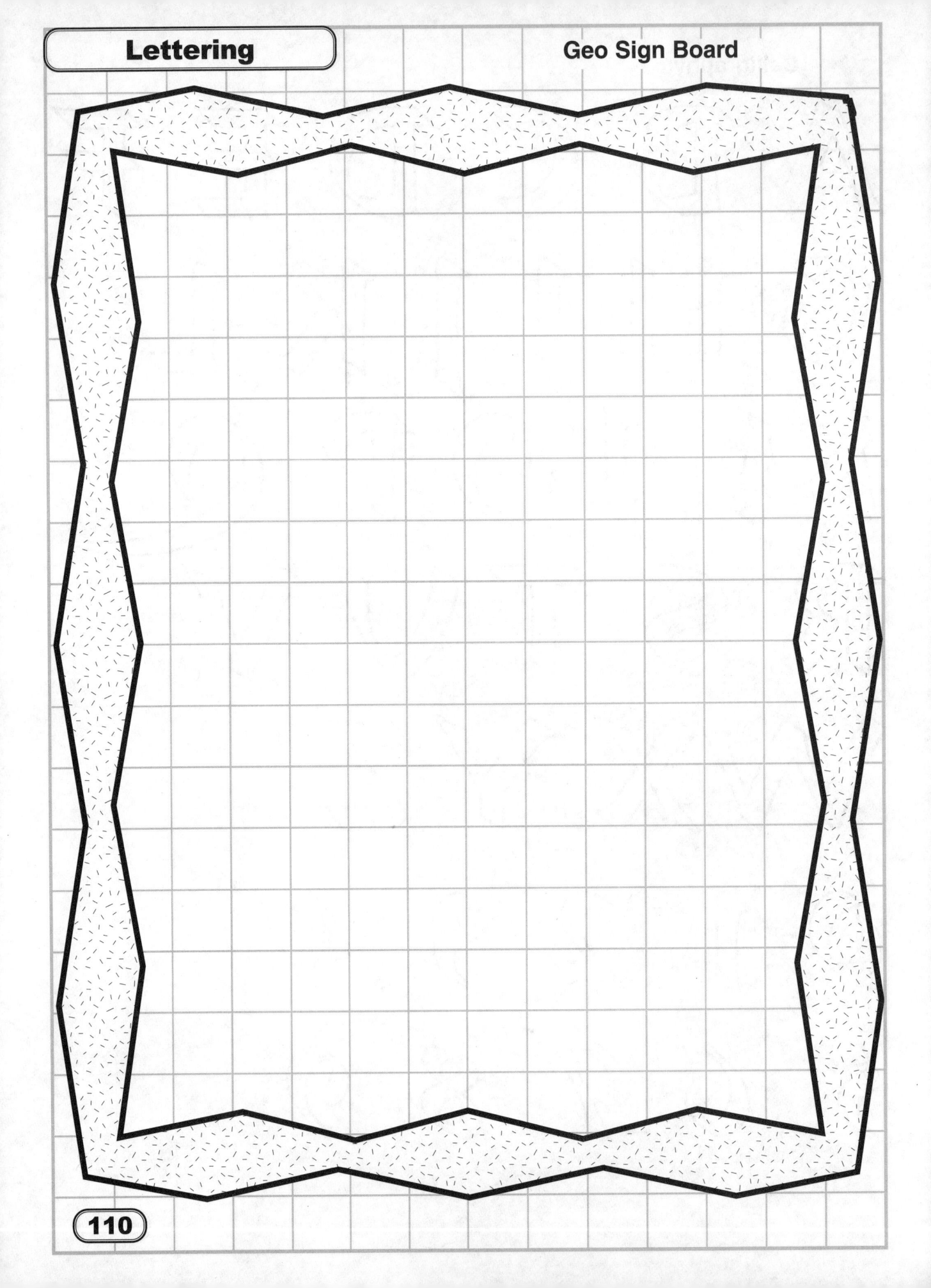

Lettering Geo Sign Board

110 Lettering

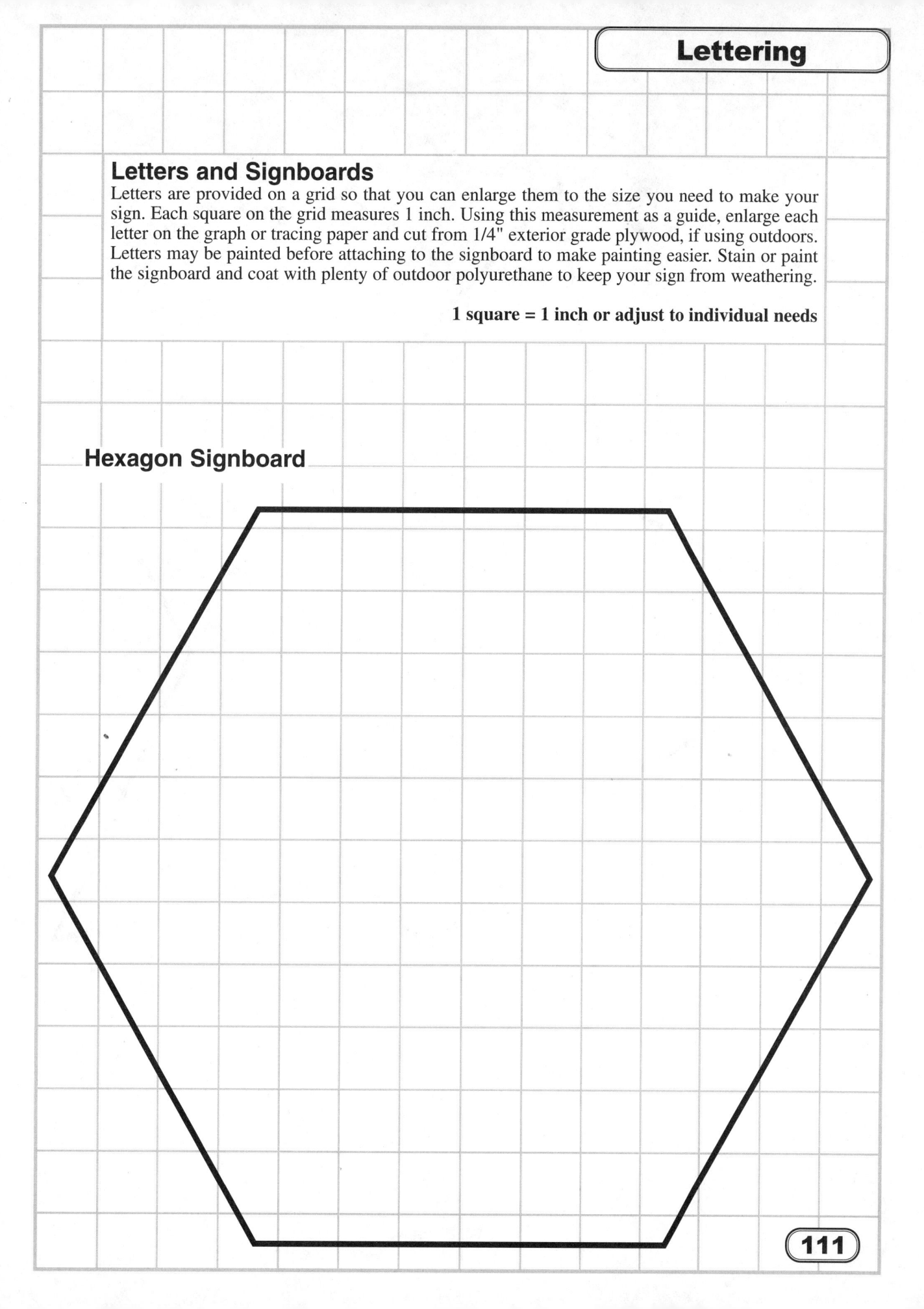

Lettering

Letters and Signboards

Letters are provided on a grid so that you can enlarge them to the size you need to make your sign. Each square on the grid measures 1 inch. Using this measurement as a guide, enlarge each letter on the graph or tracing paper and cut from 1/4" exterior grade plywood, if using outdoors. Letters may be painted before attaching to the signboard to make painting easier. Stain or paint the signboard and coat with plenty of outdoor polyurethane to keep your sign from weathering.

1 square = 1 inch or adjust to individual needs

Hexagon Signboard

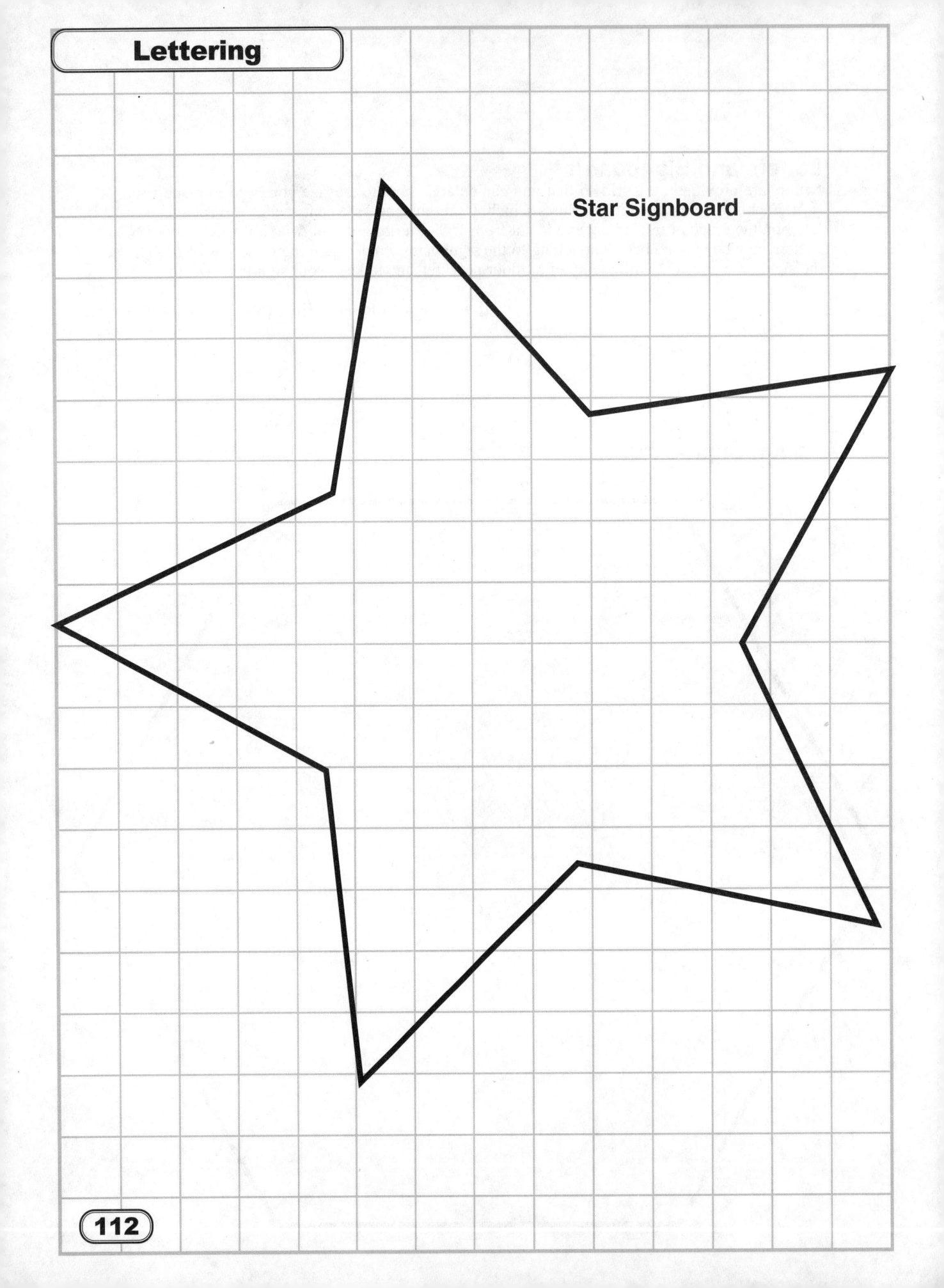

Lettering

Star Signboard

— CHAPTER TEN —
Outdoor Projects

Cockatiel House Number Sign

Cut this exotic bird and sign from 1/2" wood. Sand well. Paint with acrylics. Seal with several coats of weather resistant polyurethane. Insert screw eyes as shown into the branch and sign; connect with a small chain. Attach a hanger to the back.

Actual Size

Bird
(Cut 1)

Sign
(Cut 1)

3218

Outdoor Projects

Victorian Glider Swing

Advanced skill level

Materials Needed

Base:
- ❑ 50 linear feet of wood 1" x 4", or an equivalent amount of 3/4" oak or other hardwood

Swing:
- ❑ 20 linear feet of wood 1" x 4" (or 1" x 3" if you can find it), or an equivalent amount of 3/4" oak or other hardwood
- ❑ Eight 8' lengths of wood 1" x 2", or equivalent 3/4" oak or hardwood (No waste allowance is included, so purchase longer 1" x 2"s if the ends are not perfect.)

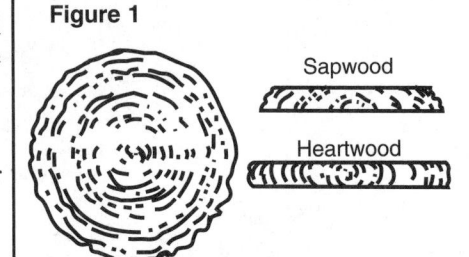

Miscellaneous:
Note: All hardware should be galvanized, or made of brass, bronze, or stainless steel.
- ❑ Eight eyebolts with a shank length of 2"
- ❑ Eight flat washers, eight hex nuts, and eight cap nuts to fit the eyebolts
- ❑ 1 1/2" long flathead wood screws, and 2d finishing nails
- ❑ Four 8" lengths of heavy chain (be sure chain is strong enough to support the weight of several adults.)
- ❑ Eight connecting links (optional) at least as heavy as the chain
- ❑ Waterproof wood glue; wood filler; wood preservative (optional); Danish oil or other finishing materials of your choice; waterproofing wood sealer (optional)

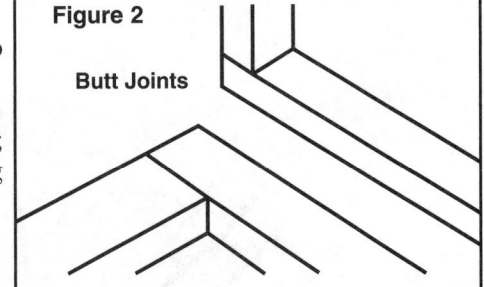

Tools Needed
- ❑ Table or circular saw
- ❑ Saber, band or jig saw
- ❑ Power drill
- ❑ Bits: a bit that matches diameter of eyebolt shanks; pilot/countersink bit for wood screws; plug cutter attachment to match size of countersink bit (optional); 2 1/2" circle cutter attachment (optional)
- ❑ Hand mortise chisel, or keyhole saw, or mortise-chisel bit for drill press
- ❑ Pipe or bar clamps

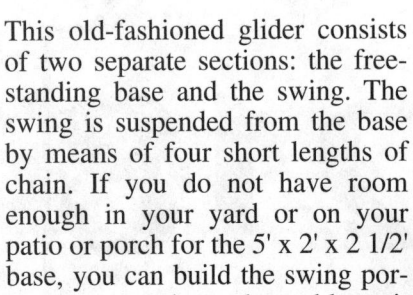

This old-fashioned glider consists of two separate sections: the free-standing base and the swing. The swing is suspended from the base by means of four short lengths of chain. If you do not have room enough in your yard or on your patio or porch for the 5' x 2' x 2 1/2' base, you can build the swing portion only, and hang it from your porch ceiling or from a friendly

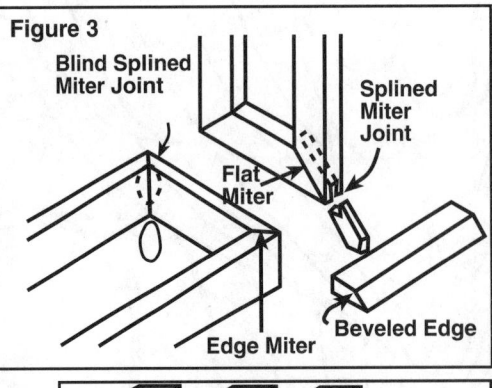

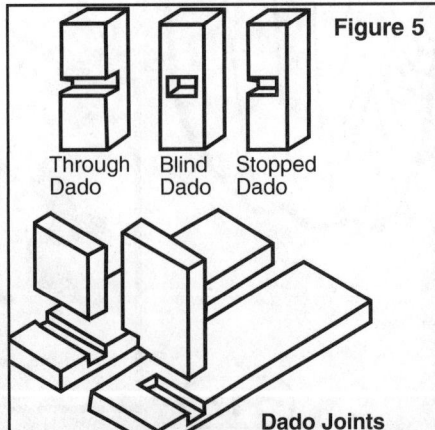

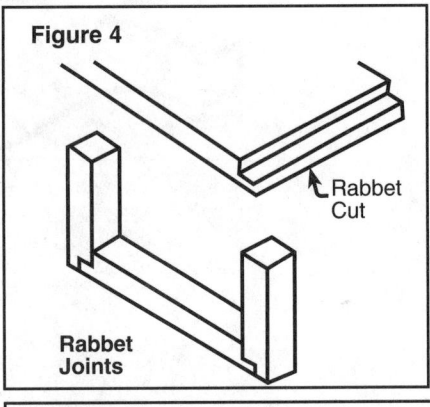

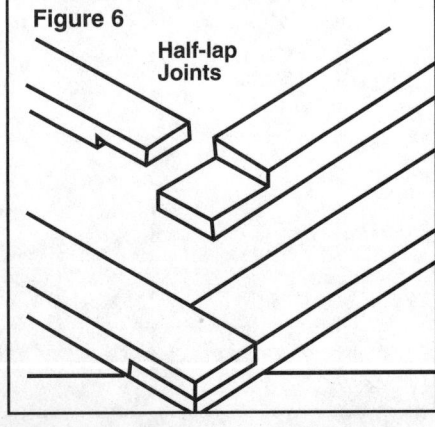

Figure 1 — Sapwood, Heartwood

Figure 2 — Butt Joints

Figure 3 — Blind Splined Miter Joint, Splined Miter Joint, Flat Miter, Edge Miter, Beveled Edge

Figure 4 — Rabbet Cut, Rabbet Joints

Figure 5 — Through Dado, Blind Dado, Stopped Dado, Dado Joints

Figure 6 — Half-lap Joints

114

old tree.

Although this project carries an "advanced" skill rating, it really is not difficult to build. The trickiest part is cutting the interlocking joints of the base section.

We have divided the instructions into three main sections: (1) building the base, (2) building the swing, and (3) finishing and final assembly. For joints secured with screws, countersink the screws and cover the heads with plugs cut from matching stock. Recess all nails and cover with wood filler.

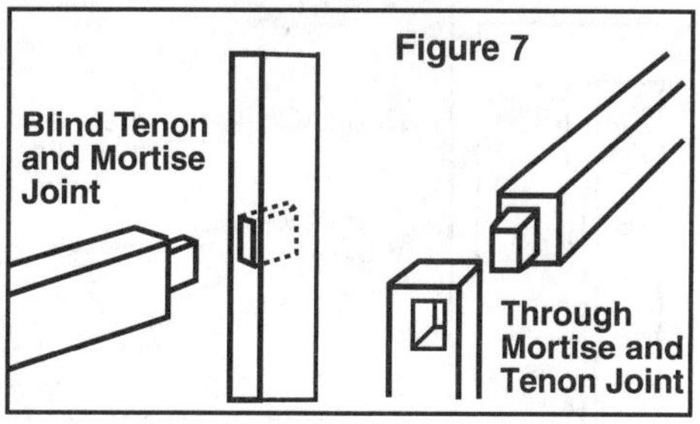

Outdoor Projects

Figure 7
Blind Tenon and Mortise Joint
Through Mortise and Tenon Joint

The Base
The base section is shown fully assembled in Figure I on page 117. It consists of two mirror image end sections, which are connected by three long braces. The pegged mortise-and-tenon joints allow you to disassemble the base for storage or transport. If you do not feel confident enough to cut the interlocking mortises and tenons, you can simply cut the braces shorter than specified, and permanently attach them to the end sections using glue and screws.

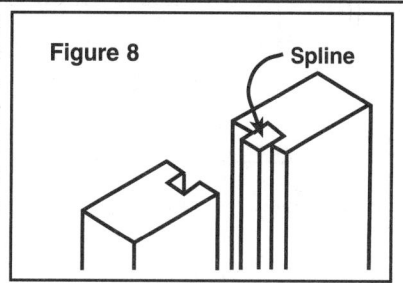

Figure 8 — Spline

Figure 9

The instructions for the base are presented in two sections: (1) cutting the parts, and (2) assembly. We suggest that you read through the instructions before beginning work.

Cutting the Parts
1. Dimensions for the base parts are listed in this step. For the E, F, G, I, J, and K's, use the patterns provided. All parts are cut from 1" x 4" wood or equivalent hardwood. We suggest that you begin by cutting the longest ones (the H and L braces), and work your way down to the smallest ones, so you'll be sure to get the most out of your wood stock. Label each part with its identifying code, for reference during assembly.

Code	Description	Dimensions	Quantity
A	Armrest Support	3 3/4" x 25"	2
B	Leg	3 3/4" x 24"	4
C	Foot	3 1/2" x 30"	4
D	Center Spacer	3 1/2" x 11"	2
E	Front Spacer	use pattern	2
F	Back spacer	use pattern	2
G	Armrest	use pattern	2
H	Lower Brace	3 1/2" x 62"	1
I	Peg	use pattern	6
J	Support Block	use pattern	2
K	Support Block	use pattern	2
L	Upper Brace	2 1/2" x 60"	2

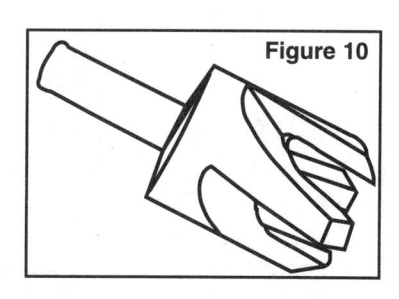

Figure 10

2. Each B leg is mortised as shown in Figure A, to accommodate an upper brace tenon (see the assembly diagram, Figure I). Draw the outlines of the mortise on one of the B legs, referring to Figure A for size and placement. The mortise is centered between the long edges, but note that it is closer to one end than the other. Cut the mortise and mark the upper end of the B leg, so you won't get it upside down later on during assembly. Mortise each B leg in the same manner, using the first one as a pattern.

3. Each C foot is modified as shown in Figure B. (The mortise will accommodate the lower brace tenon, as shown in the assembly diagram, Figure 1.) You can use an E or F spacer as a pattern to round off the two top corners, being careful not to reduce the 30" length of the lower edge. Measure and mark the outlines of the mortise, referring to Figure B for size and placement. The mortise should be centered between the long upper and lower edges, but note that it is closer to one end than the other. Mark the front end of the C foot, as shown, for reference during assembly. Use the modified C foot as a guide to round

Figure 12
Jig
Stock

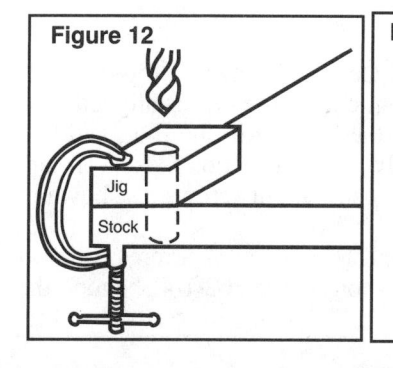

Figure 11

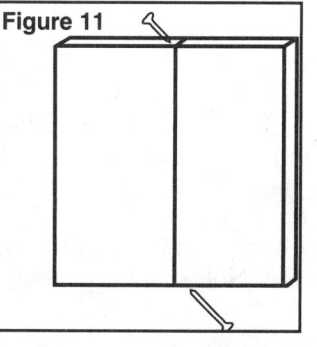

115

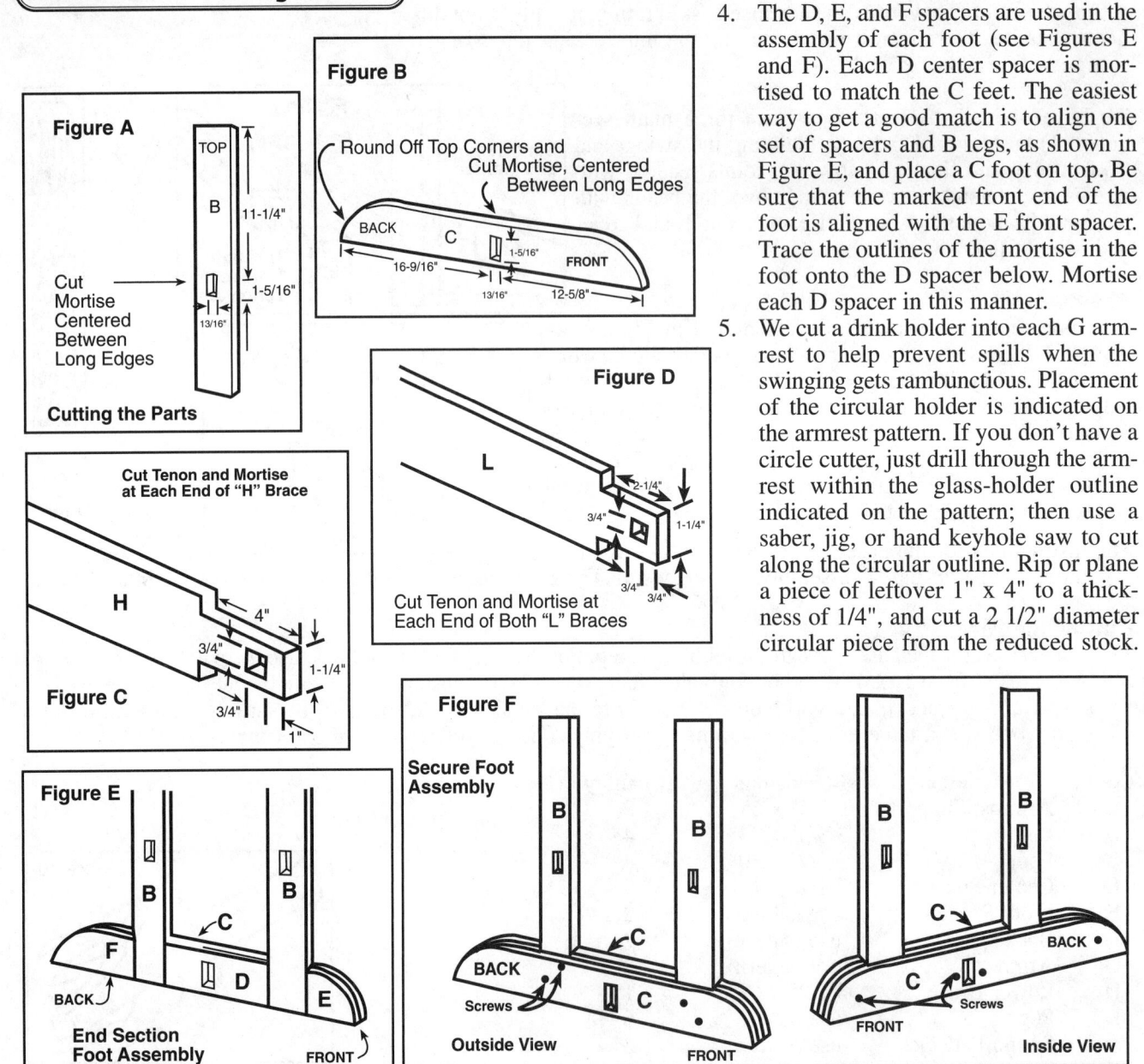

Outdoor Projects

Figure A — Cutting the Parts
- TOP
- B
- 11-1/4"
- 1-5/16"
- 13/16"
- Cut Mortise Centered Between Long Edges

Figure B
- Round Off Top Corners and Cut Mortise, Centered Between Long Edges
- BACK, C, FRONT
- 16-9/16", 1-5/16", 13/16", 12-5/8"

Figure C — Cut Tenon and Mortise at Each End of "H" Brace
- H
- 4", 3/4", 3/4", 1", 1-1/4"

Figure D — Cut Tenon and Mortise at Each End of Both "L" Braces
- L
- 2-1/4", 3/4", 1-1/4", 3/4", 3/4"

Figure E — End Section Foot Assembly
- B, B, C, F, D, E
- BACK, FRONT

Figure F — Secure Foot Assembly
- Outside View: B, B, C, BACK, Screws, C, FRONT
- Inside View: B, B, C, Screws, FRONT, C, BACK

---

off and mortise the three remaining C feet.

4. The D, E, and F spacers are used in the assembly of each foot (see Figures E and F). Each D center spacer is mortised to match the C feet. The easiest way to get a good match is to align one set of spacers and B legs, as shown in Figure E, and place a C foot on top. Be sure that the marked front end of the foot is aligned with the E front spacer. Trace the outlines of the mortise in the foot onto the D spacer below. Mortise each D spacer in this manner.

5. We cut a drink holder into each G armrest to help prevent spills when the swinging gets rambunctious. Placement of the circular holder is indicated on the armrest pattern. If you don't have a circle cutter, just drill through the armrest within the glass-holder outline indicated on the pattern; then use a saber, jig, or hand keyhole saw to cut along the circular outline. Rip or plane a piece of leftover 1" x 4" to a thickness of 1/4", and cut a 2 1/2" diameter circular piece from the reduced stock.

Glue the plug into the hole in the armrest, flush with the bottom surface. Modify both G armrests in this manner. Note that the armrests will be mirror images of each other when they are attached to the end sections (see top-view diagram, inset to Figure I), so be sure to glue the glass-holder plugs flush with opposite surfaces of the two armrests.

6. The H lower brace requires a tenon at each end, as shown in Figure C. Note that the tenon is mortised to accommodate a peg.

7. Both L upper braces require a tenon at each end, as shown in Figure D. Here again, each tenon is mortised to accommodate a peg, as shown.

Assembly

1. To begin assembling one end section (Figure E), place a C foot on a flat surface and arrange on top of it two B legs and a D, E, and F spacer, as shown. Notes: Be sure that the marked front end of the foot is aligned with the E front spacer; that the D spacer is turned so the mortise is aligned with the mortise in the foot; and that each B leg is turned with the marked upper end at the top. Glue the assembly. Place a second C foot on top, with the marked front end at the front, and glue in place. Secure the assembly using eight screws, as shown in Figure F: four inserted from one side and four from the other.

2. The top of the end section is assembled as shown in Figures G and H. Glue an A armrest support to one side of the two B legs, flush at the top. Note that the support should extend 2 1/4" beyond the

front leg, and 3 1/2" beyond the back leg. Secure by inserting two screws through each leg into the support.

3. Drill a hole through each B leg and on through the A armrest support, using a bit that matches the diameter of the eyebolt shanks. Placement of the holes is shown in Figure G. We enlarged each hole at the leg end, to create a recess for the washer and hex nut. Insert an eyebolt through each hole, from the armrest support side. Secure on the leg side using a washer, hex nut, and cap nut.
4. Add the G armrest and J and K decorative support blocks as shown in Figure H. Note that the straight edge of the armrest is flush with the outer surface of the A support. The armrest should extend just slightly beyond the support at the front end. Glue the assembly. Secure the armrest using two screws inserted into the A support. Secure each decorative support block using finishing nails.
5. Repeat the procedures described in Steps 1 through 4 to assemble a second end section. Note that it should be a mirror image of the first one, so place the A support on the opposite side of the legs, in relation to the front end of the foot assembly. The straight edge of the armrest will face the opposite direction also (see Figure I).
6. For the final assembly (Figure I), align the two end sections about 6 feet apart. Be sure that each one is turned as shown. Place the H lower brace and the two L upper braces between the end sections. Do not use glue in any of these joints, or you will not be able to disassemble the base.

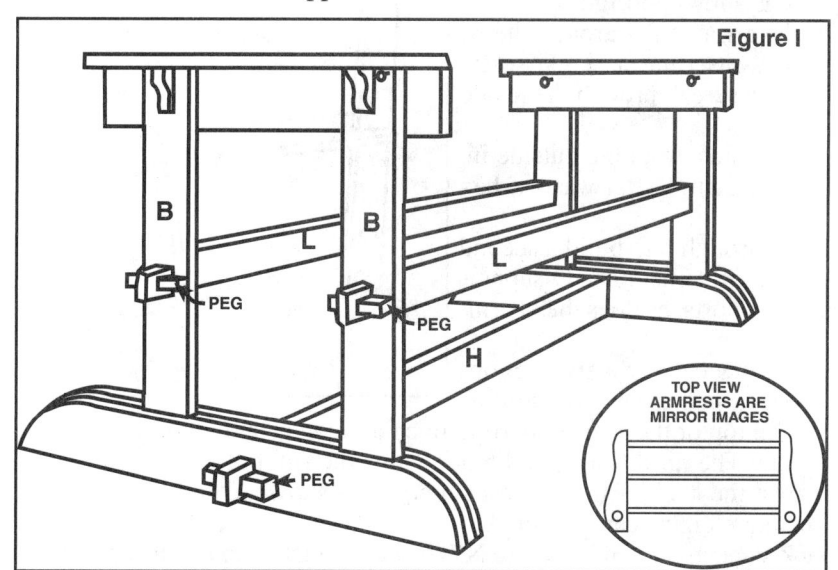

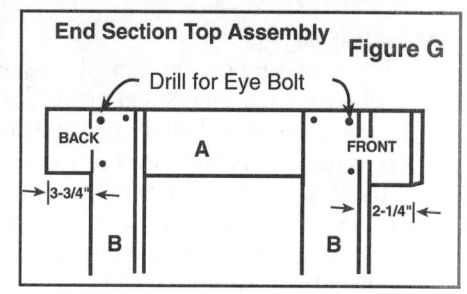

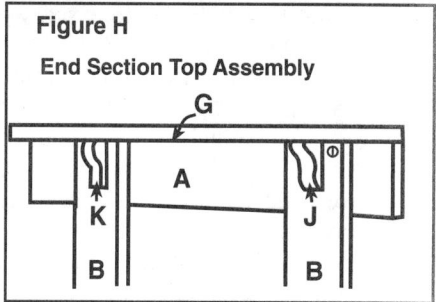

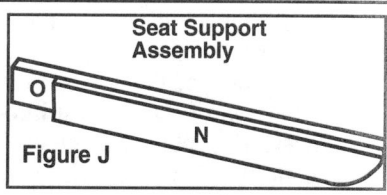

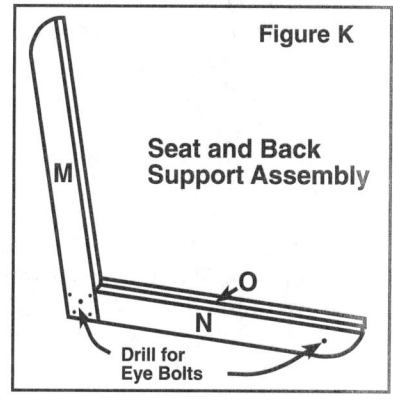

Insert the brace tenons through the respective mortises in the foot and legs of one end section, and then through the other end section. It may be necessary to sand the mortises slightly, to get the tenons to fit. Secure each joint with a peg, as shown.

The Swing

The swing consists of two mirror image end sections (Figure M), connected by seat and back slats (Figure N).

Cutting the Parts

1. Cutting instructions for the swing end section parts are listed in this step. Patterns for all parts are provided on page 114. All parts are cut from 1" x 4" wood or equivalent hardwood. Label each part with its identifying code, for reference during assembly.

Code	Description	Dimensions	Quantity
M	Back Support	use pattern	2
N	Seat Support	use pattern	2
O	Seat Support	use pattern	2
P	Armrest	use pattern	2
Q	Armrest Support	use pattern	2

2. Cut 16 slats from wood 1" x 2" or equivalent hardwood, each 1 1/2" x 48".

Outdoor Projects

Assembly

1. The seat support portion of one end section is shown in Figure J. Glue together one N and one O support, flush at the contoured front ends, as shown. Secure by inserting two screws through the O support into the N support. For future reference, the O support is on the inside surface of the end section.
2. Glue an M back support to the seat support assembly as shown in Figure K. Note that the assembly does not form a 90-degree angle, but rather a slightly wider one, so the back will tilt at a comfortable sitting angle. Insert four screws through the M support into the O support.
3. Drill two holes through the assembled seat and back supports where indicated in Figure K, using a bit that matches the diameter of the eyebolt shanks. Do not install the bolts just yet.
4. Glue a Q armrest support to the inside surface of the assembly, 6" from the front end, as shown in Figure L. Secure by inserting a screw through the lower extension of the Q support into the O seat support, as shown in the detail diagram.
5. Glue a P armrest to the Q and M supports as shown in Figure M. Note that the groove at the back end of the armrest fits around the M support. Secure the armrest at the front by inserting a single screw down into the Q support. At the back, insert a screw through the inside extension of the armrest into the M support.
6. Insert an eyebolt though each of the drilled holes, from the outside in, as shown in Figure M. Secure on the inside using a flat washer, hex nut, and cap nut.
7. Repeat the procedures described in steps 1 through 6 to build a second end section, making it a mirror image of the first one. (The O support goes on the opposite sides of the N and M supports, as does the Q armrest support.)
8. The assembled swing is shown in Figure N. Place the two end sections about 4 feet apart. Make sure they are both turned as shown, with the O seat supports facing center. Place a slat on top of the seat supports. Attach a second slat in the same manner, allowing a 3/4" space between the two slats. The third slat should butt against the front of the Q armrest supports, and the fourth slat should butt against the back of the armrest supports, as shown. Continue to add seat slats, allowing a 3/4" space between. There are eight seat slats in all.
9. The eight remaining slats are used as back slats, as shown in Figure N. They are attached to the upright M supports in the same manner as you did the seat slats.

Finishing and Final Assembly

1. Sand the assembled base and swing, and apply your chosen finishing materials.
2. The connecting links are used to join the four chains to the glider base and swing. If you did not purchase connecting links, follow the procedures described in this step, but in place of the connecting links you will have to pry open a link of the chain itself, to connect it to the eyebolt. Join an 8" length of chain to each of the eyebolts on the base section. Secure the opposite end of each chain to the corresponding eyebolt on the swing. Notes: Be sure that the front of the swing faces the same direction as the front ends of the base armrests and feet. It may be necessary to adjust the swing, by attaching the connecting links to higher links of the chains, to get the swing to sit level and high enough above the upper braces of the base.
3. If you built the swing to be hung from your porch ceiling or a tree, you will need quite a bit more chain. The amount will depend, of course, on the height of the ceiling or branch. For each side of the swing, measure from the desired height of the top of the armrest to the ceiling or branch, and add about 3 more feet to form an inverted V-shape at the bottom. If the swing will be hung from a tree, you may wish to wrap the chain around the branch instead of inserting hangers into it. If so, add a bit more to accommodate the circumference of the branch. In addition to the chain, you'll need a total of eight connecting links (optional) and two heavy-duty hangers to join the chains to the ceiling. Many hardware and home centers carry packaged porch swing chain that's already assembled in the proper configuration.

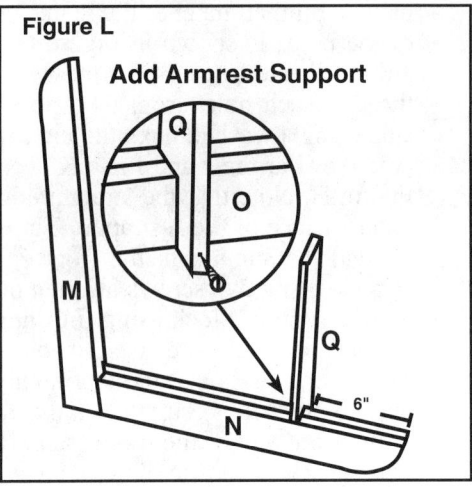

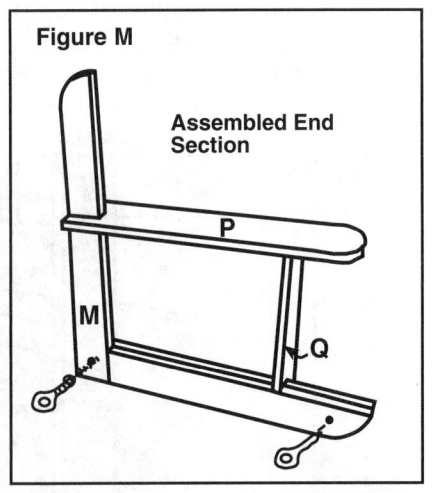

Outdoor Projects

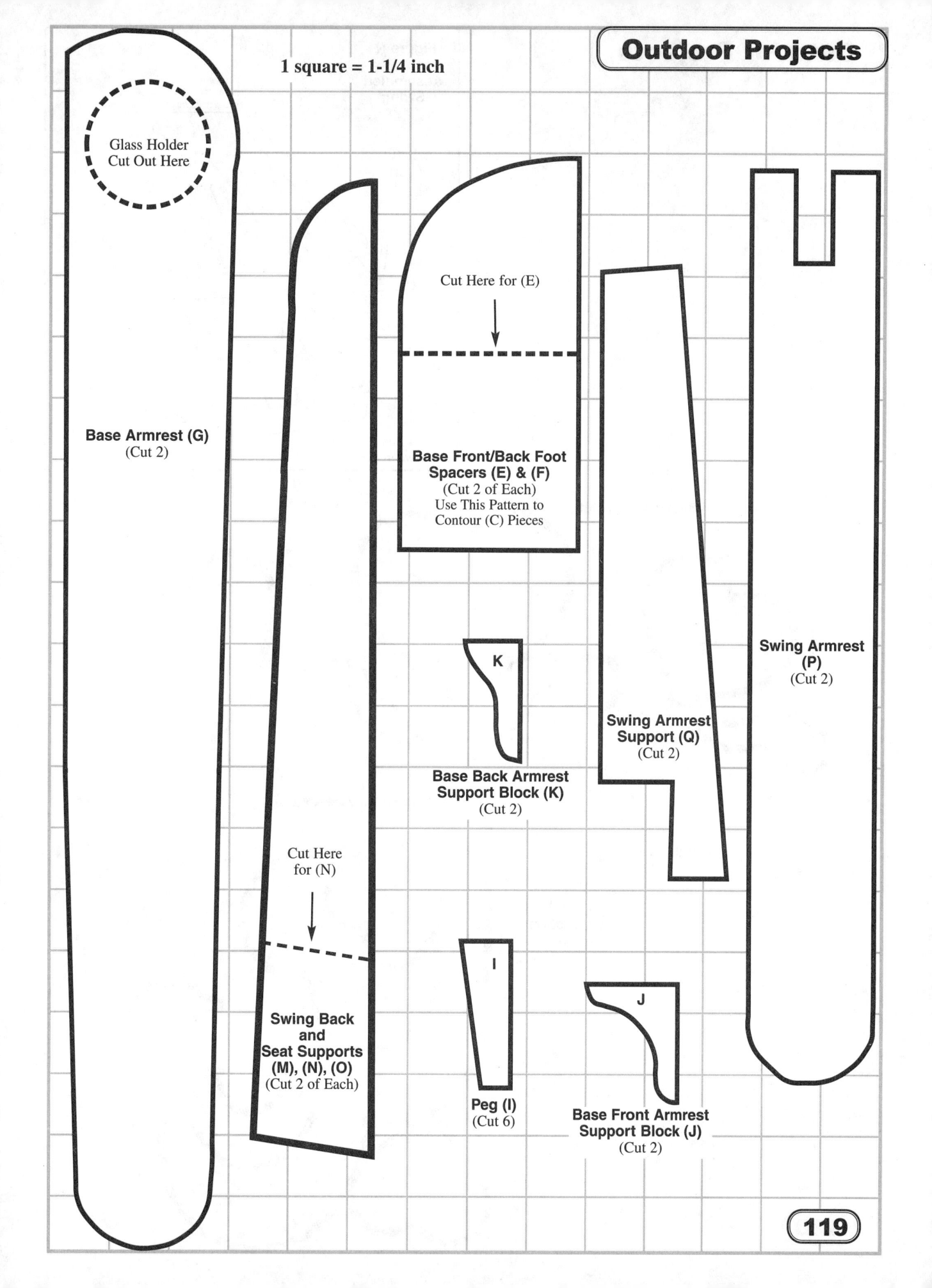

1 square = 1-1/4 inch

Glass Holder Cut Out Here

Base Armrest (G)
(Cut 2)

Cut Here for (E)

Base Front/Back Foot Spacers (E) & (F)
(Cut 2 of Each)
Use This Pattern to Contour (C) Pieces

K

Base Back Armrest Support Block (K)
(Cut 2)

Swing Armrest Support (Q)
(Cut 2)

Swing Armrest (P)
(Cut 2)

Cut Here for (N)

Swing Back and Seat Supports (M), (N), (O)
(Cut 2 of Each)

I

Peg (I)
(Cut 6)

J

Base Front Armrest Support Block (J)
(Cut 2)

119

Outdoor Projects

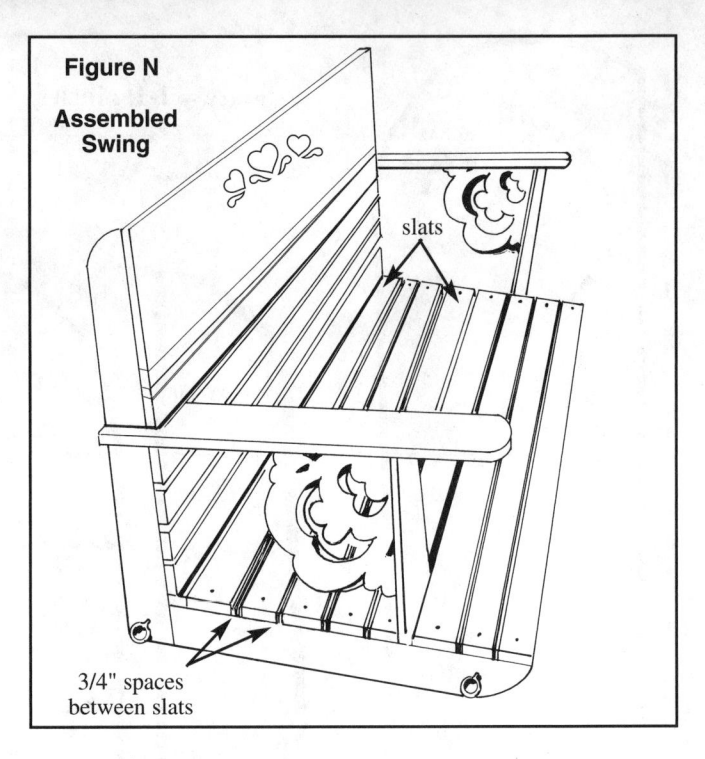

Figure N
Assembled Swing

slats

3/4" spaces between slats

Backrest Cut Out

Actual Size

Armrest Decoration
(Cut 2)

120

Outdoor Projects

Wings (Cut 2)
Body (Cut 1)
Butterfly Mailbox Reflector

House (Cut 1)
House Mailbox Reflector (Cut 1)

Daisy (Cut 1)
Daisy Mailbox Reflector (Cut 1)

Welcome Driveway Reflector (Cut 1)

Mailbox and Driveway Reflectors

Your friends will never miss your driveway again because you'll have a unique reflector attached to your mailbox, fence post or on a dowel inserted into the ground. Cut the pattern from 1/2" outdoor grade plywood. Sand and paint with acrylic paints. Seal with an outdoor grade polyurethane. Cut self-adhesive reflective tape into a circle and attach onto reflector. If available in your area, use an adhesive backed or screw-type reflector.

Actual Size

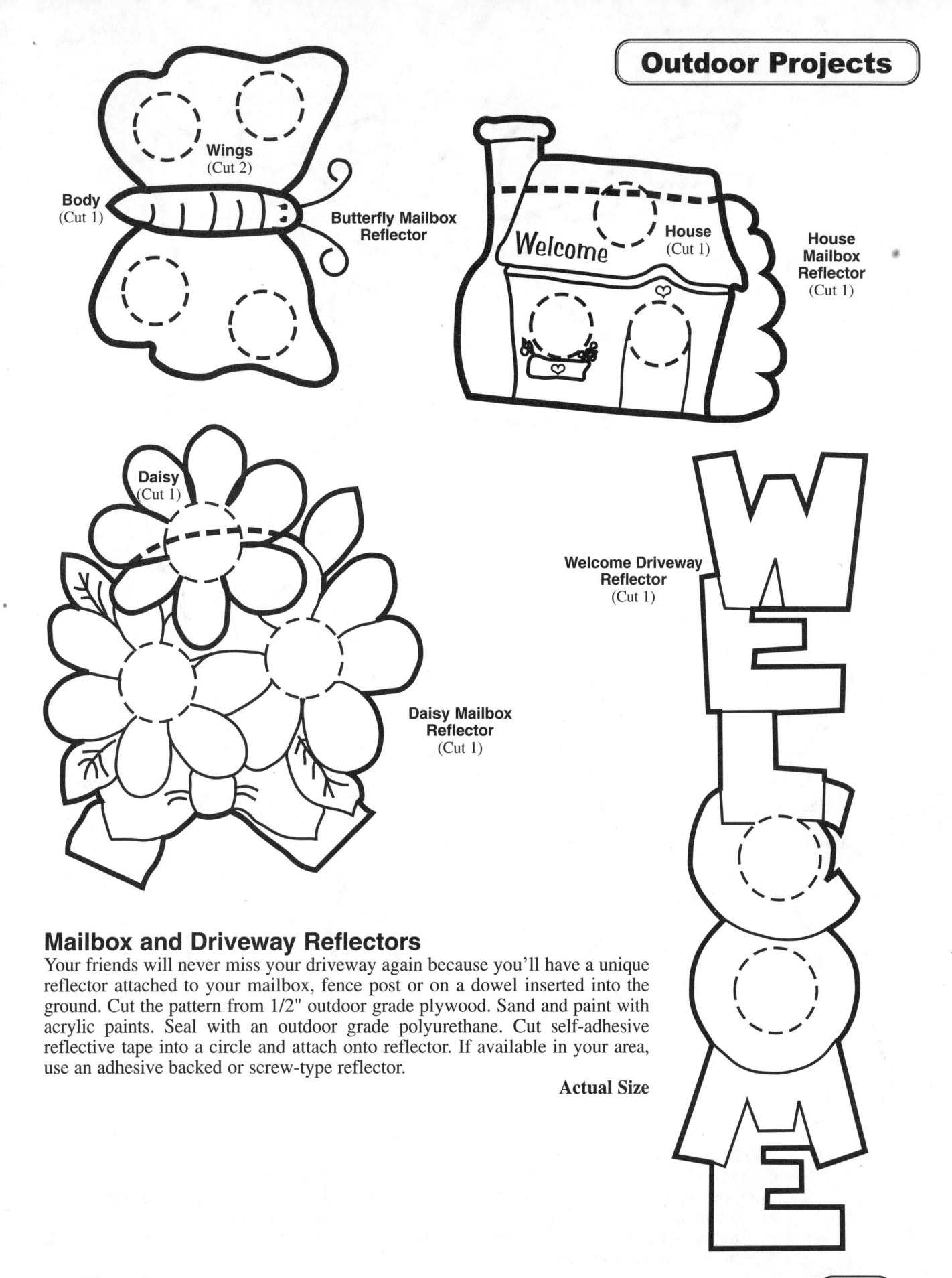

Outdoor Projects

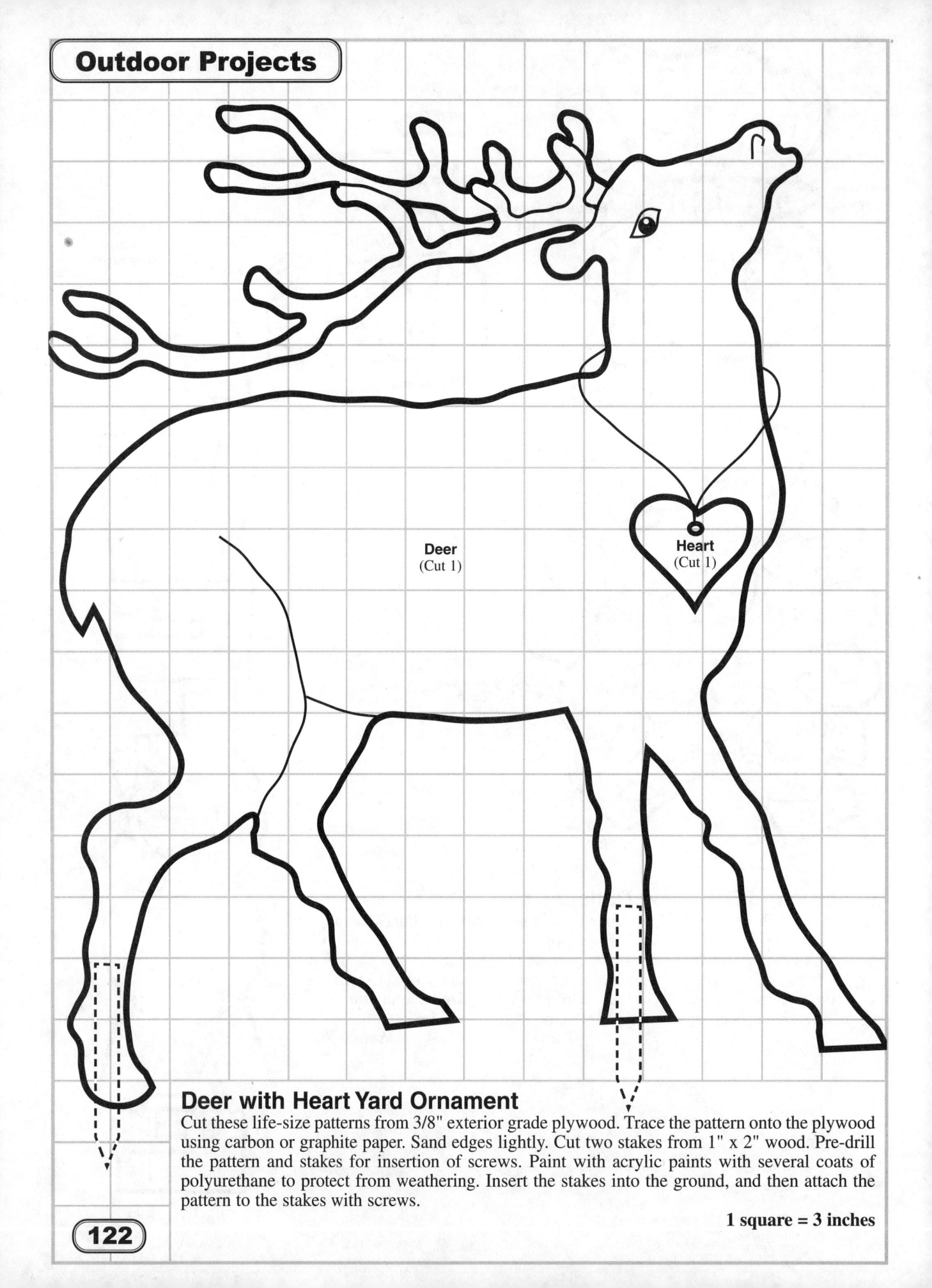

Deer with Heart Yard Ornament
Cut these life-size patterns from 3/8" exterior grade plywood. Trace the pattern onto the plywood using carbon or graphite paper. Sand edges lightly. Cut two stakes from 1" x 2" wood. Pre-drill the pattern and stakes for insertion of screws. Paint with acrylic paints with several coats of polyurethane to protect from weathering. Insert the stakes into the ground, and then attach the pattern to the stakes with screws.

Deer (Cut 1)

Heart (Cut 1)

1 square = 3 inches

CHAPTER ELEVEN
Peg Racks and Shelves

Sunflower and Bird Shelf
(Cut 1)

Bird placement

Shelf Placement

Brace Placement

Brace Placement

Shelf
(Cut 1)

Shelf Brace
(Cut 2)

Wing
(Cut 1)

Bird
(Cut 1)

Small Sunflower And Bird Shelf

Cut the shelf pieces from 1/2" wood. Sand all of the pieces. Glue and nail the shelf and brace to the back. Paint and seal with acrylics. Attach a hanger to the back

1 square = 1 inch

123

Peg Racks/Shelves

God Bless Our Cabin Peg Rack

Cut this pattern from 1/2" wood. Drill a hole at each "X" for insertion of dowels. Sand the pattern. Paint and seal with acrylics. Attach a sawtooth hanger on the back.

Actual Size

Drill Here

Peg Rack (Cut 1)

GOD BLESS OUR CABIN

Drill Here

Peg Racks/Shelves

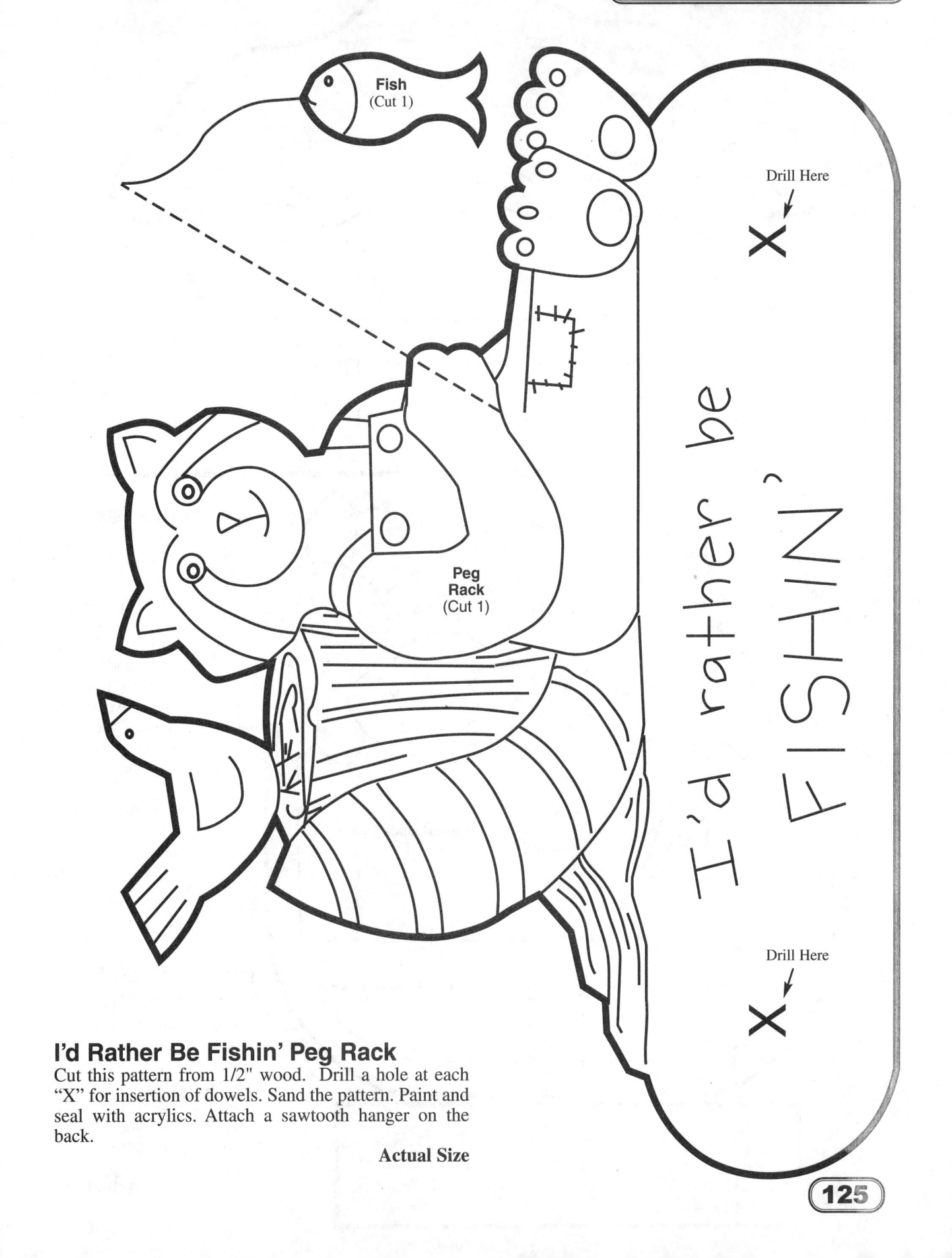

Fish (Cut 1)

Peg Rack (Cut 1)

Drill Here

Drill Here

I'd rather be FISHIN'

I'd Rather Be Fishin' Peg Rack
Cut this pattern from 1/2" wood. Drill a hole at each "X" for insertion of dowels. Sand the pattern. Paint and seal with acrylics. Attach a sawtooth hanger on the back.

Actual Size

125

Peg Racks/Shelves

Apple
(Cut 1)

Peg Rack
(Cut 1)

Drill Here
Drill Here

APPLE PIE

Shelf Brace
(Cut 1)

Shelf Back
(Cut 1)

Shelf Placement

Brace Placement

Shelf
(Cut 1)

Apple Pie Peg Rack

Cut the base from 1/2" wood. Cut the apple from 1/4" wood. Drill a hole at each "X" for insertion of dowels. Sand the pattern. Paint and seal with acrylics. Attach the apple to the base with yellow wood glue. Attach a sawtooth hanger on the back.

Actual Size

Blackbird and Sunflower Shelf

Cut this pattern from 1/2" wood. Sand the pattern. Paint and seal with acrylics. Attach the brace and shelf from the back with countersink wood screws. Attach a sawtooth hanger on the back.

Actual Size

Peg Racks/Shelves

Welcome Friends Peg Rack
Cut this pattern from 1/2" wood. Drill small holes as indicated for insertion of 19 gauge wire. Drill holes at "X"s for insertion of shaker pegs. Sand the pattern. Paint and seal with acrylics. Tie a bow around metal wire handle. Hang by the handle.

Actual Size

Peg Racks/Shelves

Shelf
Cut 1

Bow placement

Shelf Support placement

Bow placement

Shelf Support
(Cut 1)

Kaitlin

Bow
(Cut 2 from 3/4" wood)

Cutout

Bow and Heart Shelf

Personalize this shelf for a little girl's room or leave the name off and enjoy it in any other room in your home. Cut the pieces from 3/4" wood. Allow the shelf to hang over the support 2" on each end. Sand well. Attach pieces with # 10 wood screws. Stain or paint with acrylics. Seal with an acrylic brush-on or spray varnish.

1 square = 1 inch

Double Display Shelf
Directions on next page

Double Display Shelf Blackbird
(Cut 1)

Bird's Wing
(Cut 1)

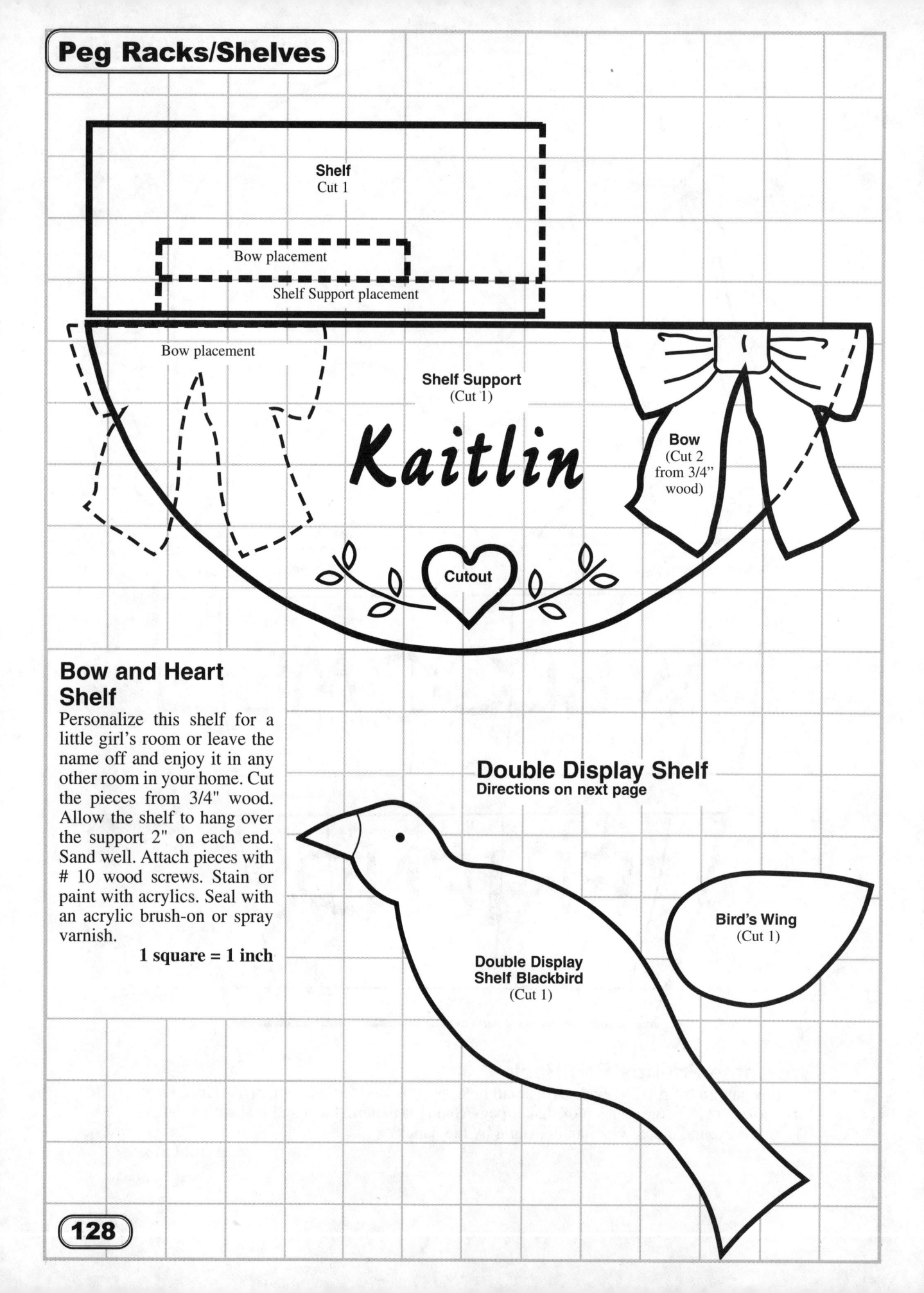

128

Peg Racks/Shelves

Double Display Shelf Back
(Cut 1)

Shelf Placement

Brace Placement

Shelf Placement

Brace Placement

Shelf
(Cut 1)

Shelf Brace
(Cut 1)

Double Display Shelf
Cut the back, shelves and brackets from 1/2" wood. Cut the blackbird from 1/4" wood and the wing from 1/8" wood. Attach shelves and brackets with glue and wood screws. Sand all of the pieces. Attach the blackbird and wing from the previous page with glue. Paint and seal with acrylics.

1 square = 1 inch

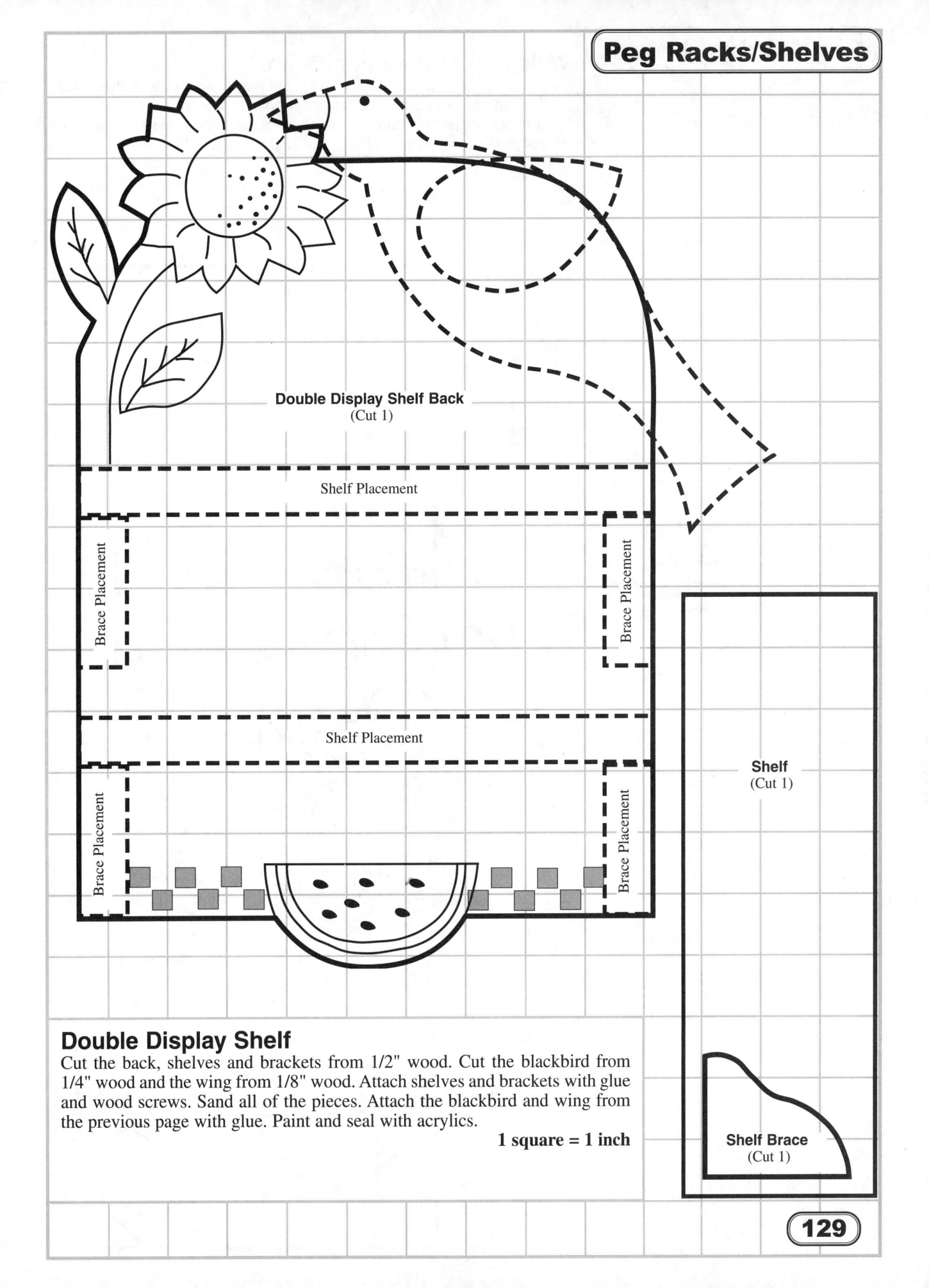

Peg Racks/Shelves

Welcome Aboard Peg Board

Suitable for hanging coats, scarves, caps, etc. Cut the back from 1/2" wood. Cut the heavier lined rocks, sailboat and wave from 1/4" wood. Drill holes for pegs in places indicated. Sand well. Glue the accessory pieces onto the backboard. Paint and seal using acrylics. Attach a hanger to the back.

1 square = 1 inch

Welcome Aboard Base
(Cut 1)

Sailboat on Waves
(Cut 1)

placement of sailboat

Rock
(Cut 1)

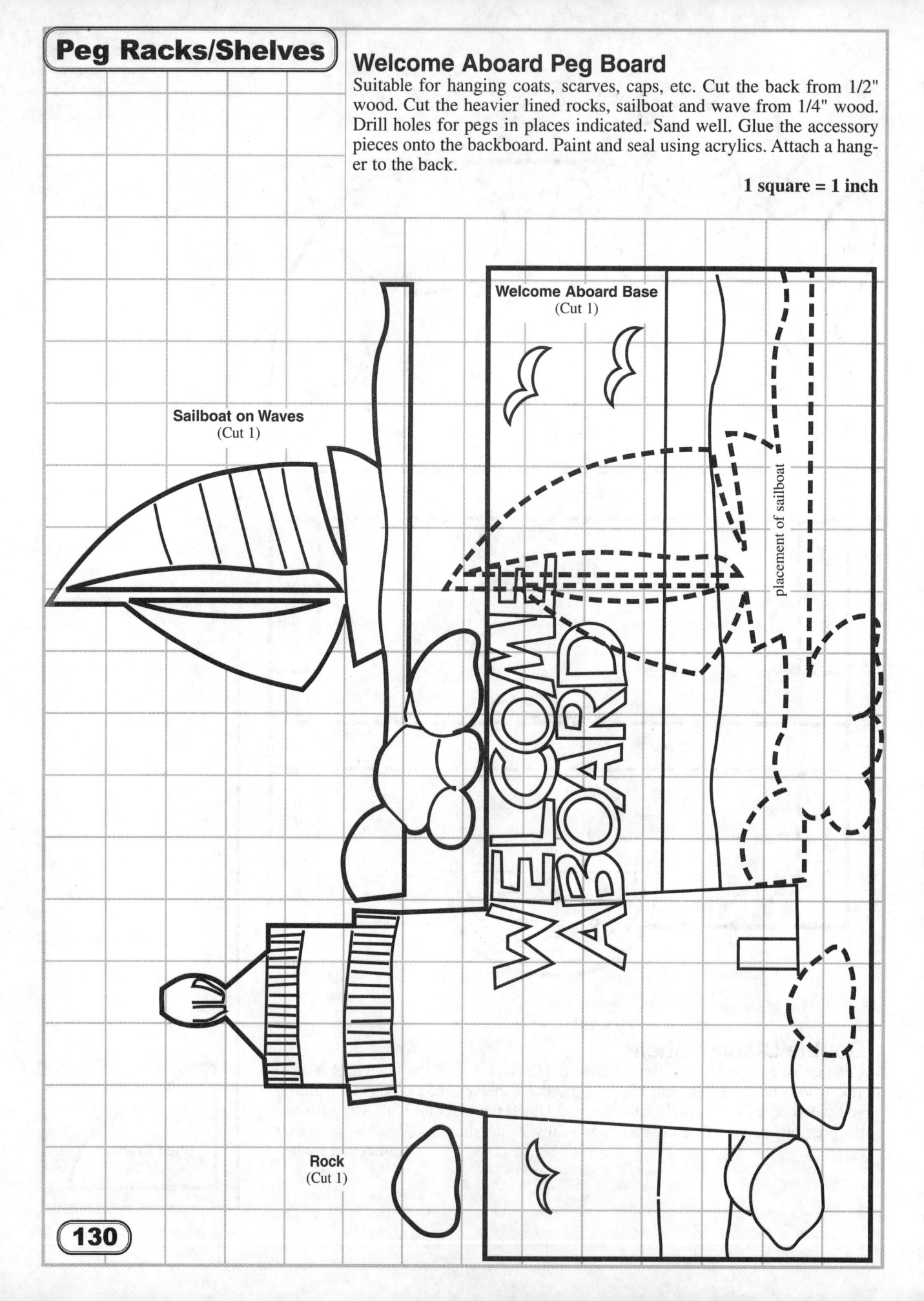

130

CHAPTER TWELVE
Plaques

Basket Of Apples Intarsia Plaque

Cut 2 patterns, 1 full pattern using 1/8" plywood, and 1 using 3/4" wood. Trace the design onto the 3/4" wood and cut the individual pieces. Round the top edges of all the cut-out pieces. Paint with acrylic paints. There is no need to paint the 1/8" cut-out. Allow the paint to dry. Attach all of the pieces to the 1/8" back with wood glue. Seal with an acrylic spray sealer. Attach a hanger to the back.

1 square = 1 inch

Base (Cut 1)

Placement for apple & bowl

AN APPLE A DAY

Apple Bowl (Cut 1)

Plaques

"A" Is For Apple Intarsia Plaque

Cut 2 patterns using the outside black line that goes around the entire plaque, 1 using 1/8" plywood, and 1 using 3/4" wood. Trace the design onto the 3/4" wood and cut the individual pieces. Round the top edges of all the cut-out pieces. Paint with acrylic paints. There is no need to paint the 1/8" cut-out. Allow the paint to dry. Attach all of the pieces to the 1/8" back with wood glue. Seal with an acrylic spray sealer. Attach a hanger to the back.

Actual Size

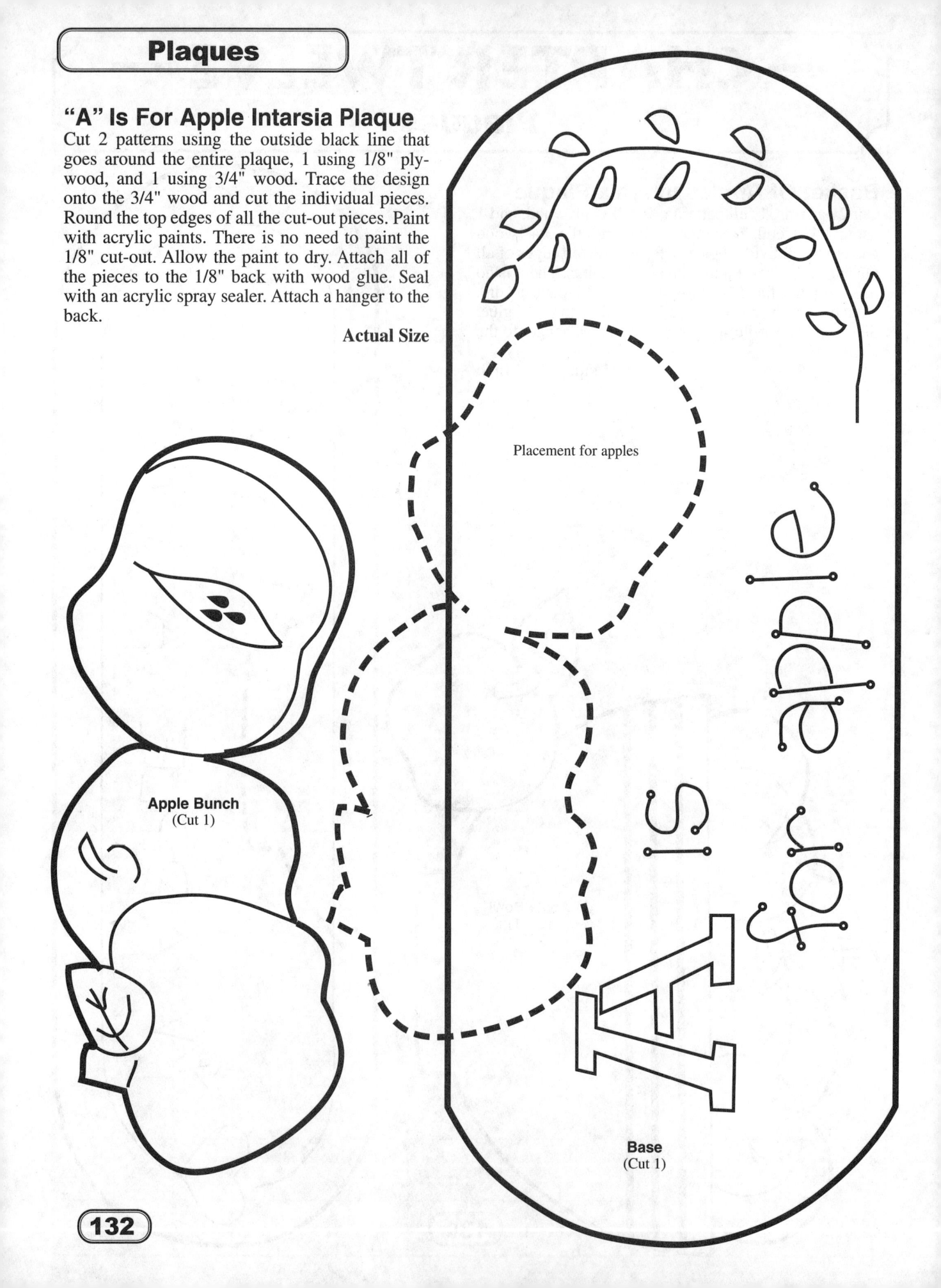

Placement for apples

A is for apple

Apple Bunch
(Cut 1)

Base
(Cut 1)

132

Plaques

Placement for kisses

CHOCOLATE SPOKEN HERE

Base
(Cut 1)

"Kiss"
(Cut 3)

Chocolate Spoken Here Intarsia Plaque
Cut 2 patterns using the outside black line that goes around the entire plaque, 1 using 1/8" plywood, and 1 using 3/4" wood. Trace the design of the individual pieces onto the 3/4" wood and cut the individual pieces. Round the top edges of all the cut-out pieces. Paint with acrylic paints. There is no need to paint the 1/8" cut-out. Allow the paint to dry. Attach all of the pieces to the 1/8" back with wood glue. Seal with an acrylic spray sealer. Attach a hanger to the back.

Actual Size

Plaques

"Missing My Mind" Plaque
Cut the plaque and hanging sign from 3/4" wood. Drill 1/8" holes in each one as shown. Sand. Paint and seal with acrylics. Attach together with raffia.

Actual Size

Girl (Cut 1)

Base (Cut 1)

OF ALL THE THINGS I'VE LOST ...

Drill 1/8" Holes Here

Sign (Cut 1)

Drill 1/8" Holes Here

I MISS MY MIND THE MOST

Plaques

Intarsia-Style Rooster Wall Hanging
Using 1/8" plywood cut the entire pattern as one piece for the backing. Trace the design onto 3/4" wood and cut the individual pieces. Round the top edges of all the cut-out pieces. Paint with acrylic paints. No need to paint the 1/8" cut-out. Allow the paint to dry. Attach all of the pieces to the 1/8" back with wood glue. Seal with an acrylic spray sealer. Attach a hanger to the back.

Actual Size

Plaques

"A Man's Got to Believe in Something" Fishing Sign

Cut the sign and fish from 3/4" wood. Drill holes as indicated. Sand. Transfer the design using graphite or carbon paper. Paint with acrylic paints. Seal with an acrylic spray sealer. Attach the fish to the sign with a couple of 5" long pieces of 19 gauge wire. Attach a hanger to the back of the sign.

Actual Size

Base
(Cut 1)

A MAN'S GOT TO BELIEVE IN SOMETHING ...

Drill holes

I believe I'll go fishin' ...

Drill holes

Fish
(Cut 1)

136

Plaques

Cat And Fish Dinner Welcome Sign

Cut the Welcome sign from 3/4" wood. Sand the pieces. As an alternative, the cat and bowl of fish can be cut as separate pieces from 1/2" wood and glued to the sign using yellow wood glue. Paint and seal using acrylics.

Actual Size

137

Plaques

Drill here

Drill here

Heart
(Cut 1)

Apple
(Cut 1)

Heart And Apple Welcome Sign
Cut the apple and heart from 1/2" wood. Drill small holes into the heart and apple as shown. Sand. Paint and spray with acrylics. Hang the heart in the center of the apple using ribbon or raffia. Attach a sawtooth hanger to the back.

Actual Size

Plaques

Apple
(Cut 1)

Cut out or cut from 1/4" wood and glue to apple

Heart And Apple Hanging Welcome Sign

Cut the apple and hanging sign from 1/2" wood. Cut the heart out of the apple or cut a heart from 1/4" wood and glue to the apple with wood glue for a 3-D effect. Drill holes as indicated. Sand well. Paint and seal using acrylics. Hang the sign from the apple with raffia.

Actual Size

Sign
(Cut 1)

WELCOME

Plaques

Intarsia-Style Sun Wall Hanging
Cut 2 patterns, 1 of the entire pattern using 1/8" plywood, and 1 of the individual pieces using 3/4" wood. Trace the design onto the 3/4" wood and cut the pieces. Define the lines of the nose and eyebrow with your scroll saw. Round the top edges of all the cut-out pieces. Paint with acrylic paints. Paint the sun's rays in 2 shades of yellow, the face in 3 shades of yellow, the clouds white with pale blue outlines and the background deep blue. No need to paint the 1/8" cut-out. Allow the paint to dry. Attach all of the pieces to the 1/8" back with wood glue. Seal with an acrylic spray sealer. Attach a hanger to the back.

Actual Size

Plaques

Little Girl Welcome Sign
Cut the girl from 1/2" wood. Cut the welcome sign and fingers from 1/4" wood. Sand, then transfer the detail using graphite paper. Paint with acrylics. Attach the fingers to the sign and the sign to the girl using yellow wood glue. Attach a saw-toothed hanger to the back.

Actual Size

Plaques

All Creatures Plaque
Directions on next page

Butterfly (Cut 1)

Cardinal (Cut 1)

Frog (Cut 1)

Base (Cut 1)

Sun & Clouds (Cut 1)

All Creatures Great & Small The LORD GOD Made Them All

Turtle (Cut 1)

Butterfly (Cut 1)

Robin (Cut 1)

142

Plaques

Dog
(Cut 1)

Dog's Tail
(Cut 1)

A much loved but very ferocious dog lives here

Heart
(Cut 1)

Paw
(Cut 1)

Paw
(Cut 1)

Ferocious Dog Plaque
Cut the dog from 1/2" wood. Cut the heart and tail from 1/4" wood and the paws from 1/8" wood. Sand, then transfer the detail using graphite paper. Paint with acrylic paints. Attach the paws to the heart and then attach the heart and tail to the dog using yellow wood glue. Seal with a spray or brush on varnish. Attach a saw-toothed hanger to the back.

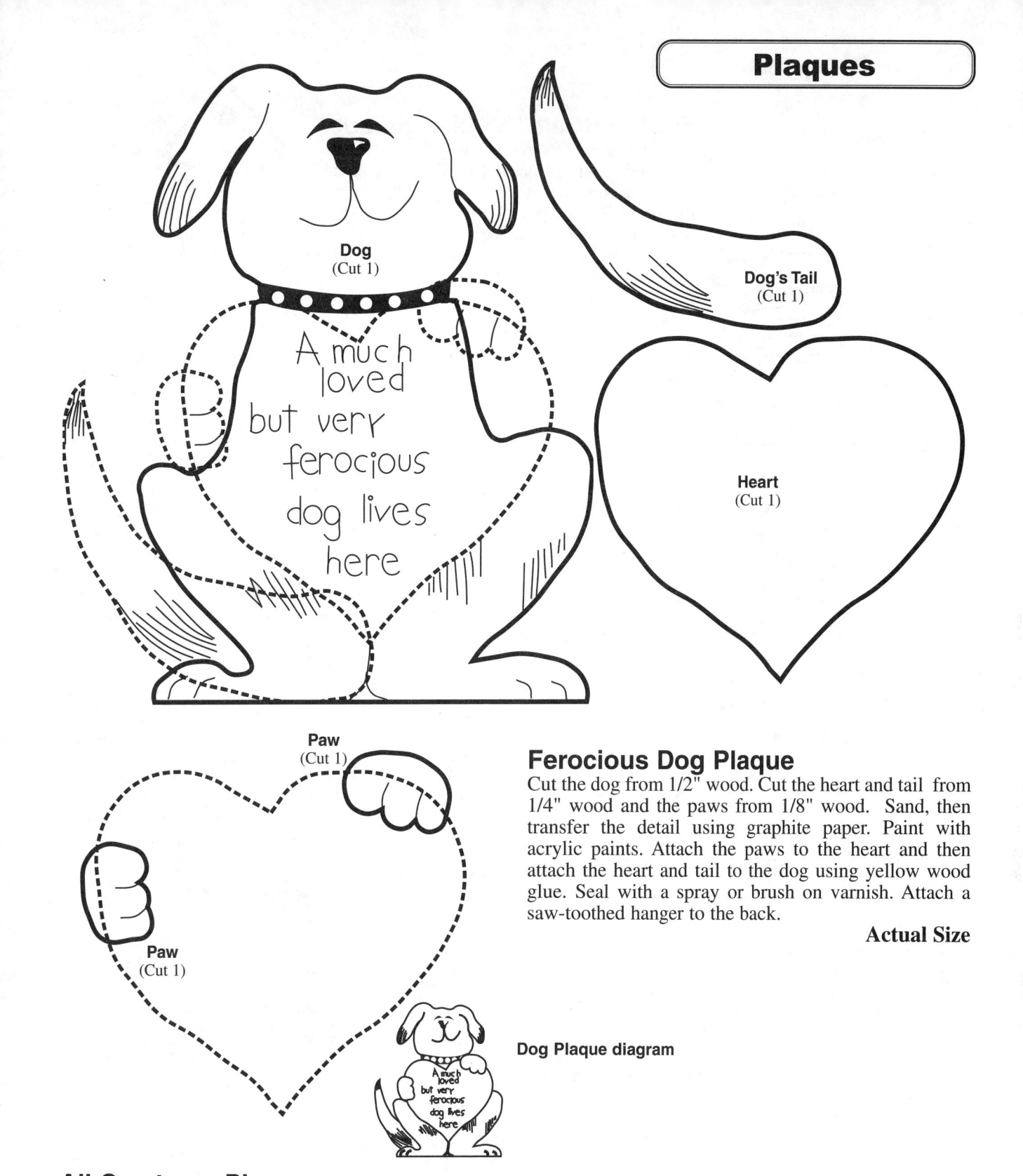

Actual Size

Dog Plaque diagram

All Creatures Plaque
(from previous page)
Cut the base (use dotted line) from 1/2" wood. Cut the animals from 1/4" wood. Drill small holes at the top of the plaque as indicated. Sand, then transfer the detail using graphite paper. Paint with acrylic paints. Attach the animals to the sign using yellow wood glue. Seal with a spray or brush on varnish. Insert wire, ribbon or cord through holes for hanging.

Actual Size

143

Plaques

Sewing Room "Mobile" Plaque
Cut each piece from 1/4" wood. Drill holes as indicated for insertion of 18 gauge wire or raffia. Sand, then transfer the detail using graphite paper. Paint with acrylic paints and seal with a spray or brush on varnish. Hang using the wire or raffia.

Actual size

Spool (Cut 1)

Scissors (Cut 1)

Cloth (Cut 1)

Heart (Cut 1)

I ♥ to sew!

Schoolhouse (Cut 1)

SCHOOL

Flag (Cut 1)

Slate (Cut 1)

$\frac{\begin{array}{r}1\\+1\end{array}}{2}$ ABC

Apple (Cut 1)

A+ teacher

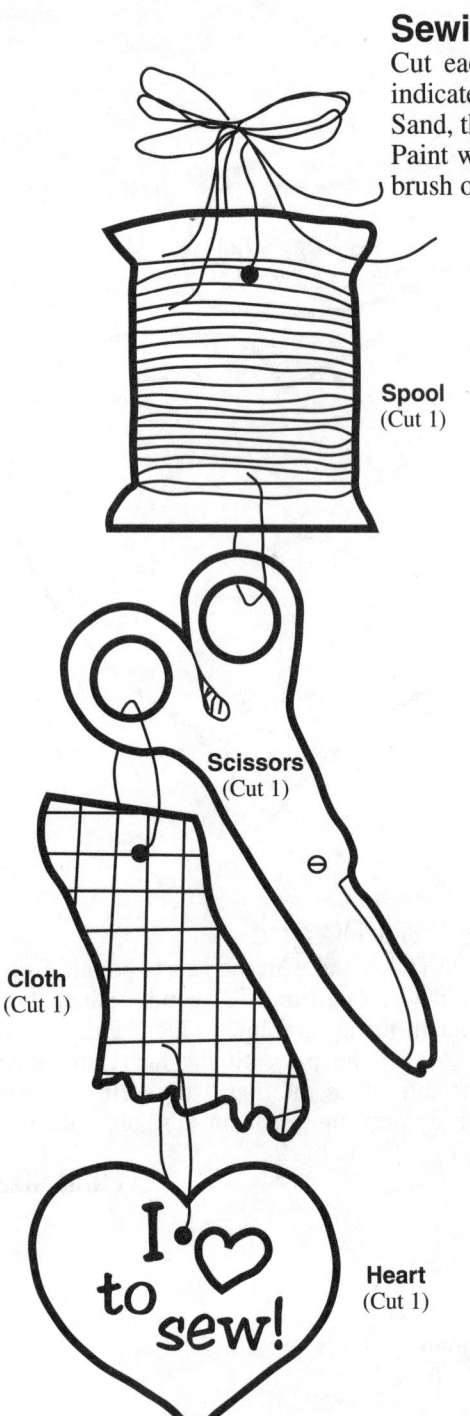

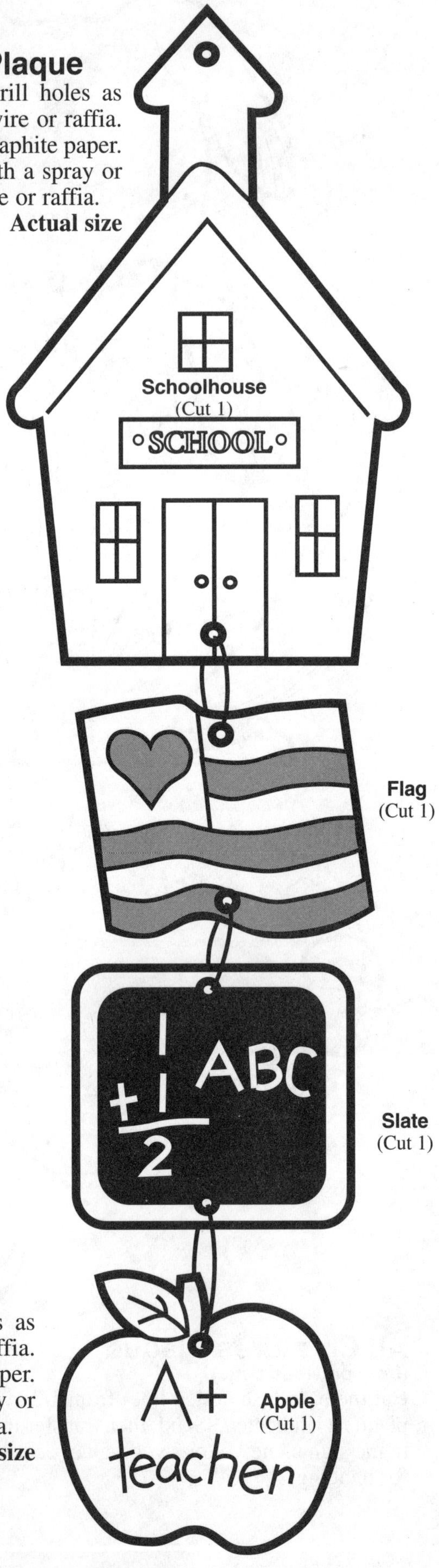

Teacher "Mobile" Plaque
Cut each piece from 1/4" wood. Drill holes as indicated for insertion of 18 gauge wire or raffia. Sand, then transfer the detail using graphite paper. Paint with acrylic paints and seal with a spray or brush on varnish. Hang using the wire or raffia.

Actual size

CHAPTER THIRTEEN
Wall Brackets

Ornate Bracket

Celestial Bracket

Decorative Shelf and Corner Brackets

These brackets can be very simple stained or painted or more intricate using various techniques such as woodcarving and wood burning. Cut all brackets from 3/4" or 1/2" wood. Some designs require inside cuts and others may require dowels. Designs on the face of the brackets can either be cut out or cut from 1/4" wood and attached with yellow wood glue for a 3-D effect. Transfer detail using graphite paper and either stain or paint with acrylic paints. Seal with a spray or brush on varnish.

Actual Size

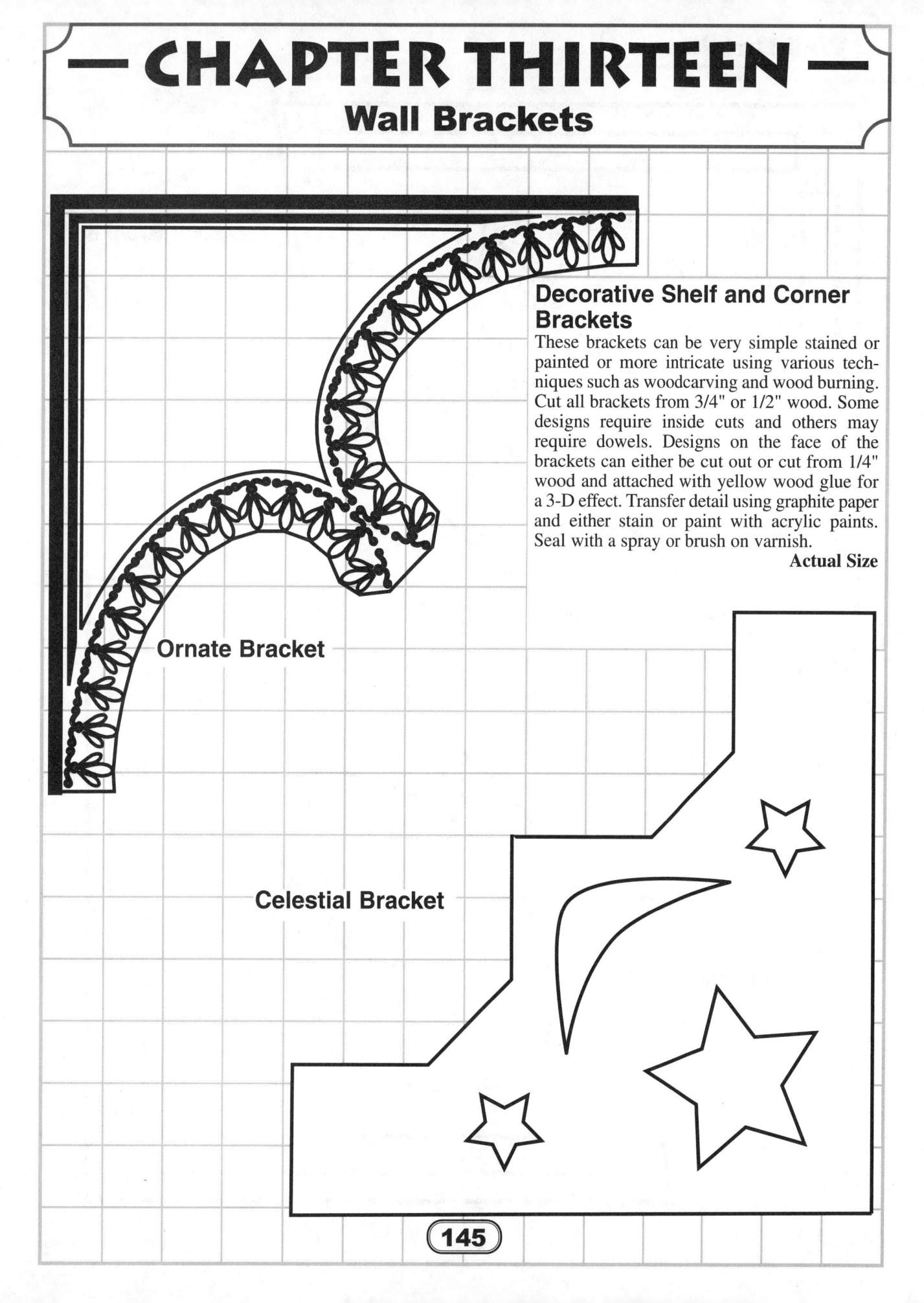

Wall Brackets

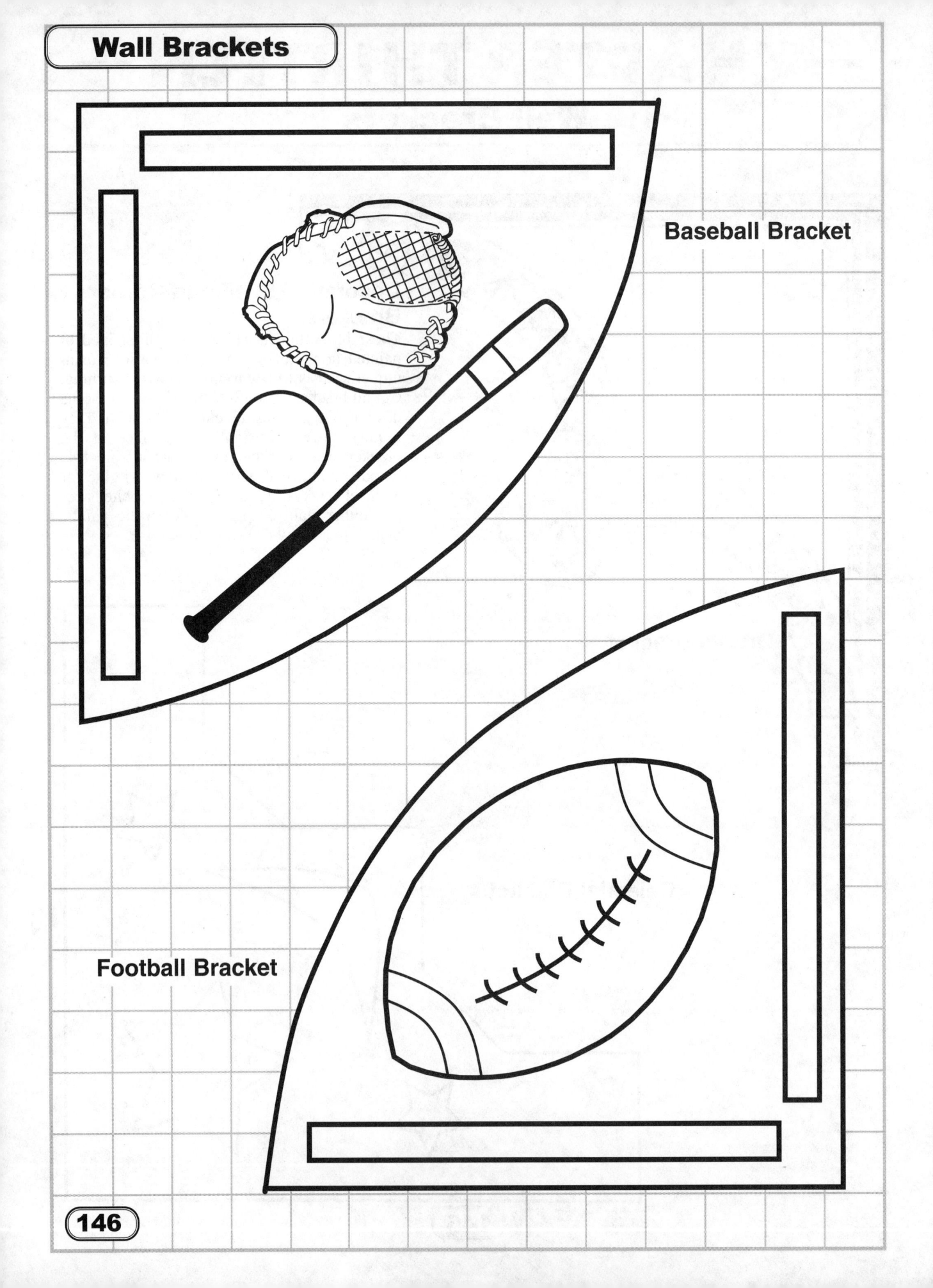

Baseball Bracket

Football Bracket

146

Wall Brackets

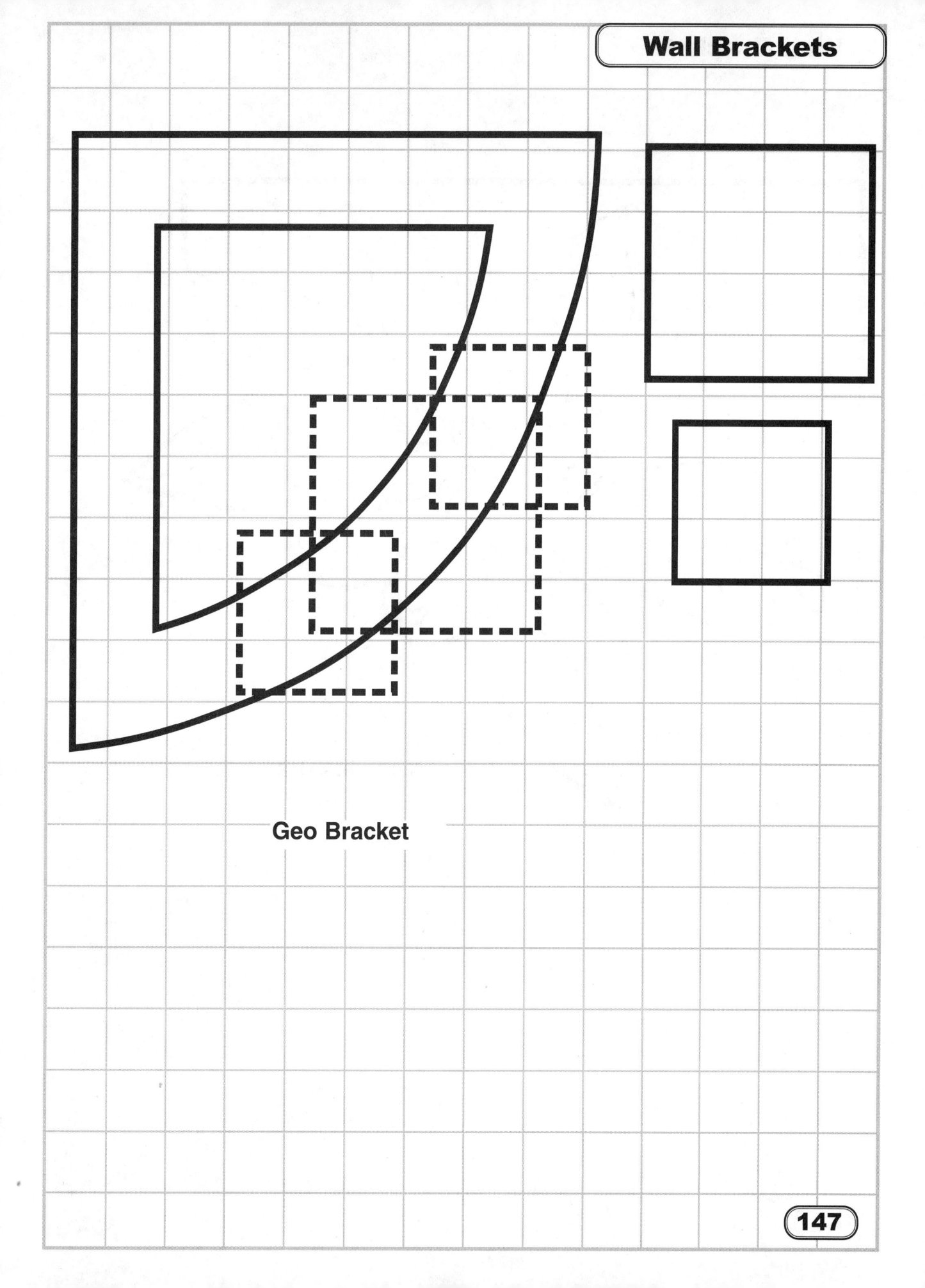

Geo Bracket

147

Wall Brackets

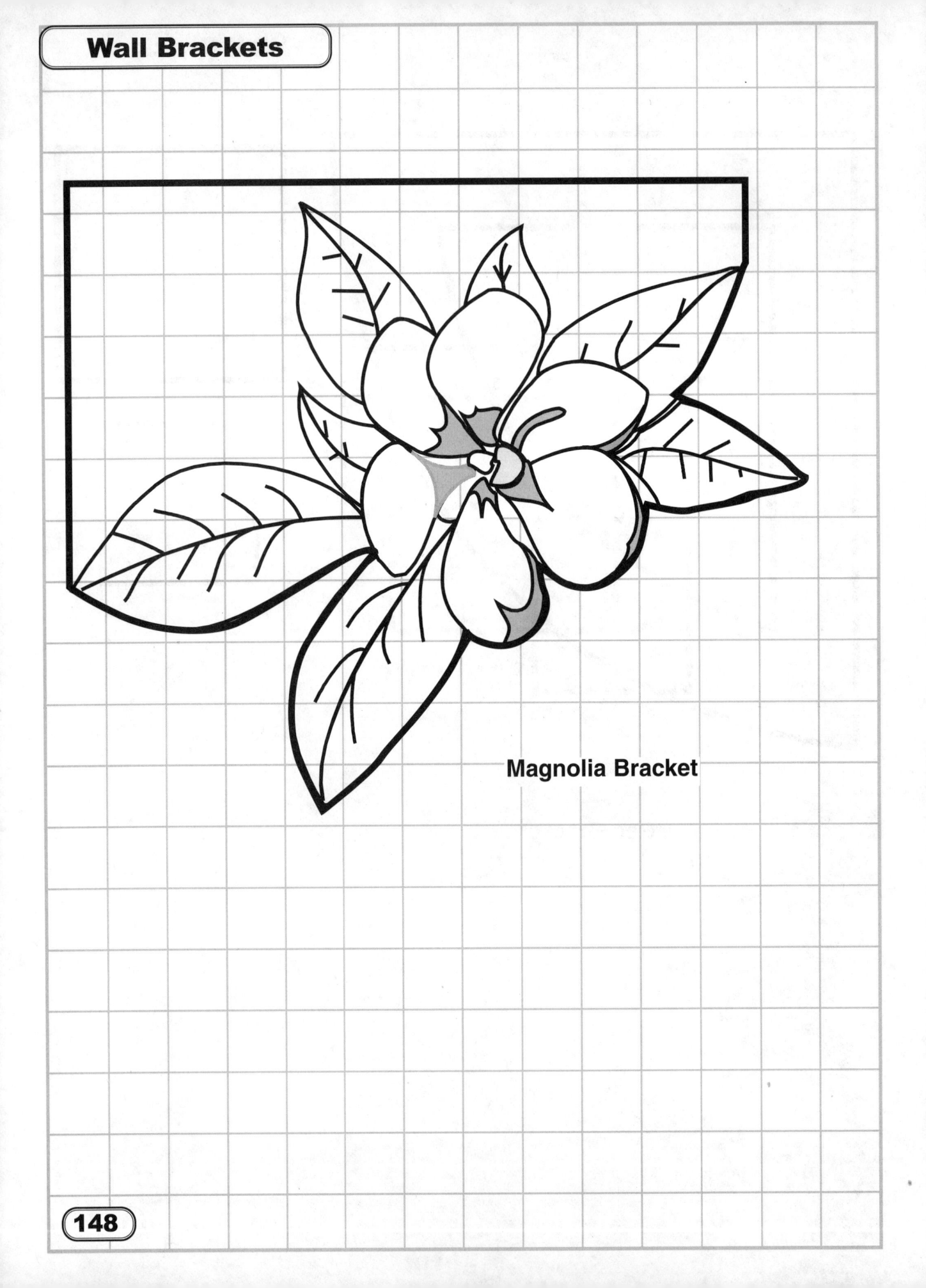

Magnolia Bracket

148

CHAPTER FOURTEEN
Western

Home, Home On The Range Peg-Board
Cut the peg-board using 1/2" wood. Drill a hole at each X for insertion of a peg. Sand well. Paint and seal with acrylics.

Actual Size

Drill Here For Peg

Drill Here For Peg

149

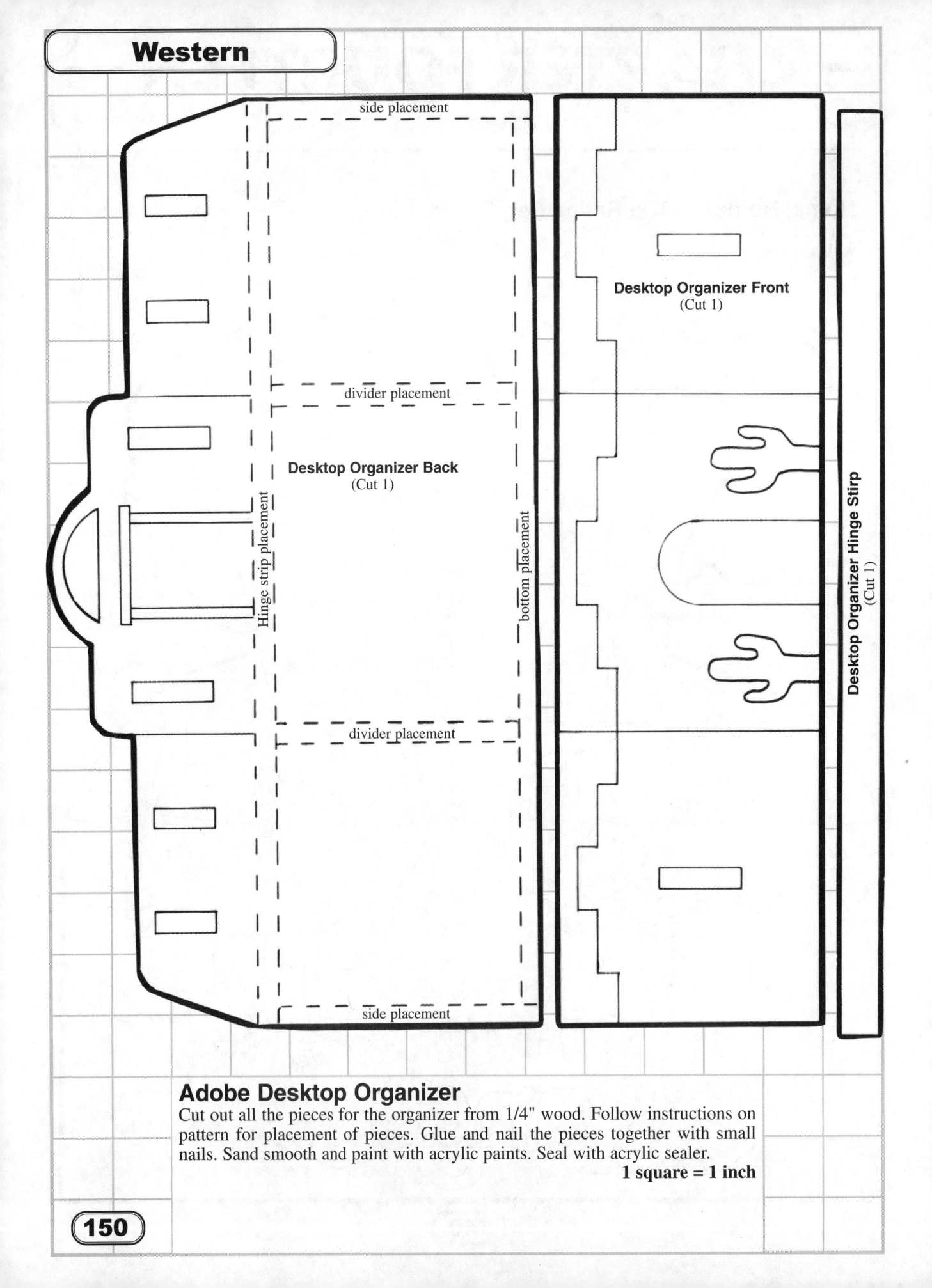

Western

side placement

Desktop Organizer Front
(Cut 1)

divider placement

Desktop Organizer Back
(Cut 1)

Hinge strip placement

bottom placement

Desktop Organizer Hinge Stirp
(Cut 1)

divider placement

side placement

Adobe Desktop Organizer
Cut out all the pieces for the organizer from 1/4" wood. Follow instructions on pattern for placement of pieces. Glue and nail the pieces together with small nails. Sand smooth and paint with acrylic paints. Seal with acrylic sealer.

1 square = 1 inch

Western

Desktop Organizer Continued

Desktop Organizer Bottom
(Cut 1)

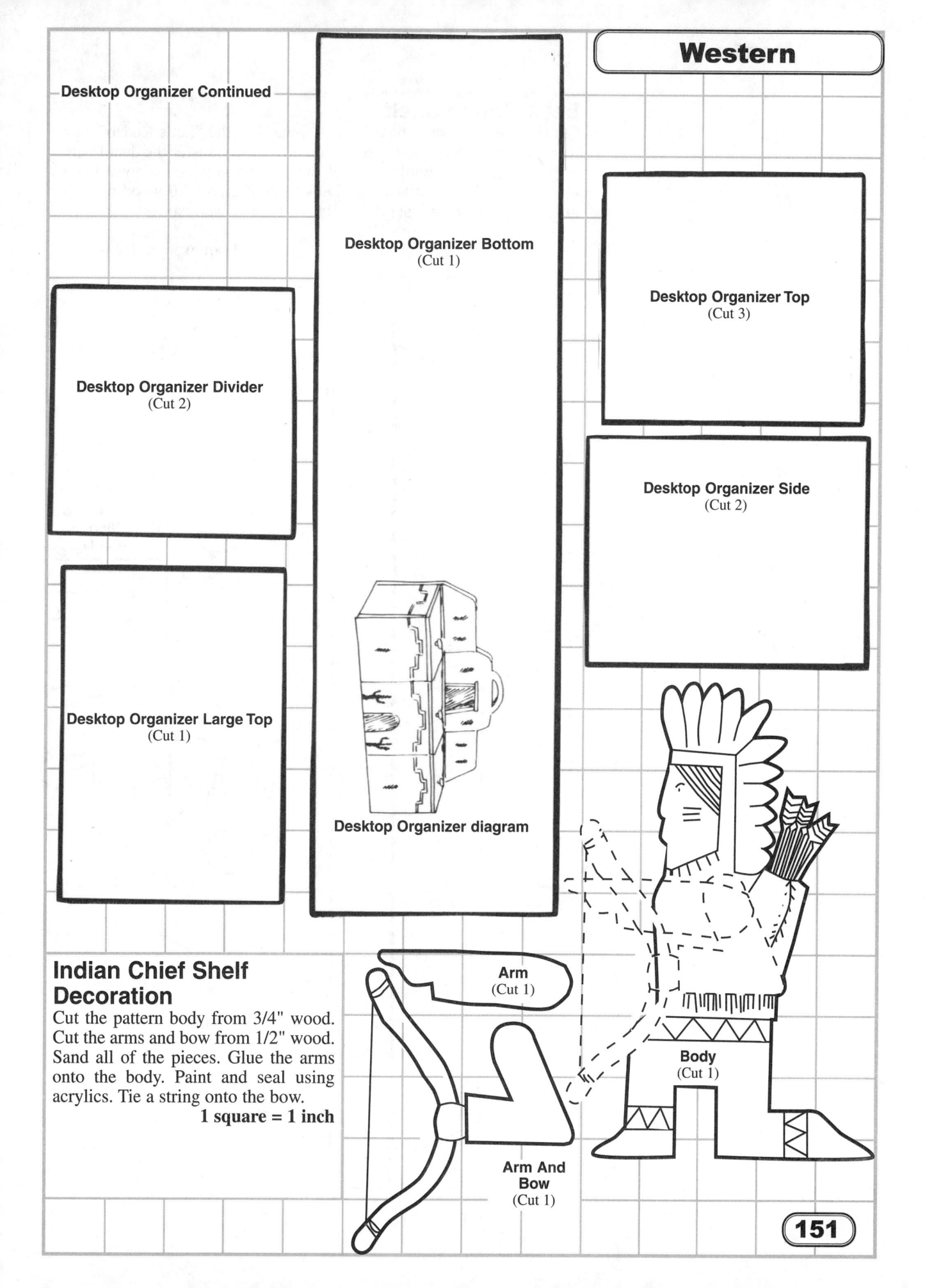

Desktop Organizer Top
(Cut 3)

Desktop Organizer Divider
(Cut 2)

Desktop Organizer Side
(Cut 2)

Desktop Organizer Large Top
(Cut 1)

Desktop Organizer diagram

Indian Chief Shelf Decoration

Cut the pattern body from 3/4" wood. Cut the arms and bow from 1/2" wood. Sand all of the pieces. Glue the arms onto the body. Paint and seal using acrylics. Tie a string onto the bow.

1 square = 1 inch

Arm (Cut 1)

Arm And Bow (Cut 1)

Body (Cut 1)

Western

"Let's Rodeo" Shelf diagram

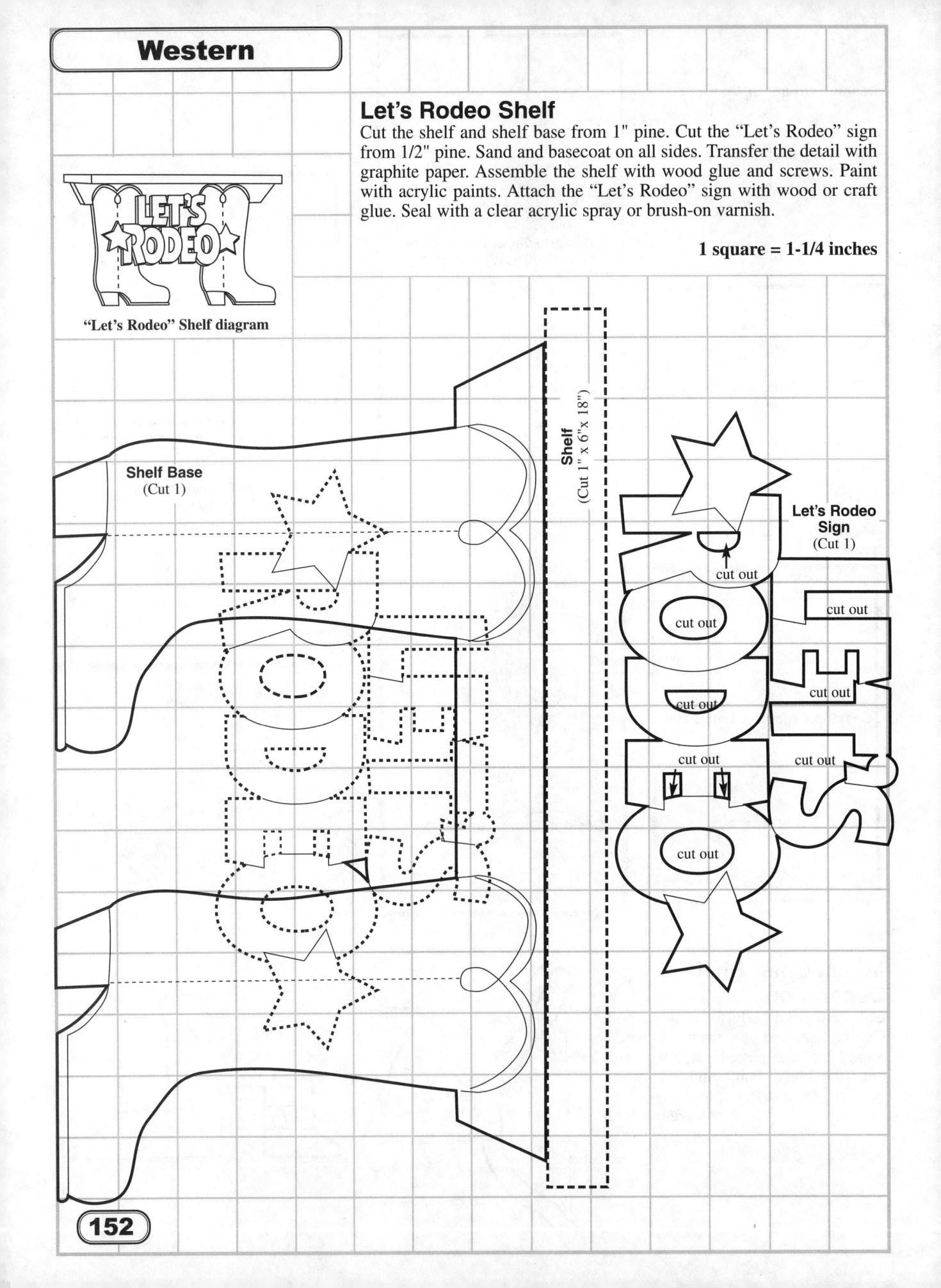

Let's Rodeo Shelf

Cut the shelf and shelf base from 1" pine. Cut the "Let's Rodeo" sign from 1/2" pine. Sand and basecoat on all sides. Transfer the detail with graphite paper. Assemble the shelf with wood glue and screws. Paint with acrylic paints. Attach the "Let's Rodeo" sign with wood or craft glue. Seal with a clear acrylic spray or brush-on varnish.

1 square = 1-1/4 inches

Shelf Base (Cut 1)

Shelf (Cut 1" x 6" x 18")

Let's Rodeo Sign (Cut 1)

cut out

152 Western

Western

Cactus Peg Board Towel Holder

Cut out the towel holder from wood. Drill holes at places marked with an "X" for pegs. Sand and paint with acrylic paints.

1 square = 1 inch

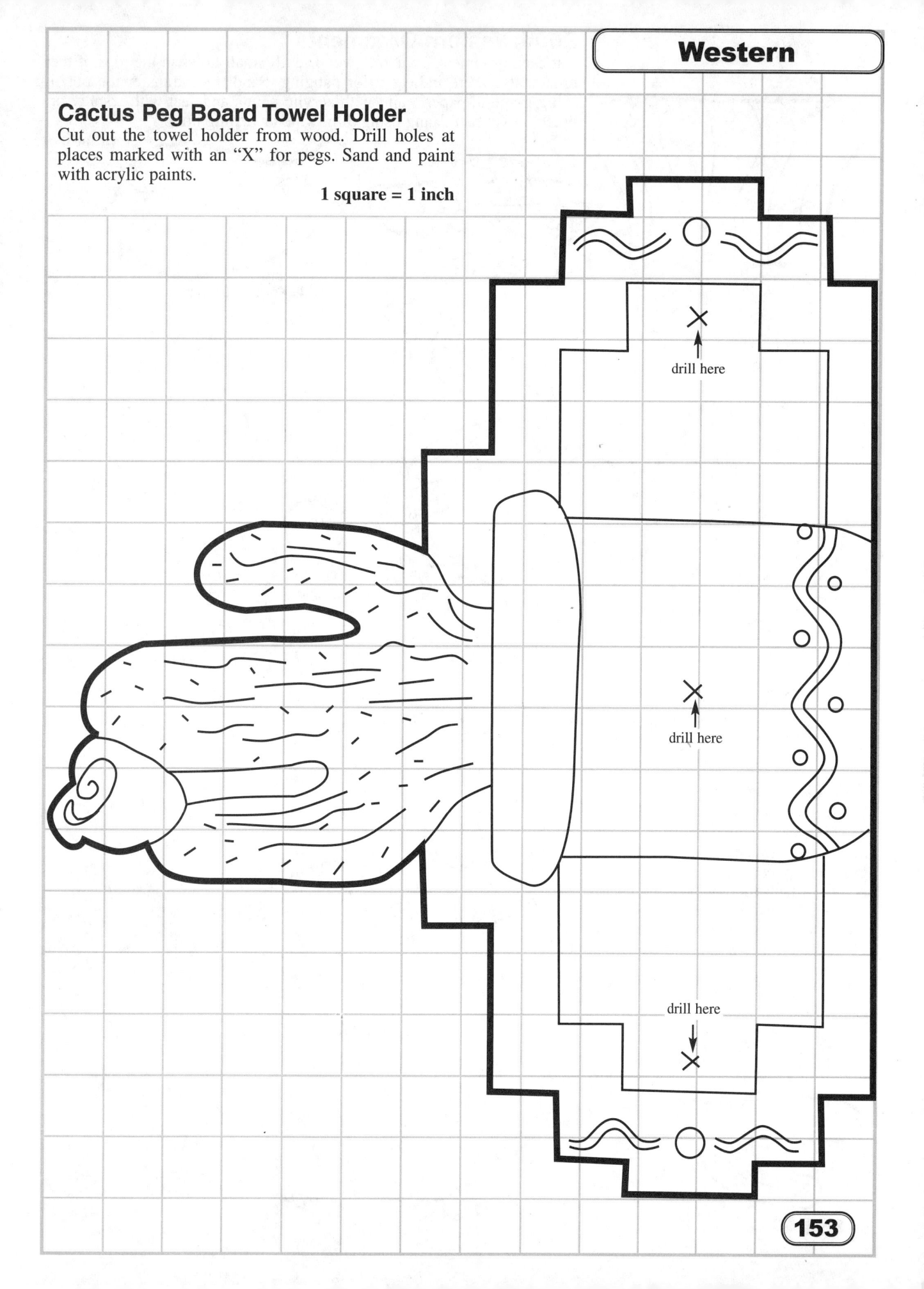

drill here

drill here

drill here

153

Western

Southwestern Ornaments

Cut each ornament from 1/4" wood. Drill small holes in the tops of the ornaments where indicated for hanging. Sand, then transfer the detail using graphite paper. Paint with acrylic paints and seal with a spray or brush on varnish. Hang using thin twine or fishing line.

Actual Size

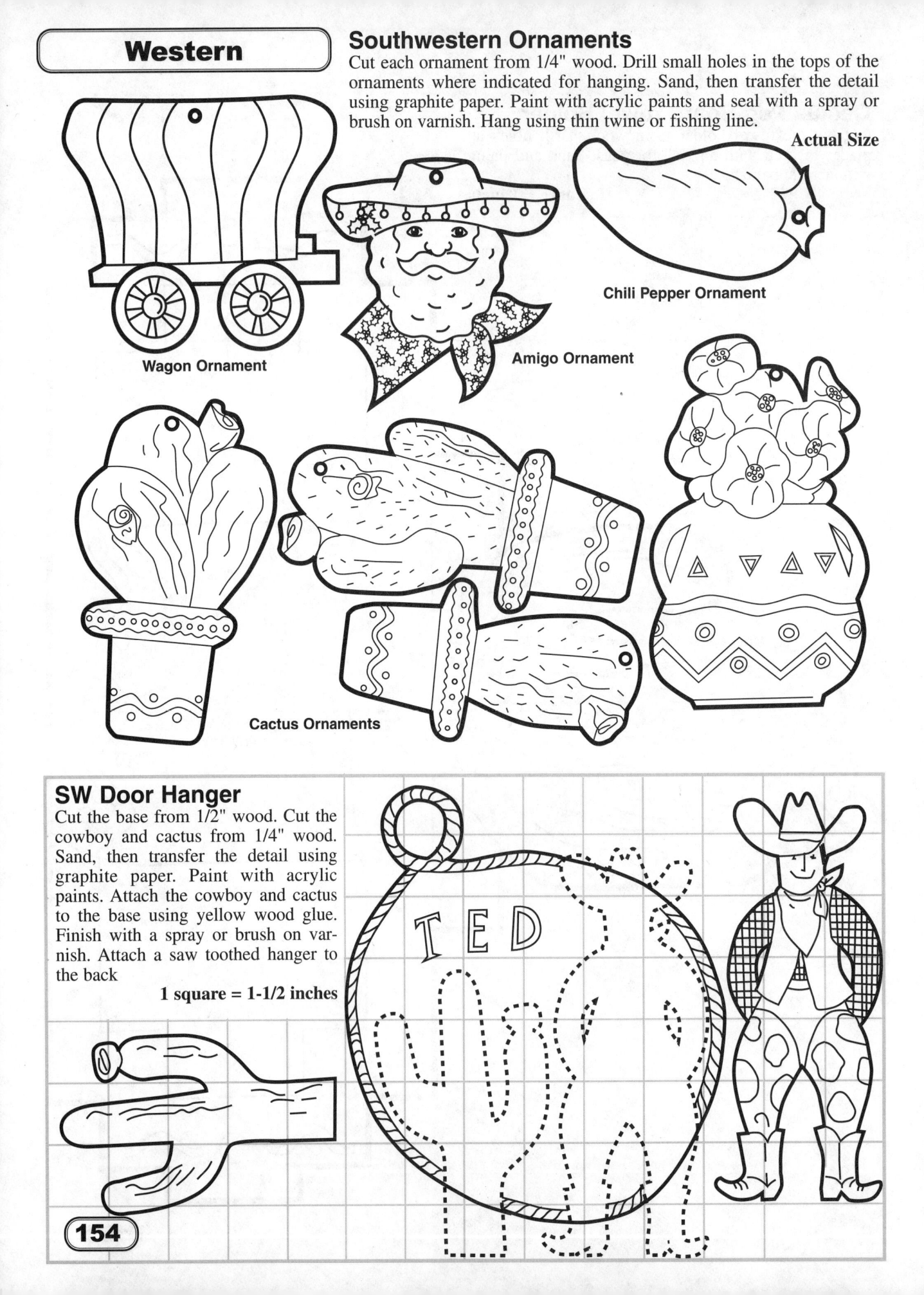

Wagon Ornament

Amigo Ornament

Chili Pepper Ornament

Cactus Ornaments

SW Door Hanger

Cut the base from 1/2" wood. Cut the cowboy and cactus from 1/4" wood. Sand, then transfer the detail using graphite paper. Paint with acrylic paints. Attach the cowboy and cactus to the base using yellow wood glue. Finish with a spray or brush on varnish. Attach a saw toothed hanger to the back

1 square = 1-1/2 inches

154

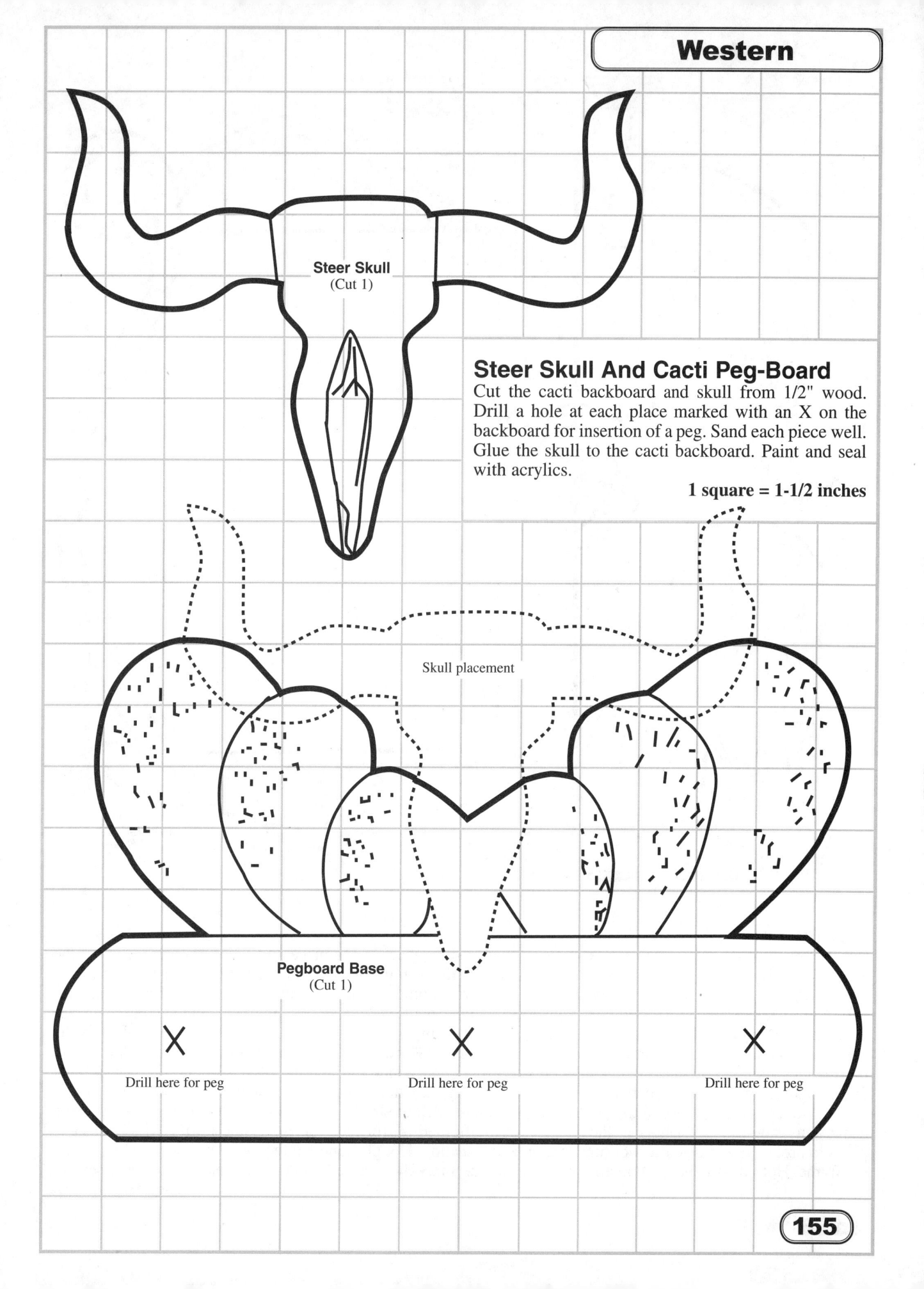

Western

Steer Skull
(Cut 1)

Steer Skull And Cacti Peg-Board
Cut the cacti backboard and skull from 1/2" wood. Drill a hole at each place marked with an X on the backboard for insertion of a peg. Sand each piece well. Glue the skull to the cacti backboard. Paint and seal with acrylics.

1 square = 1-1/2 inches

Skull placement

Pegboard Base
(Cut 1)

Drill here for peg   Drill here for peg   Drill here for peg

Western

Frame (Cut 1)

Hat placement

Hat (Cut 1)

Cut out

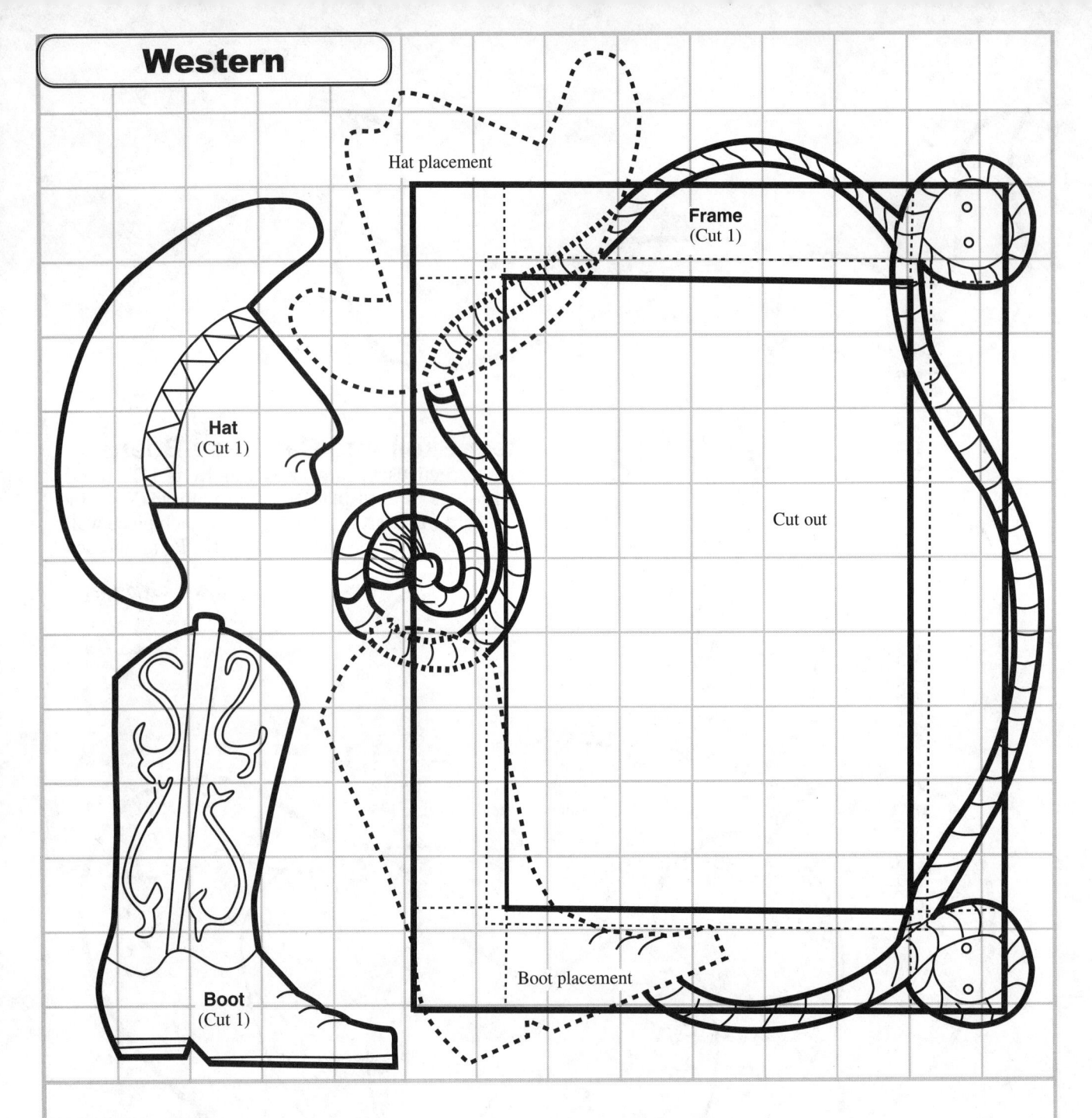

Boot (Cut 1)

Boot placement

Western Mirror

Cut the frame of the mirror using 1" x 4" wood. Cut 2 side pieces, 1 top piece and 1 bottom piece. Rabbet the ends of each board 3/8" x 3 1/2" so that the boards will fit flush when assembled. Rabbet the inside edges 1/2" wide x 1/8" deep to accept an 1/8" deep mirror. The mirror should fit flush with the back once the frame is assembled. Cut a back for the mirror from 1/8" plywood. Cut the hat and boot from 1/8" plywood. Sand all of the pieces. Assemble the frame with wood glue and finishing nails. Allow to dry. Place the frame face side down. Dry fit the 1/8" plywood back over the frame. Predrill 2 small holes 1 1/8" from the outside edge of the frame at the top and bottom and 3 small holes 1 1/8" from the outside edge at each side through the plywood and 3/8" through the frame. Stain or paint the frame, hat and boot. Allow to dry. Lay the frame face down and insert the mirror. Place the back over the mirror. Align the predrilled holes and attach the back to the frame with 1/4" screws. Attach a heavy-duty saw-toothed hanger to the back. Turn the framed mirror face up. Cover the mirror with a sheet of paper to protect it while you're working on gluing and sealing. Hot glue about 6 feet of hemp rope as shown onto the frame. Hot glue the hat and boot in place as shown. Spray the finished product with an acrylic spray sealer.

1 square = 1 inch

Buffalo Peg-Board

Cut the peg-board using 1/2" wood. Drill a hole at each X for insertion of a peg. Sand well. Paint and seal with acrylics.

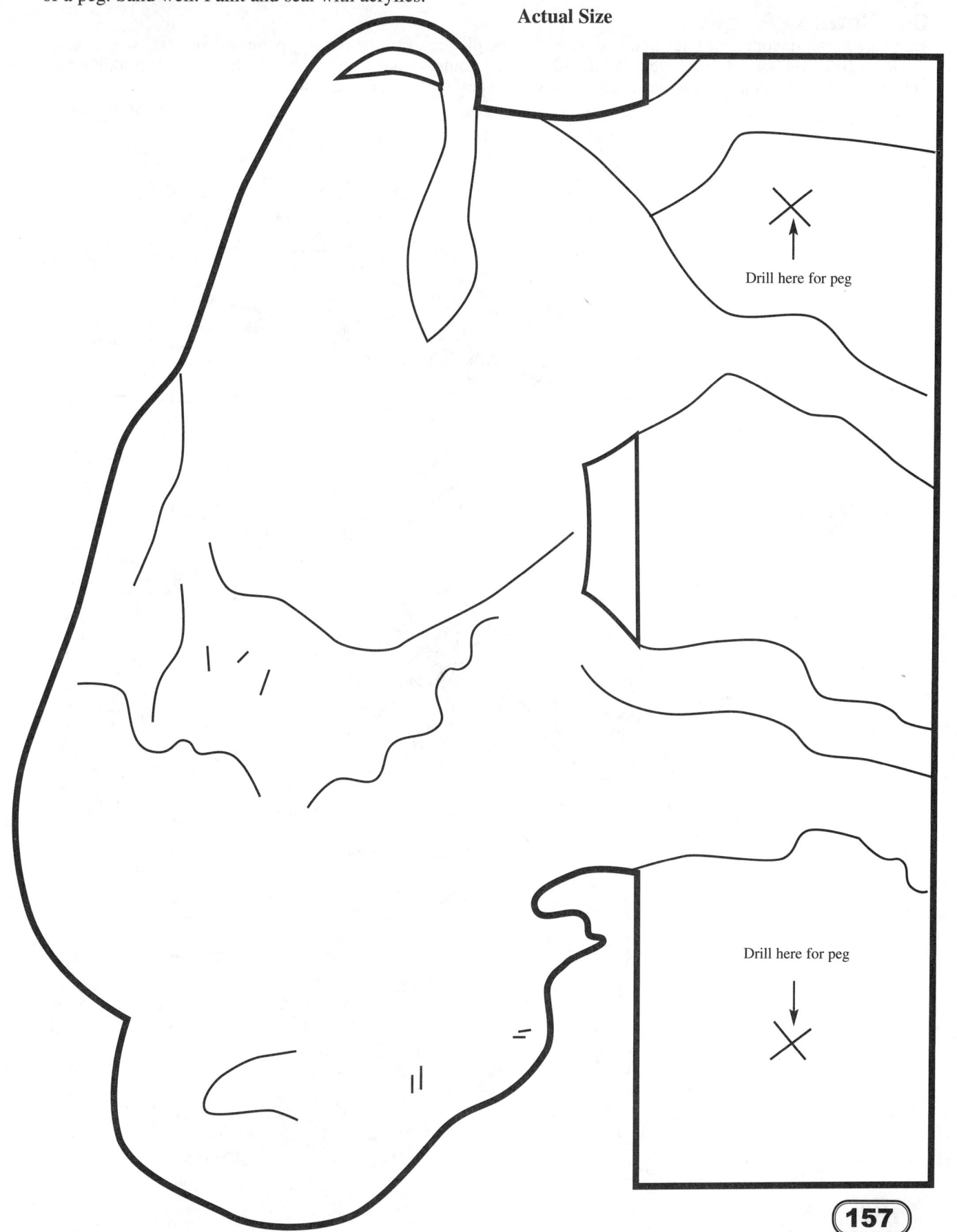

Actual Size

Western

Drill here for peg

Drill here for peg

157

Western

3-D Cowboy Plaques
Decorate a wall in your little buckaroo's room with these plaques. Cut the cowboy patterns from 1/2" wood. Cut the arms from 1/4" wood. Sand well. Paint with acrylic paints. Using wood glue, attach each of the additional cut pieces to the main pattern as indicated. Seal with a spray or brush on varnish.

Actual Size

INDEX

3-D Decorations 11-20
   "I Love Apples" Mobile 14
   Amish Home and Family 12
   Capering Cat on a Stand 16
   Kittens and Pumpkins Windowsill Sitter 19
   Layered Village 18
   Mama And Baby Bunny 11
   Over the Door Fishing Boy 16
   Over the Door Frog Decoration 16
   Ribbons and Hearts Carousel 17
   Sleepy Time Rabbit 20
   Teacher Garland 20

A

Amish patterns 12
Angel 72, 77, 80, 86, 90
Apples 14, 131-132, 138, 139

B

Beagle 13
Bean Bag Baby Victorian House Holder 47
Bears 32, 46, 81
Bird 142
Birdhouses 22-26
   Barn Birdhouse 25
   Lighthouse Birdhouse 21
   Lovebird Design Birdhouse 26
   Schoolhouse Birdhouse 22
   Sunflower Shelf Sitter Birdhouse 24
Blackbirds 67, 71, 73, 97, 123, 126, 128, 129
Buffalo 157
Bulldog 13
Bunny 11, 67, 70, 86, 94
Butterfly 142

C

Cabinet 87
Cactus 150, 153, 154-155
Cats 16, 137
Cat On A Stand 16
Chairs 32
Checkerboards 34
Chest of Drawers 59
Chicken 34
Church 18
Clocks 49
   "A Stitch in Time" Clock 50
   Bird and Sunflower Clock 49
   Comical Cat Clock 52
   Ornate Boudoir Clock 52
   Tiny Village Clock 51
Coat Tree 56
Coffee Table 57
Cow 100
Cowboy 152, 154, 156, 158
Cradle 62

D

Dalmatian 13
Deer Yard Ornament 122
Dinosaurs 36, 41, 45, 48
Dog 143
Dragons 36
Driveway Reflectors 121
   Welcome Driveway Reflector 121
Ducks 45

E

Elephants 46

F

Feeders 23
   Squirrel Feeder 23
Fish 16, 136
Fishing Boy 16
Flamingo 68
Fox Terrier 13
Frame 98
Frog 16, 46, 142
Furniture 53
   Adirondack Rocker 53
   Child's Chest of Drawers 59
   Cradle 59
   Dressing Screen 58
   Heart & Vine Coat Tree 56
   Treetop Coffee Table 57
   TV/VCR Stand 65

G

Games 34, 35
Garden 67
   "Gardening" Angel 72
   "Sheriff" Scarecrow and Wagon 74
   Flamingo Whirligig 68
   Golfer Whirligig 69
   Grandpa Bunny 67
   Grandpa Bunny Garden Welcome 70
   Little Worm Garden Sign 74
   Mary, the Bird Lady 71
   No Old Crows Garden Sign 73
   Owl Whirligig 68
   Think, Dream, Plan, Hoe Garden Sign 73
   Woodpecker Whirligig 68
Garland 20
Giraffes 46
Girls 47
Golfer 69
Grandma 98

H

Hearts 17
Holiday 75
   "And to All a Good Night" Decoration 75
   "Let It Snow" Hanging 83
   "NOEL Angel" Sill Sitter 86
   Christmas Angel 90
   Christmas Cabinet 87
   Christmas Countdown 91
   Deer Lawn Decoration 95
   Frosty And Freeza Snow People 84
   Heart And Star On A Dowel 83
   Little Angel Candy Holder 80
   Little Snowmen Linkables 85
   Nativity 77
   Ornaments 78
   Santa Bear Shelf Sitter 81
   Snowflakes 92
   Snowman 83, 84, 85, 89, 93
   Snowman Trio Ornaments 89
   Winter Wonderland Yard Ornament 93
Horse 17
Household Helpers 97
   "My Heart Belongs To Gramma" Picture Frame 98
   Cooking Utensil Holder 99
   Country Seed Plaque And Key Holder 97
   Cow Notepaper Holder 100
   Lamb Notepaper Holder 100
   Little School House Calendar 102
   Moose Notepaper Holder 101
   Potato & Onion Bin 103
   Sugar Packet Caddy 101

I

Indian 151
Intarsia 50, 133
   "A" Is For Apple 132
   Basket Of Apples Plaque 131
   "A Stitch in Time" Clock 50
   "Chocolate Spoken Here" Plaque 133
   Comical Cat Clock 52
   Rooster Wall Hanging 135
   Sun Wall Hanging 140

K

Kittens 19, 34
Koalas 15

L

Lamb 100
Lettering 107
   Block 108
   Calligraphy 109
   Sherwood 107
Lighthouse 130
Lions 46

M

Mailbox Reflectors 121
   Butterfly Mailbox Reflector 121
   Daisy Mailbox Reflector 121
   House Mailbox Reflector 121
Merry-Go-Round 17
Mirror 156
Mobile 14, 144
Monkey 46
Moose 101

N

Nativity 76, 77
Night lights 36
Noah's Ark 44, 46

O

Ornaments 78, 154
Outdoor Projects 113
   Cockatiel House Number Sign 113
   Deer with Heart Yard Ornament 122
   Victorian Glider Swing 114
Over The Door decorations 16
Owl 68

Index

P

Paper And Pencil Holders 36
Pattern 6
   Sizing of 6
   Transferring of 7
Peg Rack 47, 149, 152, 153, 155, 157
Peg Racks 123
   Apple Pie Peg Rack 126
   God Bless Our Cabin Peg Rack 124
   Home on the Range Peg Rack 149
   I'd Rather Be Fishin' Peg Rack 125
   Welcome Aboard Peg Board 130
   Welcome Friends Peg Rack 127
Pigs 13, 15
   Flying Pig Wire-wing Angel 13
   3-D Pig Shelf Decorations 15
Plaque 158
Plaques 131
   "A Man's Got to Believe in Something" Fishing Sign 136
   "Missing My Mind" Plaque 134
   All Creatures Plaque 142
   Cat And Fish Dinner Welcome Sign 137
   Ferocious Dog Plaque 143
   Heart And Apple Hanging Welcome Sign 139
   Heart And Apple Welcome Sign 138
   Intarsia 131
      "A" Is For Apple Intarsia Plaque 132
      Basket Of Apples Plaque 131
      Chocolate Spoken Here Intarsia Plaque 133
      Intarsia-Style Rooster Wall Hanging 135
      Intarsia-Style Sun Wall Hanging 140
   Little Girl Welcome Sign 141
   Sewing Room "Mobile" Plaque 144
   Teacher "Mobile" Plaque 144
Playhouse 35
Post Office 18
Pull Toys 45, 46
Pumpkins 19
Puzzles 46

R

Rabbit 20
Rabbits 46
Raccoon 125
Rocking Horses 37, 38

S

Safety 5
   Common Sense for Saws 5
   Rules for 5
Sailboat 130
Santa 75, 91
Scarecrow 74, 88
Seasonal 75
   "I Love Spring" Bunny 94
   Holiday Welcome Sign 81
   Hopping Bunny On A Stand 86
   Scarecrow Autumn Yard Ornament 88
Sheepdog 13
Shelf Decorations 15
Shelves 123
   Blackbird and Sunflower Shelf 126
   Bow and Heart Shelf 128
   Double Display Shelf 129
   Small Sunflower And Bird Shelf 123
Shops 18
Sign Board 110
   Geo 110
   Hexagon 111
   Star 112
Snowflakes 92
Snowman 83, 84, 85, 89, 93, 95-96
Southwestern, *See Western*
Stacking Animals 13
Star 83
Steer 155
Sun 142
Sunflower 49, 71, 73, 97, 99, 101, 106, 123, 126, 129

T

Teacher 20, 144
Tic-Tac-Toe 34
Tools 5
   Care of 5
   Equipping Your Workshop 5
Townhouse 18
Toys 27-48
   Book Ends 31
   Bulletin Boards 30
   Cork Boards 30
   Dinosaurs 30
   Doll Clothes 28, 29
   Dolls 27
   Elizabeth And Jonathan Victorian Dress-up Dolls 27
   Kittens 30
   Mittens 30
   Mobile 44
   Noah's ark 31
   Plaques 30
   Rocking Dinosaur 41
   Rocking Horse 37
Turtle 142
TV/VCR Stand 65

V

Village 18

W

Wall Brackets 145
   Baseball Bracket 146
   Celestial Bracket 145
   Football Bracket 146
   Geo Bracket 147
   Magnolia Bracket 148
   Ornate Bracket 145
Watermelon 97, 99, 101, 123, 129
Welcome 139, 141
Western 149
   3-D Cowboy Plaques 158
   Adobe Desktop Organizer 150
   Buffalo Peg-Board 157
   Cactus Peg Board Towel Holder 153
   Home, Home On The Range Peg-Board 150
   Indian Chief Shelf Decoration 151
   "Let's Rodeo" Shelf 152
   Southwestern Ornaments 154
   Steer Skull And Cacti Peg-Board 155
   SW Door Hanger 154
   Western Mirror 156
Whirligig 68
   Flamingo Whirligig 68
   Golfer Whirligig 69
   Owl Whirligig 68
   Woodpecker Whirligig 68
Windowsill Decorations 19
Wood 5
   Creating a Profitable Hobby 9
   Finishing 8
      Decorative Finishing Items 9
   Joining 7
      Joining with Glue 8
   Purchasing 5
   Selection of 6
Woodpecker 68